T0367125

THE

PUBLICATIONS
OF THE
SURTEES SOCIETY
VOL. CLXXXVII

THE

PUBLICATIONS

OF THE

SURTEES SOCIETY

ESTABLISHED IN THE YEAR
M.DCCC.XXXIV

VOL. CLXXXVII

FOR THE YEAR MCMLXXII

At a COUNCIL MEETING of the SURTEES SOCIETY, held in Durham Castle on 9 December 1974, Mr. C. R. Hudleston in the chair, it was ORDERED—

'That Dr. C. J. Kitching's edition of The 1559 Royal Visitation of the Northern Province of the English Church should be printed as a volume of the Society's publications.'

and

'That an expression of the Council's gratitude to the Marc Fitch Fund for a substantial grant towards the costs of publication should be included in this volume.'

A. J. PIPER
Secretary

THE
ROYAL VISITATION
OF 1559

Act Book for the Northern Province

TRANSCRIBED AND EDITED WITH AN INTRODUCTION BY

C. J. KITCHING, B.A., Ph.D.

Assistant Keeper of Public Records

PRINTED FOR THE SOCIETY BY
NORTHUMBERLAND PRESS LIMITED
GATESHEAD
1975

From the original in the Public Record Office,
State Papers Domestic, Elizabeth I: SP 12/10*

TABLE OF CONTENTS

PREFACE

Many colleagues and friends have helped in the production of this edition by giving freely of their time, advice and individual expertise. My interest in the Act Book was first kindled by Dr David Loades of Durham University who also very kindly read a draft of the Introduction. The late Mrs Norah Gurney and her colleagues at the Borthwick Institute in York patiently answered many questions about the records there. I am greatly indebted to Dr Nicholas Cox of the Public Record Office who read the complete transcript of the Latin passages and helped to monitor scribal errors of both the sixteenth and the twentieth centuries. Such errors as may remain are the responsibility, respectively, of Thomas Percy, notary public, and myself! Miss Catherine Burling generously typed the complicated index.

I am most grateful to the Editor of the Surtees Society and to the Northumberland Press for the great pains they have taken in seeing this particularly difficult text through the press. But above all a particular word of thanks must be given to the Marc Fitch Fund for a substantial grant in aid of this publication.

Public Record Office   C.J.K.

November 1974

ABBREVIATIONS USED IN THE FOOTNOTES

Aveling   J. C. H. Aveling, *Catholic Recusancy in the City of York, 1558–1791.* (Catholic Record Society 1970)

BIHR   *Bulletin of the Institute of Historical Research*

BM   British Museum

Borthwick   University of York, Borthwick Institute of Historical Research

EHR   *English Historical Review*

Frere   W. H. Frere, *Visitation Articles and Injunctions* (3 vols., Alcuin Club Collections, xiv, xv, xvi, 1910; 2nd vol. in conjunction with W. M. Kennedy.)

Gee   *The Elizabethan Clergy and the Settlement of Religion, 1558–1564* (Oxford, 1898)

LP   *Letters and Papers Foreign and Domestic of the reign of Henry VIII* ed. J. S. Brewer and others, (2nd edition, 21 vols., London 1920.)

PRO   Public Record Office

Venn   J. A. Venn, *Alumni Cantabrigienses* (4 vols., Cambridge, 1922–7)

INTRODUCTION

THE ROYAL VISITATION OF 1535

A royal visitation of the church in England was first contemplated in 1535 to give substance to the newly defined Supremacy of Henry VIII and to remove any lingering allegiance of clergy and people to the spiritual authority of Rome.

Henry VIII entrusted to Thomas Cromwell, his vicegerent and vicar-general in matters spiritual, the power to conduct such a visitation, and there was a temporary inhibition of ecclesiastical jurisdiction in September 1535.[1] This, however, was short-lived, and from the following month licences were already being issued to archdeacons and bishops to resume their right to prove wills and grant administrations for estates valued at less than £200, and to ordain clergy. The inhibition has been seen as a necessary move, (the king taking to himself for a time all spiritual authority, suspending clerical jurisdiction, and then gradually restoring it as a royal grant), to remove any doubt about the source of authority within the English church.[2] But there is hardly any evidence to suggest that the royal visitors-general conducted a *parochial* visitation at this time. In the northern province, Legh and Layton were on tour early in 1536, and their work continued until at least the summer. They visited all the cathedrals including that at York which was not a monastic foundation, but the rest of their concern seems to have been exclusively with the monasteries,[3] and the only book of *comperta*[4] contains no parochial business. During their stay in each diocese, ecclesiastical jurisdiction was suspended, which led to some protest from the bishops, particularly from Tunstall of Durham. The visitors gave the bishops Injunctions for their cathedrals but during most if not all their visitation, the general Royal Injunctions were not yet available. When these were published in the summer of 1536, with the clear intention that they should be presented to the clergy of each deanery by Cromwell's commissaries undertaking the general visitation, Legh and Layton had already finished their monastic business in the province, and there is no trace of any other commissaries returning to enforce the Injunctions in that year. It may very well be that Cromwell had quite enough business arising from the visitation of the monasteries and from his probate jurisdiction over estates valued at more than £200, and therefore left to the diocesans, for the moment, the responsibility of circulating and enforcing the Injunctions of 1536. A clause in the 1537 Injunctions issued by Bishop Lee for the diocese of Coventry and Lichfield suggests that the visitors there had, at least in some places, presented the Royal Injunctions,[5] but he goes on to give the clergy of the diocese until the following Lammas to obtain copies, which were not yet widely known or available. Other episcopal Injunctions from various dioceses confirm that the enforcement of the 1536 Royal Injunctions was initially undertaken by the diocesans.[6]

On 27th March 1538, however, Thomas Legh issued a further inhibition through Archbishop Lee, to the clergy of the northern province, announcing his intention of visiting them in the following month. This was carelessly and incompletely copied into the archbishop's register at a later date,[7] and the timetable is therefore partly obscured, but the outline is:

Thu 4th April: Guisborough priory (for clergy of the deanery of . . .)
Fri (no entry)
Sat 6th April: Rievaulx abbey
Mon   —   Fountains
Wed   —   York (? St. Mary's)
Thu (no entry)
Fri   —   Selby
Sat 13th April: St. Oswald's
Mon   —   Roche

This important document ordered all clergy of whatever position, all church wardens and two or three other worthy persons from each parish to attend, deanery by deanery, at the centres specified. All were to swear oaths of fealty and obedience to the king, denouncing the Pope and his jurisdiction in accordance with the Act of Succession,[8] and to subscribe their names having thus sworn. Then the clergy were to show all letters of ordination, dispensation, institution and the like, together with the foundation deeds of all chantries. The laymen were to make presentments of matters (and persons) deemed to be in need of reform. Executors of persons dying during the visitation were to present the wills for probate. Procurations for the visitation were to be paid, and scribes and apparitors were to be in attendance from dawn each day during the sessions (*mane et diluculo singulorum dierum*). The objectives and logistics of this visitation are revealed in this document as nowhere else. The commissary was empowered to conduct in the king's name a visitation on a scale larger than had ever been attempted even by an archbishop before, including not only most of the functions of a provincial visitation, but also the reception of oaths of allegiance. The inhibition was published by the vicar-general, William Cliffe, but apart from a glimpse of George Palmes, archdeacon of York, sitting on 7th May as Legh's commissary to hear a matrimonial cause,[9] there is no other known record of the visitation. The inhibition was relaxed, the whole province apparently having been visited, on 7th July, 1538.[10]

Three months later, in October, Cromwell issued some much more challenging Injunctions, instituting parish registers for baptisms, marriages and burials, and striking a harder blow against images, pilgrimages and shrines than in 1536.[11] But there was no more talk of parochial visitation under Henry VIII, though the visitation of the monasteries, and more particularly the surveys of the chantries (for which returns were required from each parish and the commissioners visited selected centres in each diocese to which representatives of the clergy and laity were summoned) kept the crown firmly in touch with the local church.

THE ROYAL VISITATION OF 1547

At the beginning of Edward VI's reign, with a new regime and the publication of still more radical Injunctions in 1547, a thorough national visitation was again launched in order to enquire into the spiritual health of the nation.[12] For this visitation we have more tangible evidence. On 4th May writs were dispatched to inhibit ecclesiastical jurisdiction and preaching. The one sent to Archbishop Holgate for publication throughout the northern province survives,[13] passed under the sign manual with the counter-signatures of eight Privy Councillors including Somerset and Cranmer. There was some initial delay before the visitations began in August. A copy[14] of the list of 'the appointments of the circuites, commissaries preachers and registers for the Kinges Majesties visitation in Auguste Anno 1547', divides the country into six circuits by dioceses, one for the northern province and five for the southern thus:

1. York, Durham, Carlisle, Chester
2. Westminster, London, Norwich, Ely
3. Rochester, Canterbury, Winchester, Chichester
4. Salisbury, Exeter, Bath & Wells, Bristol, Gloucester
5. Peterborough, Lincoln, Oxford, Coventry & Lichfield
6. Worcester, Hereford, Llandaff, St David's, Bangor, St Asaph

This time the task was not left to one man. The commissaries proposed for the northern circuit were the Dean of Westminster (William Benson), and Sir John Hercy, with Nicholas Ridley as preacher and Edward Plankeney as registrar. Whilst the local evidence of the visitation having taken place is irrefutable, its sparsity must again be lamented. There is record of the visitation at York Minster, before Roger Tonge, DD (one of Edward VI's chaplains), Hercy, William Moreton esq. and Edmund Farley, whilst at Doncaster, Hercy was absent, though the other commissaries appeared, aided by the local knowledge and talent of Thomas Gargrave, John Hearne and John Markham.[15]

The visitors sent out in advance of their arrival in each deanery a set of Articles of enquiry in four sections, to be answered respectively by bishops, archdeacons and their officials; by other clergy; by laity; and by chantry priests. They encouraged the reporting of many errors of omission and commission after self-examination, rather than having the clergy report on the laity and vice-versa. The Injunctions have been widely discussed, and need not again be rehearsed. At the mother church of each diocese, the visitors delivered the now customary special Injunctions, and those for the Dean and Chapter of York, dated 26th October and 1st November, copied by the registrar for the visitation, survive. Unfortunately no detailed register of the visitation acts seems to have survived for any of the six areas,[16] though we can be sure that the visitors gained much useful local information to hand on to the chantry commissioners who followed them only a few months later.

PLANS FOR THE ROYAL VISITATION OF 1559

During Mary's reign it was necessary, despite the queen's firm belief in papal authority, to use the royal supremacy for a while as a means of enforcing a return to the old religious practices. With this intention the queen issued a new set of Articles, but it is significant that the diocesans were left to enforce them, and no attempt was made to conduct a royal visitation. However, the events of the reign and the religious apprehensions and manoeuvrings of the first year of Elizabeth made it inevitable that another visitation should be promoted to check the damage caused to the Protestant reforms by the temporary revival of allegiance to Rome, to redress the wrong done to clergy evicted by Mary because they were married, and to set out afresh the independent authority of the crown over the English church.

It was first necessary to devise and promulgate new Acts of Uniformity and Supremacy together with a revised Prayer Book and further Royal Injunctions. These, however, were formidable preliminaries[17]—more so than the crown had originally expected. Preparations for the third major set of religious reforms in little more than a decade could not be lightly undertaken, and there was more than spiritual authority at stake for the clergy who would be asked to accept the settlement. Those instituted in Mary's reign following the deprivation of married predecessors must have already feared for their future careers. Even if they were safe on this count, they must have cast a wary eye in the direction of the returning Protestant exiles for whom posts had to be found. A delicate situation thus faced Elizabeth quite apart from the major problems of authority and doctrine. But it was clear from the outset that the minimum requirement for the clergy of the new regime had to be an ostensible acceptance of the royal supremacy and of the Prayer Book and Injunctions when eventually formulated. That most would be demanded of those with the highest offices in the church was equally plain, for royal authority would be ineffective, or at least incomplete, if those controlling ecclesiastical jurisdiction did not openly accept and promote the settlement. Archbishops, bishops, archdeacons, vicars-general and deans—the key figures through whom the royal authority would be exercised—constituted a more important sector to control first than the clergy at large, and we shall see that the latter were given more time to reconsider any initial inclination to reject the terms of the settlement. At a parochial level the crown could not afford to be too severe until there was a plentiful supply of clergy available to replace any who might be dismissed.

The Acts of Supremacy and Uniformity finally passed at the end of April, 1559.

On 23rd May the Privy Council was first commissioned to administer a new oath of Supremacy to priests, judges and JPs. Draft lists of commissioners for a Royal Visitation were drawn up,[18] using the 1547 circuits as model, and on St John Baptist's day (24th June) when the new Prayer Book became mandatory, Letters Patent[19] were issued to establish the six circuits and their commissioners.

Three days earlier, two of the northern bishops, Oglethorpe (Carlisle) and Scott (Chester) had been deprived for refusing to subscribe. To Elizabeth's great disappointment Archbishop Heath followed their example and was finally removed on 7th July. Of the northern bishops therefore, only Tunstall of Durham hung on to his office long enough to receive notification of the inhibition of his episcopal jurisdiction during the visitation, and on 19th August he protested fiercely at the removal of altars and crucifixes which he had witnessed in London at the hands of the visitors there, 'because I can not my self agree to be a sacramentary nor to have any new doctrine taught in my diocese'.[20] But on 22nd August the northern visitors arrived at Southwell to begin their business and Tunstall was not finally deprived until the last day of the main visitation of his own diocese (28th September).[21] The commissioners' initial plans for the other three northern dioceses must have been addressed to the vicars-general. Before tracing the visitation itself we should consider some of the planning and preparation without which it would have been impossible.

THE VISITORS AND THEIR COMMISSION

The lists of commissioners for each circuit included the Lords Lieutenant of each county, several trusted divines (at least one being a reputed preacher), two or three lawyers and a complement of local gentry. It was never intended that the Lords Lieutenant should serve actively,[22] or that all the gentry named should be in attendance all the time. The main burden would inevitably fall on two or three of the commissioners in each circuit, to whom the responsibility for planning must have been committed. In the draft for the northern circuit it was proposed that Lever be the preacher, but this rôle was eventually filled by Edmund Scambler.[23] Otherwise there were no significant changes in the names between draft and patent. In the north the two commissioners destined to head the visitation were Edwin Sandys and Henry Harvey.

Sandys had been a leading Cambridge theologian, master of St Catharine's College and Vice-Chancellor until his removal by Mary. He fled to Strasbourg for most of her reign but returned promptly afterwards and was one of those responsible for drafting the new Prayer Book. He was renowned as a preacher and frequently receives reverential acclaim from the scribe of the visitation. In a matter of weeks after the visitation he was consecrated bishop of Worcester and later became bishop of London (1570–7) and Archbishop of York (1577–88). Although an ardent puritan he seems to have respected the right of fellow churchmen to defer their acceptance of the reformed religion, and certainly exercised his function as presiding judge of the visitation with equity and clemency.[24]

Harvey was an ideal companion: a skilled ecclesiastical lawyer who held important offices under both Edward and Mary. He seems to have regarded his profession too highly to risk it by expressing any strong partisan religious views, and whilst he was not destined for the episcopate, he did reach high office in the church.[25]

Scambler, a third product of Cambridge, was one of the courageous few who despite strongly Protestant beliefs stayed in England during Mary's reign and ministered secretly to Protestant congregations. He became one of Archbishop Parker's chaplains and, in 1561, bishop of Peterborough. A Lancastrian, he was particularly suitable as one of the northern visitors.[26]

Sandys and Harvey attended every major session of the visitation, and Scambler may also have been on hand, though he is named less frequently. In any event, the team was very strongly headed. Trusted members of the Council of the North, with important knowledge of the area covered, were also included among the number of the active visitors: Sir Thomas Gargrave, Sir Henry Gates and Lord Evers, took their turns in the areas appropriate to their interests. Two other local gentry with legal knowledge, Christopher Estofte and George Browne, were sent a special letter urging their co-operation with the visitors,[27] and both appeared as commissioners during the course of the visitation. The scribe of the whole operation was Thomas Percy, notary public, and he seems to have been represented by a deputy (John Stace) on only one occasion.[28] His official deputy named in the commission, John Hodges, may well have been in attendance, though he is never named in the Act Book.

The terms of the commission were similar to those for the earlier Royal Visitations rehearsed above. The whole province was subject to the visitors' authority, clergy and laity alike, and their powers embraced all aspects of ecclesiastical jurisdiction. Quite apart from obtaining subscriptions to the royal supremacy, the Prayer Book and Injunctions, they were to grant probate of wills, and letters of administration, and to handle testamentary causes arising; to hear instance causes and punish contumacy; to take stock of vacant benefices and admit suitable persons duly presented for institution; to examine the clergy's letters of ordination and institution, and remove unsuitable incumbents; to licence preachers, to review the cases of persons imprisoned for matters of religion, and those deprived by Mary of their benefices. They might do anything else needful for the reform of the church in the queen's name, and appoint deputies to assist them and to handle causes not completed before the end of the visitation. With presentments of church wardens also to be heard, and procurations and synodals to be collected, it is not difficult to imagine how exhausting the business must have been, and how intricate the planning of the itinerary and timetable so that all the clergy and parochial representatives could be present at some stage.

The paperwork associated with the planning has unfortunately perished, but there can be no doubt that when the scribe sent the inhibition to bishops and archdeacons for publication together with the Articles of enquiry for the visitation,[29] he enclosed, as in 1538, a timetable, leaving the provincial officials to circulate the necessary citations and arrange accommodation for the visitors and their entourage.[30] The many subsidiary documents, such as citatory mandates and schedules of penances, issued during the visitation and repeatedly mentioned in the text, were most probably destroyed after their satisfactory implementation, to reduce the bulk of material carried around the province. Stranger, however, is the loss of several important registers which were certainly compiled, notably the books of subscriptions to the supremacy,[31] the register of wills proved by the visitors, and the record of licences to preachers,[32] together with all accounting documents for the collection of the necessary procurations. These may have been returned to London with the Act Book, but it has been plausibly suggested that they were left in York, handed on to the ecclesiastical commissioners in the 1560's and have since been lost. It is therefore no mean blessing that the main Act Book has survived where so much else has perished.[33]

THE 1559 ACT BOOK: Description

The Act Book as now preserved in a single volume with the livery of the State Papers Domestic[34] was originally two separate paper volumes. The second (now fols. 168–end), much the shorter, (consisting of some twenty folios only, with a parchment cover which has survived), is a register of recognisances for the subsequent appearance of persons bound over by the visitors at a preliminary hearing. With the exception of the first few recognisances, this has only been calendared in the present edition since much of the language is mere common form. The original first volume, which has been transcribed in full, was a fair copy made after the visitation, probably from several different current registers which overlapped somewhat in content. The component parts are easily identifiable by parchment tabs separating the various sections of the volume. Section I (fols. 1–54) is the main chronicle of proceedings at each centre visited. Next comes a record of the instance causes in which clergy deprived by Mary for marriage attempted to regain their livings (fols. 57–76). This is followed by a short section listing clergy admitted to vacant benefices during the visitation (fols. 70–87), and a much larger section giving presentments of churchwardens, parish by parish and diocese by diocese, in answer to the Articles of enquiry (fols. 90–135). So many charges of immorality were to be heard in the closing stages of the visitation that they were entered in a separate account (fols. 137–147) divorced from the main chronicle of proceedings. Finally, there is a register of clerical absentees, parish by parish within each deanery. Most of these sections cover the whole time span of the visitation, so that the complete chronology can only be retrieved by piecing together information from all sections.[35] The greater part of the Act Book is in the customary technical Latin typical of the church courts, and sometimes an '&c' replaces a whole phrase or formula familiar to the scribe, leaving the sense obscure to the modern reader. Such cryptic abbreviations have occasionally been explained in the footnotes. The churchwardens' presentments and the text of the recognisances are the only substantial portions of the book written in English, save for occasional *verbatim* reports of important testimony and denials of the royal supremacy.

Whilst there were no indexes in the two original volumes, they were clearly intended as works of references, and in general there are marginal annotations of the names of key persons or places recorded in the adjacent paragraphs. The sectional divisions of the main volume, and the chronological arrangement, further make for easy reference, and the eye is led down each page to the beginning of each new statement by the use of bold lettering to pick out the first word or words of important phrases. In short the Act Book, beautifully presented, is a model of clarity rarely excelled among sixteenth century records.

Nevertheless, the sad loss of subscription books and of the records of the queen's commissioners sitting in London to hear cases referred by the provincial visitors means that the Act Book leaves several tantalising queries about the final outcome of cases heard by the northern visitors. On its own, it fails to answer some of the most important questions we should like to ask: how many clergy were deprived as a result of the visitation, and how many merely had their livings sequestrated during their lifetime; how many of those bound over to appear were actually summoned before the ecclesiastical commissioners sitting in London; how many of the laity presented by churchwardens escaped with no more than a caution; how many of the clerical absentees eventually subscribed and before whom? These are severe limitations, yet they cannot blind us to the fact that the 1559 Act Book for the northern province tells us a great deal about every aspect of the church in English society at this critical period—perhaps more than any other single text. It is particularly notable for 'naming names': clergy and laity, present and absent; patrons of livings; non-residents; apparitors, and so on. A glance at the index alone will show the strength of the Act Book in this respect.

The value of this source material has, of course, long been realised, and much of the pioneer work is still of great value.[36] Many of the questions posed above have been at least tentatively answered, and it is no part of the present editor's intention to cover extensively such ground as has already been explored. But the Act Book has been used almost exclusively to answer one question: the number of persons deprived as a result of the visitation, (and indeed more work still needs to be done in this field). The text, printed *in extenso* for the first time, brings to light many more details of the procedure and nature of the visitation than have been ascertainable from earlier studies based on it.

VISITATION PROCEDURE

The procedure for the full sessions of the visitation may be briefly set out. The commissioners arrived at the appointed church and public prayers were offered. A sermon was preached, then they adjourned to the place set apart for the session: usually the choir or chancel. The commission was read aloud,[37] and if the session was being conducted by surrogates in place of Sandys and Harvey, their letters of surrogation were also read. The archdeacon or his official certified that the citatory mandate had been received and published, and then the names of those cited to appear were read out, and absentees declared contumacious. Next, the Registrar read the Articles (circulated in advance) and Injunctions, and the churchwardens of each parish swore that they would make diligent written answers of the matters contained, after which they were dismissed until the time appointed to deliver their presentments and show inventories of their church goods. This might be in the afternoon of the same day, or, as at Chester,[38] the following day. The clergy were also ordered to appear again at an appointed hour to show their letters of ordination and institution, and other muniments, and to be individually examined.[39] At cathedrals and colleges, the statutes had to be shown, and special Injunctions were presented.[40] This, with minor local variations, was the pattern of events, though further sessions were called to handle the many other aspects of the visitation: litigation and probate prominent among them. It was frequently necessary to order parties to appear again at a later stage in the visitation to continue a cause, because of the commissioners' limited time at each port of call. This factor made the Royal Visitation a somewhat slow and inefficient vehicle for ecclesiastical suits.

As we should expect, there were no Sunday sessions, and Michaelmas day was also respected as a feast, but rather surprisingly the visitation continued on the feasts of St Bartholomew (24th August), St Matthew (21st September) and St Luke (18th October). Sandys and Harvey appeared at all main sessions but appointed surrogates on three occasions. Thomas Percy was in attendance as registrar except for the session at Alnwick and possibly part of that at Tarvin. In each case, surrogation was only adopted under some peculiar circumstances. At Durham Bernard Gilpin and Scambler were deputed to visit one of the prebendaries in his own house because he had a broken leg.[41] Gilpin and two assistants were dispatched to hold a session at Alnwick because it was thought 'safer' that the commissioners should not go into this remote northern territory,[42] and presumably such a detour would have delayed their progress into Carlisle and deprived them of a welcome Michaelmas rest in Durham. Rumours of plague in the city of Chester led them to depute Scambler again to hold a session at Tarvin,[43] but the fact that Scambler and Percy were able to go for a final session only two days later in Chester itself, strongly suggests that the real reason for their surrogacy on this occasion was that the principal commissioners, weary of their labours, and at length at the end of their tour, wanted to return again to London.[44]

It was also necessary to appoint deputies to observe the performance of penances imposed by the commissioners, and to clear up any remaining business. There are several indications of later sessions having taken place.[45] In Tunstall's register under the date 8th October, 1559 we find the appointment of Gilpin and Roger

Watson to serve as surrogates for the Durham diocese with Christopher Chaytor as scribe.[46] If the Act Book is to be believed, sessions were held in Manchester on 31st October and Newcastle on 18th December, after the visitors had departed. Many more cases were referred by the commissioners to the ecclesiastical commission sitting in London. There is no evidence of the delegation of powers to the mayors of towns visited, as at Gloucester, Exeter and Southampton in other circuits.[47]

The sermon was a crucial part of the main sessions, setting out, one presumes, the full justification for the visitation. No text used for these orations has survived, but the registrar repeatedly stresses the sincerity and devotion with which they were delivered. Sandys regarded this as one of his own primary duties, and preached at most of the major centres: 10 or more sermons in all. Scambler, the official preacher was in the pulpit on at least five occasions, and the remaining preachers were aspiring and trusted churchmen.[48]

THE VISITATION OF THE CLERGY

A good deal has already been published about the sequestration of livings and deprivation of clergy in the early years of Elizabeth. The supply of clergy was critically low following a fall in the number of those ordained in the 1550s and an unusually high mortality rate in the years immediately preceeding the visitation,[49] so that wholesale evictions would have ruined the church.

In theory, all clergy had been cited to attend the visitation, but large numbers of parochial clergy failed to appear and were pronounced contumacious, *pena reservata*. Such detailed research as has been done, however, shows that very few of the absentees were subsequently deprived.[50] Nobody was punished *ipso facto* for non-appearance, and it must be assumed that the surrogates clearing up business after the visitors had gone received further subscriptions from clergy originally absent. Some absenteeism was certainly attributable to sickness, whilst among the pluralist higher clergy it was inevitable, and often excusable since many of them would in any case meet the visitors personally at another stage of the visitation by virtue of other promotions they held. Some commissioned other clergy to stand proxy for them and explain their absence. John Rokeby, vicar-general of York, could hardly be expected to turn up at Southwell where he held a prebend if he were still to make plans for the visitors' future accommodation and attend to his business on the Council of the North; he therefore ordered Robert Cressy, Official of the archdeacon of Nottingham, to appear for him. Robert Pursglove, another Southwell prebendary who was also suffragan bishop of Hull, and George Palmes, a fellow prebendary at York, both used Cressy's services.[51] At York, Scambler himself stood proxy for one of the prebendaries. But such proctors were not allowed to subscribe on behalf of their clients, who could at best defer the day of reckoning by this means while avoiding any charge of contumacy. Personal subscriptions would be required of them in the end.

Among those who did attend the visitation, the parochial clergy offered least resistance, whilst many of the higher officials who had run the Marian church were naturally more conscience-stricken following the stand made by their bishops against the settlement. But the visitors expected some degree of soul-searching and gave each person who refused to subscribe a second, third and often a fourth opportunity. Some felt that they could accept the royal supremacy but not the Prayer Book and Injunctions. A few, after due reflection, decided to subscribe, but the majority of those who had once raised the courage to refuse held firmly to their decision. When the visitors were satisfied that there was no hope of subscription, they sequestrated the livings of the offenders and took from them a bond to appear again before them or before the resident commissioners in London when called to attend.[52] Thereafter the Act Book is silent on the outcome of the proceedings.

Although the visitors were empowered to deprive, this was an expedient used only five times against non-subscribers, and then always stressed in the most solemn manner in the text, to show the gravity of the judgement. In each such case a written definitive sentence was passed explaining their action, and as we should expect, it was the obstinate men in the highest positions who suffered this penalty: George Palmes (archdeacon of York and commissary of the Exchequer Court there), Roger Mershall (sub-dean of York), Thomas Sedgwick (Regius Professor of Divinity at Cambridge and vicar of Gainsford), Anthony Salvyn, (master of Sherburn Hospital and vicar-general of the Durham diocese), and William Carter (archdeacon of Northumberland).[53] At York, Pursglove and Downes, while rejecting the Prayer Book, accepted the supremacy and for the moment merely had their livings sequestrated by the Visitors. More surprisingly, if the record is correct, Thomas Robertson, dean of Durham who vigorously asserted papal supremacy, and five like-minded prebendaries,[54] only had their livings sequestrated. Those who refused to subscribe but did not assert papal supremacy in this way seem to have suffered exactly the same penalty. They included all save one of the remaining prebendaries and minor canons of Durham, though no trouble was encountered at Carlisle and little at Chester.[55]

Boyes of Otley was the first person recorded as taking a stand against subscription, and was bound over to report to the London commissioners at St Paul's.[56] Three other West Riding clergy followed his lead, and they were perhaps suspected of a local conspiracy to demur, for they were put in the charge of a royal constable who was to see them brought safely to York to appear again.[57] This is the only reference to formal arrests being made, and in other cases the recognisances were probably regarded as sufficient security. These bonds make interesting reading both because of the network of implied social relationships between the bonded man and his sureties, and because of the variation in the sums required of the different offenders. The Register of recognisances is not quite complete, since the Act Book itself records nine lesser clergy at Durham who collectively refused to subscribe and were bound over, yet they are not recorded in the Register. The original bonds were evidently returned to Chancery, but have now disappeared.[58] Of those registered only three out of twenty-eight refer to laymen, and none of these have anything to do with the supremacy. Indeed there is no sign that the laity were required to swear the oath of supremacy during this visitation.[59] As for the clergy, Gee's assertion[60] that the sums demanded were smaller for those who accepted the supremacy is quite wrong. At York, Pursglove accepted the supremacy and had to pledge £200, whilst Mershall rejected it and only pledged £100. At Durham Crawforth accepted, but pledged £200, the same sum as Cliffe and Nicholas Marley who both asserted papal supremacy. In fact little equity seems to have prevailed in the imposition of these penalties, save that the mere parish clergy only pledged £40:

Table of clerical recognisances (excluding sums pledged by sureties)

£ Pledged	Name
500	*Robertson
300	Bennet, *Dalton, *Tuttyn, *A. Salvyn, Carter, Sedgwick *Bullock, Hart
200	Palmes, Pursglove, Crawforth, S. Marley, *Cliffe, *N. Marley
100	Mershall, Downes, Whitehead
500	Boyes (for self plus sureties)
40	Jennings, More, Thompson, R. Salvyn

* asserted papal supremacy

By implication, the persons who stood surety in these bonds must have been present before the visitors, though this raises a question of procedure: were those refusing to subscribe warned at the first refusal that they would require sureties for appearance if they persisted? Personal friends and relatives figure largely among the sureties,[61] whilst notaries and lawyers occasionally appear.[62] Richard Goldthorpe, MP for York, was one of those standing surety for Palmes, and Oswald Wilkinson, keeper of York Castle also appears in the list.[63] Most of the remaining sureties are obscure country gentry and yeomen, and we must not assume that their religious sympathies were with the persons for whom they stood.

Sequestration was not always a penalty. Vacant livings had to be put in the charge of sequestrators so that they were not diminished during the interregnum before the advent of the next incumbent. The sequestrators, usually two in number, were often laymen appointed by the visitors from among the parishioners. They held office until their authority was formally revoked, but had to render account of their administration, perhaps to the rural dean, though this is never made explicit.[64]

It is equally true that deprivation was not always a penalty for a wilful offence. The incumbents of 28 livings, removed by Mary for having married under the Edwardian dispensation, pleaded for restitution before the visitors, and the sitting incumbents, who had committed no offence, were certainly deprived in 21 cases, and possibly in another two. One case ended when the plaintiff died, and four others did not come to a conclusion, for reasons unspecified. According to the terms of the commission, the dispossessed clergy became candidates for pensions in compensation, or for further preferment provided that they subscribed to the Elizabethan settlement. This is another field where research needs to be continued.

Procedure in causes of restitution necessarily had to be summary if the visitors were to cope with all the business scheduled. The party seeking restitution must have had to inform the registrar in advance, since the record clearly states that the adverse party was formally cited to attend by means of a written citation delivered to him personally or affixed to the door of his church. The citations, delivered by apparitors,[65] contained a brief statement of the petition for restitution, often in the form of articles: that the petitioner had been properly instituted, that he had been deprived solely for marriage, that he should therefore be restored, and so on. On the day of the hearing, the visitors first ascertained from the apparitor that the citation had been delivered. Either party in the cause might be represented by a proctor to save his personal attendance before the visitors, and if so the proctor was duly sworn and admitted, having shown his written proxy. John Stace appears to have been a resident proctor for the visitation, employable primarily by the petitioners and used by them in 14 out of the 28 cases. He appeared once for one adverse party,[66] but only when the petitioner was personally present. The adverse parties were rarely represented by proctors.[67] If the adverse party or his proctor failed to attend he was declared contumacious and the cause was adjourned for a further citation to be delivered, but eventually the visitors proceeded *in contumaciam* by allowing the contents of the original citation to be used as a summary petition, judging the petitioner's case on this alone, and finally passing sentence in his favour. Since the absent party was deprived by virtue of the judgement, there was no need for any separate penalty for his non-appearance. Where both parties appeared, the adverse party was asked to reply orally to the matter explained in the citation, and his *verbatim* answers were generally recorded in the Act Book. He was also allowed to submit *materiam exceptoriam* in writing, attempting to prove his own claim to the benefice, whereupon the petitioner would in turn be required to give answer. The judge was evidently able to ask supplementary questions, (for instance whether the petitioner's deprivation was indeed solely for marriage),[68] and witnesses were allowed to testify in support of either side. The letters of institution of both parties, and sometimes the record of the Marian deprivation from the diocesan court, were produced in evidence.

With all the other business of the visitation there is no wonder that these causes, to run their full course without prejudice to either party, had to be adjourned several times before the definitive sentence was reached. The protracted dispute over the rectory of Settrington was heard first at Auckland, next at Northwich a month later, and then transferred to the Court of Delegates because the adverse party, John Thornton, appealed against his deprivation. Another battle, for Kirkby in Cleveland, was fought at Durham, Newcastle and Chester before being referred to the London commissioners. These, however, were the extreme cases, and by contrast some of the sitting incumbents voluntarily yielded their benefices.[69]

The visitors were not concerned exclusively with removing the Marian clergy. A whole section of the Act Book[70] is devoted to the institution of clergy presented by patrons to vacant livings during the visitation. These are distinct from the vacancies reported in the main chronicle of the visitation and the church-wardens' presentments. The list gives also the names of patrons. Only 3 of the 33 vacancies were in the royal gift, so there was no opportunity for 'packing' the north with favourers of the reformed religion. Two of the commissioners, Harvey and Evers, each presented to one of the vacant livings. Thirty of the vacancies were in the diocese of York and 3 in Chester including Romaldkirk, a royal living held *in commendam* with the bishopric of Carlisle. The award of this living to John Best therefore foreshadowed his promotion to the episcopate. Bishop Tunstall was still in office when the visitors reached Northallerton, and he presented John Pearson to the vicarage of Osmotherly. This important section of the Act Book seems to have largely escaped Gee's attention.

THE VISITATION OF THE LAITY

Interspersed throughout the main chronicle of the visitation are reports of laymen presented to the visitors for judgement on moral offences. There is also a separate section[71] devoted to similar cases left over for the surrogates to hear. As the accused parties were present for judgement, presumably duly cited, we must assume that they had been delated by apparitors and churchwardens for being the most notorious offenders within their parishes. There was some selection involved, however, for when the wardens made their formal presentments many more moral offenders were included, yet not cited to appear for judgement, and it may be that they were simply referred to the next session of the local courts. There had probably not been sufficient time to apply for citations against all suspect parties, and it is certain that the visitors could not hear every potential case of this kind.[72]

Table of moral causes heard by the visitors:

Session at	no. of causes	folio
Southwell	1	5v
Blyth	1	8r
Pontefract	1	10r (promoted cause)
Halifax	1	12r
York	10	22r–24v
Northallerton	2	27v–28v
Newcastle	10	40r–41r
Alnwick	1	43v
Chester	9	137v–139r
Manchester	34	139r–146v

The large number of these causes in the Chester diocese is hard to explain, save for the extra time available there to prepare presentments. But there are other oddities in the figures. The parish of Whitgift alone accounted for half of the causes heard at York, and there were no such presentments at all for the diocese of Carlisle. Even the Chester figures are accounted for by a handful of parishes. Certainly no meaningful conclusions about the distribution of offenders can be drawn from these statistics, whose erratic nature is reflected among the moral presentments which did not proceed to judgement. Nor should we assume any 'purge' to be taking place in 1559, for cases of sexual incontinence, adultery, fornication, bigamy, incest and the like had dominated the church courts for centuries and their continued proliferation speaks volumes against the ineffectiveness of the courts' censures.[73]

Those presented for judgement offered remarkably little resistance, though two women were excommunicated for failing to attend.[74] Most of the accused openly admitted their offences. Indeed, one woman admitted to a bigamous marriage and produced the parish priest as a witness that he had officiated at both the happy ceremonies![75] In the face of such confessions, the visitors imposed a penance to be done on or before a specified date. Whilst there was some variation in the severity of the penalty according to the seriousness of the crime, the culprits were at least required to make a public declaration of their offences, (from a 'schedule' given to them by the court), either in church at service time or in some other public place where there were certain to be crowds.[76] Often if a man and woman were both judged culpable, the man did penance in the market place, the woman in the church. In addition they usually had to appear in church on one or more Sundays or feast days, barefoot, clad in the simplest woollen or linen garments (*lineis sive laneis*) to be seen to be contrite. The father of illegitimate children could be ordered to support them,[77] and offenders might further be required to pay a sum to the poor chest, or to give bread or clothes to the poor.[78]

A certificate that the penance had been performed was to be given to the rural dean or a named surrogate within a specified period.[79] Ralph Winnington of Stockport petitioned against doing penance in the parish church and was ordered instead to pay 6/8 in cash and 13/4 in bread to the poor,[80] which gives some idea of the relative value of humiliation. Having carried out their penance the couple were usually ordered never to meet again except in public places with at least two people present.

Sometimes a party tried to use an alleged prior contract of marriage as a means of evading punishment, but this did not always convince the visitors.[81] In one case, anxious to terminate their sitting and cut short the business, they allowed the curates of two parishes to witness a solemnization of the matrimony as an alternative to the culprits' doing penance.[82] The man had already fathered five illegitimate children by the same woman. Other entries confirm that marriage was an alternative to penance,[83] and if there was any doubt of the parties' good faith, the commissioners might demand sureties for the marriage.[84] Several charges were dismissed after the parties had pledged marriage by a given date.[85] John Rede of Stockport offered to marry his partner before Christmas, but was given the choice of marrying her before the end of three weeks or doing penance:[86] which option he adopted is not disclosed.

In the rare event of the accused denying the offence he was called on to purge himself by producing a number of his near neighbours to swear that he was telling the truth. Such compurgation could not be accomplished before the visitors left, so they assigned deputies to witness the act. At Northallerton it was left to the rural dean, who had to summon the parties.[87]

A major item on the agenda at each centre of visitation was the reception of presentments by churchwardens and representatives of each parish in answer to the Articles of enquiry circulated in advance. The returns were submitted in writing for the benefit of the registrar, and the negative returns which must have constituted a majority of the answers were ignored when the presentments were written up.

The Articles of 1559,[88] like those of 1547, though couched in the form of questions to be answered left no doubt of the crown's attitude on each topic mooted. They were, in fact, a clear policy blueprint for the new Protestant regime, and sought to measure the extent to which the demeanour of clergy and people fell short of the implied ideal which ran somewhat as follows. The clergy should be resident and diligent in their ministry, providing soundly educated deputies if they had to be absent from their benefices. They should have due dispensation if holding more than one benefice, and should not indulge in simony. Apart from the obvious duties of administering the sacraments and visiting the sick they should exhort their parishioners to be loyal to the queen, to attend only the parish church, to see their children educated in the Christian faith, to learn the Creed and the Lord's Prayer in English and read the Bible and *Paraphrases* if possible; to help the poor, to delate moral offenders and to protect the church goods. The clergy should also see that the services prescribed by the Prayer Book—and only those—were duly and decorously performed at suitable hours, with sermons and/or readings in English from the scriptures. Images, pilgrimages and all vestiges of superstitious practices should be abolished, and no masses could be tolerated, nor beads, nor seditious books. For their part the laity should co-operate in all these ventures, relieving the poor, reporting persons suspect of heresy or moral offences, or of hindering the ministry by abusing the clergy, causing disturbances during the sermon or keeping shops open during services as a rival attraction. Together, the clergy and people should keep the church fabric in repair and maintain the parish register and the poor box.

The wardens, then, were asked to report on the known failings of their parish under any of these headings, and a few statistics were also required, notably details of books burnt, of persons persecuted or dispossessed by Mary, of vacant livings and of the number of deaths in the year preceding the visitation.

Although the presentments which resulted, if we consider the province as a whole, touch on most of the Articles at some point, it is clear that no single parish conducted any really thorough scrutiny on every Article, and the returns tend to concentrate on a few aspects only. They must therefore be interpreted with great care. The large number of negative returns and omissions must also be remembered. It is impossible to believe that no parish in the city of Durham, and only one in the city of York could find anything to report, yet such would be the conclusion if the returns were taken at face value. By contrast, several areas were really thorough in their enquiries on moral offences, South Yorkshire, Tyneside and Cheshire producing the biggest crop of culprits, as in the moral causes discussed above.[89] Much seems to have depended upon the diligence and initiative of individual wardens and apparitors. The belief of the wardens of Clitheroe that common fornicators 'doo muche hurte in the contrye'[90] was by no means universally shared. No reliable statistics can therefore be produced to show the real distribution of particular offences, but it is instructive to note the nature of the offences reported.

Similar caution is needed in interpreting the comments on church fabric and goods. The whole story is certainly not revealed, and there are also exaggerations and inaccuracies in what is reported. 'Decay' might mean anything from a small hole in the roof to a state of collapse, and the frequency of reported dilapidations is not necessarily a cause for surprise or alarm. No true picture of the impact of Mary's attempts to restore the old religious practices emerges, though there are isolated reports of the retention of images by churches or individuals, as we should expect so soon after the accession of Elizabeth, before her Injunctions had had time to become widely accepted. Apart from the removal of fixtures and fittings of the old religion, the provision of books for the reformed liturgy was one of the greatest problems that had to be solved. It was a slow process, whatever deadlines the crown might impose, and the returns show several parishes admitting the lack of communion books, *Paraphrases* and the like, often pleading that their original copies of suitable books had been carted off in Mary's reign and burned. It was to be years rather than months before the parishes were fully equipped with the relevant service books.[91]

By comparison with the information against laymen for moral offences, complaints against the clergy were remarkably few in the presentments, though the wardens were given the opportunity to make any protest they felt needful. Again it was in the Chester diocese that most specific charges were made.

The speed and method of the visitation necessarily meant that the impressions gained were somewhat superficial, but the visitors had discovered enough to satisfy the crown's purpose of asserting its authority over the church and its courts, and advertising the requirements of the new settlement, which could in future be enforced by the church courts themselves, supplemented by the various ecclesiastical commissions. No formal instrument putting an end to the visitation has survived, though a draft among the State Papers[92] suggests that the registered

Acts and seals used by the visitors were to be returned to the Principal Secretary. If this was generally fulfilled, there is some cause for surprise that only the northern Act Book has survived among the State Papers. The northern visitors whose progress we have been tracing finished their work on the 26th October, those in the London-Ely-Norwich circuit at about the same time, and those in the south west before 2nd November.[93] Details for the other circuits are lacking, but it seems unlikely that the visitation anywhere continued beyond the end of the year.[94]

APPENDIX I

COPY OF A LETTER SENT TO ESTOFTE AND BROWNE

PRO, SP 12/6 fol. 30

Trusty and welbeloved we grete you well. And where as we have named & appoyncted you amonges others in commission for visitacion of our clergie in the circuite northwardes, we have thought good by thies our lettres to require you as one whom we have in this behalf specially chosen & reposed trust in touching the knowlege of the common lawes of this our realme, that at suche tyme as the rest of our commissioners of that circuite shall make their repaire in to the counties or diocese where you reside, and shall signifye to yow the tyme and place of there comming thither, you do applie yourself (other busynes set aparte) to joyne with them for the execution of our said commission and to assist them therin bothe with your advise & other wise the best you may. Wherunto as we doubt not but you will have regarde considering this our pleasure, so will we consider the same towardes you, as shalbe to your reasonable contentation accordingly geven etc.

On the back of the copy is written:

M. to Mr Browne & Mr Estofte lawyers xiiij° Augusti 1559.

APPENDIX II

THE OATH ADMINISTERED TO THE CLERGY DURING THE VISITATION

You shall sweare that you shalbe faigthfull and obedient unto the Quenes Majestie, her heires and successours, and to the uttermost of your power undrestanding and learning you shall mainteign and set furth all statutes and lawes and the religion received by her Grace or her heires or successours and the Iniunctions at this present time exhibited by her Grace, her officers or Commissioners, and that you shall make true presentment of all soch thinges as arr to be presented in this visitacion, so helpe you God and by the contentes of the booke.

(Text taken from *Lambeth Palace CM XIII, 58*)

APPENDIX III   *Table of Sessions*

Key to Commissioners and Surrogates:

Commissioners	Surrogates
1. Edwin Sandys	A. Bernard Gilpin
2. Henry Harvye	B. Edmund Scambler
3. Sir Thomas Gargrave	C. William Harrison
4. Sir Henry Gates	D. Sir John Foster
5. Christopher Estofte	E. Sir Edward Fyton
6. Lord Evers	F. William Morton
7. Sir Henry Percy	G. Thomas Percy
8. George Browne	

The Sessions:

Date		Place	Preacher	Visitors (key above)
AUGUST				
Tu	22	St Mary Nottingham	Sandys	1,2,3,4
Th	24	Southwell	—	1,2
F	25	Southwell (chapter house)	—	(1,2)
Sa	26	Blyth	Blunston	1,2
M	28	Pontefract	not named	1,2,4
*W	*30	Halifax	Pilkington	1,2,3
SEPTEMBER				
M	4	Otley	Sugden	1,2,3
Tu	5	York [probate only]	—	1,2
W	6	York (chapter house)	Sandys	1,2,3,4
Th	7	York: All Saints, Pavement	Pilkington	1,2,3,4
F	8	York: St Michael, Ouse Bridge	Scambler	1,2,3,4
		York (consistory)	—	1,2,3,4
Sa	9	York (consistory)	—	1,2,3,4
M	11	Hull	Sandys	1,2,4
Tu	12	Beverley	Scambler	1,2,4,5
Th	14	Malton	not named	1,2,4
Sa	16	Northallerton	Scambler	1,2,4
M	18	Richmond	Sandys	1,2,4
Tu	19	Richmond	—	1,2,4
Th	21	Auckland (*session begun in church but adjourned to bishop's palace chapel*)	Sewell	1,2,4
Sa	23	Durham (chapter house)	Sandys	1,2,4,6,7
		Durham: (house of William Todd)	—	A,B
M	25	Durham: St Nicholas	not named	1,2,4,6,7
Tu	26	Durham (chapter house)	—	(1,2,...)
W	27	Newcastle: St Nicholas	Sandys	1,2,4,6,7
Th	28	Newcastle: St Nicholas	—	(1,2,...)
Sa	30	Alnwick	Gilpin	A,C,D
OCTOBER				
Tu	3	Carlisle (chapter house)	Sandys	1,2,8
W	4	Carlisle (chapter house)	Sandys	1,2,8
Th	5	Carlisle (chapter house)	—	1,2,8
F	6	Penrith	Sewell	(1,2,8)
M	9	Kendal	Sandys	1,2,8
Tu	10	Kendal	—	(1,2,8)
W	11	Kendal	—	(1,2,8)
Th	12	Lancaster	Gilpin	1,2,8
M	16	Wigan	Pilkington	1,2,8
W	18	Manchester (parish church)	Sandys	1,2,8
Th	19	Manchester College (chapter house)	—	(1,2,8)
F	20	Northwich	Best	1,2,8
Sa	21	Northwich	—	(1,2,8)
		Northwich (at lodgings of commissaries)	—	(1,2,8)
Tu	24	Tarvin	Scambler	B,E,F
Th	26	Chester	Scambler	B,G

Later sessions dated in the text:

Sa	28	Doncaster (*session planned but not held*)		
Tu	31	Manchester		unnamed surrogates
DECEMBER				
M	18	Newcastle		

Notes:
* The text has Wednesday, the last day of August but this is an impossible date in 1559.
Where the Visitors are recorded in brackets, the text does not specify which ones were in attendance, and the entries here are suggestions only.

APPENDIX IV

Table of presentments concerning laity

The figures include the moral causes heard, and the wardens' presentments, but exclude returns for the cathedrals of York and Chester.

OFFENCE	DIOCESE			
	YORK	DURHAM	CARLISLE	CHESTER
illegitimate children	25	15	2	55
fornication, adultery	9	10	3	125
'not handling his wife as he ought'	–	–	–	1
incontinence	2	–	–	28
harbouring moral offender	2	–	–	–
bigamy	1	1	1	1
incest	–	–	–	1
'suspicious living'	2	1	–	–
separation	3	2	–	3
whoredom	–	1	–	1
marriage without banns read	1	–	–	1
marriage to third party after banns read	2	–	–	1
concubinage	–	1	–	12
noise in church	1	–	–	–
troubling curate during service	1	–	–	–
refusal to attend service	4	–	–	3
heresy, report of burning for	–	–	–	1
unreconciled excommunicate	–	–	–	1
blasphemy	–	–	–	2
witchcraft	1	–	–	–
'calculation and conjuring'	1	–	–	–
scolds	9	–	–	–
failure to implement will	6	–	–	–
failure to repay loan from poor box	2	–	–	–
debt owed to church	–	–	–	1
keeping alehouse open during service	–	1	–	–
drunkenness	–	–	–	5
swearing	–	–	–	1

APPENDIX V

Table of presentments concerning church and clergy

These figures exclude the cathedrals of York and Carlisle, and reports of vacancies given in the main chronicle of the visitation.

OFFENCE	YORK	DURHAM	CARLISLE	CHESTER
books destroyed, removed	11	4	–	4
no communion book	4	–	–	–
no register book	6	7	4	9
images not destroyed	1	1	–	–
images secretly kept	8	–	–	2
rood still intact	1	–	–	–
no pulpit	1	–	–	–
image used for pilgrimage	1	–	–	–
no poor box	–	3	1	1
no *Paraphrases*	–	–	1	–
windows unglazed	4	–	–	–
fabric in decay	25	9	1	17
vicarage in decay	8	1	–	3
prebends' houses in decay	2	–	–	–
churchyard in decay	–	–	–	2
vacant benefice	12	–	–	2
no curate	21	2	2	2
non-residence	6	2	–	14
no gifts to poor	2	–	–	8
no Creed etc. in English	1	–	–	1
no Epistle etc. in English	–	–	–	1
no services	1	–	–	2
no hospitality	–	1	–	9
simony				1
pluralism				1
drunkenness				2
failure to declare chapters				1
negligent reading				1
harbouring incontinent person				1

Notes on this edition

In this edition spelling follows the original throughout, but punctuation has been considerably modified. In particular, proper nouns begin with capitals, and many other letters capitalised by the scribe have been reduced to lower case (e.g. church, vicar). Placenames not immediately recognisable from the form given in the text are indexed under both old and modern forms. Square brackets are used to indicate or supply words omitted by the scribe, whilst italics have been used to indicate apparent scribal errors, or in longer sections to indicate *verbatim* English interpolations in otherwise Latin paragraphs.

Visitacio Regia actualiter exercita per venerabiles viros magistros Edwinum Sandis sacre theologie doctorem et Henricum Harvy legum doctorem, Commissarios inter alios generales ad visitandum tam in capite quam in membris Ecclesias Cathedrales Civitates et Dioceses Eboracenses, Dunelmenses, Carliolenses et Cestrenses, clerum et populum earundem virtute Commissionis regie amplectentis tenorem subscriptum rite et legitime aucthorizatum. In presencia Thome Percy notarij publici scribe et registrarij prefate visitacionis eadem etiam aucthoritate assignati, Anno Domini Millesimo quingentesimo quinquagesimo nono Regnique illustrissime in Christo Principis et domine nostre Domine Elizabethe, Dei Gratia Anglie, Francie et Hibernie regine, Fidei Defensoris, Anno Primo.

Elizabetha dei gratia Anglie, Francie et Hibernie Regina, fidei defensor: Charissimis consanguineis et consiliarijs nostris Francisco Comiti de Salope, Domino Presidenti consilij nostri in partibus borealibus, et Edwardo/Comiti de Darbia, ac charissimo consanguineo nostro Thome Comiti Northumbrie, Domino guardiano sive custodi marchiarum nostrarum de le Estmarche et Mydlemarche versus Scotiam, ac predilecto et fideli nostro Willelmo Domino Evers, ac etiam dilectis et fidelibus nostris Henrico Percy, Thome Gargrave, Jacobo Croftes et Henrico Gates militibus; necnon dilectis Edwino Sandis sacre theologie doctori, Henrico Harvy legum doctori, Ricardo Bowes, Cristophoro Estofte, Georgio Browne et Ricardo Kingismyll armigeris, salutem. **Quoniam** Deus populum suum Anglicanum imperio nostro subiecit, huius regalis suscepti muneris rationem perfecte reddere non possimus nisi veram religionem et syncerum numinis divini cultum in omnibus regni nostri partibus propagaverimus; **Nos** igitur, Regalis et absolute potestatis nostre nobis in hoc regno nostro commisse respectu, quoniam utrumque regni nostri statum tam ecclesiasticum quam laicum visitare et certas pietatis ac virtutis regulas illis prescribere constituimus prefatos Franciscum Comitem de Sallope, Edwardum Comitem de Darbia, Thomam Comitem Northumbrie, Willelmum Dominum Evers, Henricum Percy; Thomam Gargrave, Jacobum Croftes, Henricum Gates, milites; Edwinum Sandis, Henricum Harvy, Ricardo Bowes,[1] Christophoro Estofte, Georgio Browne et Ricardo Kingismyll armigeri, ad infrascripta vice nomine et aucthoritate nostris exequendum vos quatuor tres aut duo vestrum ad minimum deputamus et substituimus; **Ad** visitandum igitur tam in capite quam in membris Ecclesias Cathedrales, Civitates et Dioceses Eboracenses, Dunelmenses, Carliolenses et Cestrenses, necnon quascunque alias collegiatas, parochiales et prebendales ecclesias ac loca alia ecclesiastica quecunque tam exempta quam non exempta in et per easdem Civitates et Dioceses ubilibet constituta; clerumque et populum earundem in eijsdem degentem sive residentem, deque statu ecclesiarum et locorum huiusmodi, necnon vita moribus et conversatione ac etiam qualitatibus personarum in ecclesijs et

1

locis predictis degentium sive ministrantium modis omnibus quibus id melius
aut efficatius poteritis inquirendum et/investigandum; criminosos ac suscepte
religionis subscribere obstinate et peremptorie recusantes vel quocunque alio
modo delinquentes atque culpabiles condignis penis etiam usque ad beneficiorum
dignitatum sive officiorum suorum privationem, fructuum ve redituum et pro-
ventuum ecclesiarum et locorum quibus presunt sequestrationem vel quamcunque
aliam congruam et competentem cohertionem inclusive puniendum et corrigen-
dum; atque ad probatiores vivendi mores modis omnibus quibus id melius et
efficatius poteritis reducendum; **Testamenta** quorumcunque defunctorum infra
loca predicta decedentium probandum approbandum et insinuandum; administrationesque bonorum eorundem executoribus in eijsdem testamentis nominatis
committendum, administrationesque insuper ac sequestrationes bonorum abin-
testate decedentium in debita iuris forma expediendum concedendum et
committendum; compota quoque tam executorum quam administratorum et
sequestratorum quorumcunque recipiendum examinandum et admittendum, ac
insuper eosdem executores administratores et sequestratores omnes et singulos
acquietandum relaxandum et finaliter dimittendum; **Causasque** instanciarum
quascunque examinandum et finaliter terminandum, contumaces autem et rebelles
cuiuscunque condicionis sive status fuerint si quos inveneritis tam per censuras
ecclesiasticas quam personarum apprehensionem et incarcerationem ac recog-
nitionum acceptionem ac quecunque alia iuris regni nostri remedia compescen-
dum; Necnon Iniunctiones presentibus annexas[2] personis in eijsdem nominatis
nomine nostro tradendum, aliasque Iniunctiones congruas et oportunas vice et
aucthoritate nostris eis indicendum et assignandum; penasque convenientes in
earum violatores infligendum et irrogandum; **Ecclesias** etiam et alia loca dimissa
vacare et pro vacantibus habenda fore decernendum et declarandum, pentiones
que legitimas congruas et competentes cedentibus vel resignantibus huiusmodi
assignandum et limitandum; **Presentatos** quoque ad beneficia ecclesiastica que-

cunque infra Civitates Ecclesias aut Dioceses/predictas constitutas durante
visitacione nostra huiusmodi si habiles fuerint et idonei ad eadem admittendum
ac in et de eijsdem instituendum et investiendum cum suis iuribus et pertinentijs
universis, eosque in realem actualem et corporalem possessionem eorundem
inducendum et induci faciendum atque mandandum; **Necnon** clericorum et bene-
ficiatorum quorumcunque tam pro ordinibus quam beneficijs per eos adeptis
litteras et instrumenta exigendum et recipiendum eaque diligenter examinandum
et discutiendum, et quos non sufficienter munitos in ea parte comperitis ab officio
dimittendum[3] et pro sic non munitis declarandum et pronunciandum; Synodos
quoque et capitula tam generalia quam specialia cleri et populi huiusmodi pro
executione premissorum aut reformatione quacunque faciendum et convocandum;
Procurationes et Synodalia ratione huius nostr*i* visitacionis debita petendum
exigendum et levandum, ac etiam non solventes aut solvere recusantes per
censuras ecclesiasticas compellendum cohercendum et cogendum; **Necnon**
contionandi potestatem huiusmodi personis concedendum quas ad hoc divinum
munus suscipiendum aptas esse indicaveritis. **Incarceratos** et vinculis commissos
ob religionis causam antea licet nulliter condempnatos causis incarcerationis et
condempnationis huiusmodi prius examinatis et plenarie discussis examinandum

discutiendum ac in integrum iusticia id suadente restituendum deliberandum et extra prisonam dimittendum; **Necnon** causas deprivationum examinandum ac contra statuta et ordinationes huius regni nostri Anglie vel iuris ecclesiastici ordinem deprivatos restituendum; **Ac** omnia et singula alia que circa huiusmodi visitacionis seu reformationis negocium/necessaria fuerint seu quomodolibet *f.3r.* oportuna etiam si verba magis specialia de se exigunt et requirunt faciendum et expediendum, **vobis** tribus aut duobus vestrum ut prefertur de quorum eminenti doctrina morumque et consilij gravitate ac in rebus gerendis fide et industria plurimum confidimus vices nostras committimus ac plenam in Domino, tenore presentium, concedimus facultatem cum cuiuslibet congrue et legitime co-her*titi*onis potestate; **Et** preterea certos viros prudentes ac pios assignandi et nominandi per quos de statu rerum instruemini et quorum opera presentes utemini in omnibus causis ad hanc visitacionem nostram spectantibus quantum vobis convenire videbitur. Idem viri a vobis commissarijs assignati et nominati plenam potestatem habebunt etiam post commissionis decessum et post finitum visit-acionis tempus de omnibus articulis ordinibus et institutis eiusdem visitacionis inquirendi; et violatores eorum cuiuscunque condicionis fuerint conveniendi et examinandi; et omnes querelas quatenus ullum impedimentum aut offentionem nostre visitacionis continebunt accipiendi et audiendi; et huiusmodi personas offentiones et querelas Commissarijs nostris Londini residentibus et ad ecclesias-ticarum rerum reformationem designati presentabunt et exhibebunt illis vijs et modis quibus hoc convenientissime videbunt fieri posse; **Mandantes** omnibus et singulis maioribus vicecomitibus Iusticiarijs ac quibuscunque alijs officiarijs ministris et subditis nostris quatenus vobis in et circa premissorum executionem effectualiter assistant auxilientur et suffragentur./**Ut** insuper sagacitatis diligentie *f.3v.* factorumque vestrorum omnium evidens et perpetuum specimen nobis posterisque nostris remaneat, inventaque et invenienda pro recordatorum defectu debitam reformationem correctionem ve non subterfugiant ante memorie prolabantur, Nos suprema ac regali aucthoritate nostra predicta dilectos et fideles subditos nostros Thomam Percy et Johannem Hoges et eorum deputatos per commissarios nostros approbandos notarios publicos preantea legitime existentes actorum in-strumentorum decretorum sententiarum iudiciorum censurarum ceterorumque omnium et singulorum que per vos vestrum ve aliquem in visitacione hac nostra regia peragentur iudicabuntur decernentur fient ferentur et pronunciabuntur scribas et registrarios nostros publicos et principales coniunctim et divisim ordi-navimus nominavimus et constituimus, eisque officium et officia registrarij et Scribe nostri publici cum omnibus officia predicta tangentibus eorumque depu-tatis per dictos commissarios approbandis coniunctim et divisim damus depu-tamus assignamus et decernimus per presentes. **In cuius** rei testimonium has litteras nostras fieri fecimus patentes. Teste me ipsa apud Westmonasterium, vicesimo quarto die Junij Anno Regni nostri primo.

In ecclesia parochiali Beate Marie ville de Notyngham, Ebor' diocesis, *f.4r.* die martis viz. vicesimo secundo die mensis Augusti Anno Domini Millesimo quingentesimo quinquagesimo nono, Regnique illustrissime domine nostre Domine Elizabethe Dei Gratia Anglie, Francie et Hibernie Regine, Fidei Defensoris, Primo. **Quibus die et loco**, finitis precibus expositoque ad populum sacro Dei verbo per eximium virum magistrum Edwinum Sandis sacre Theologie doctorem, prefatus Edwinus unacum Thoma Gargrave, Henrico Gates militibus, et Henrico Harvye legum doctore, cancello eiusdem ecclesie ad locum decenter ornatum simul adivere eijsdemque ibidem sedentibus Litteras Commissionales prelibate Illustrissime domine nostre Regine Sigillo magno communitas omni cum humilitate reverentia pariter et obedientia condignis receperunt, ac easdem per Thomam Percy notarium publicum scribam et registrarium antedictum publice legi fecerunt. Et incontinenti onus executionis earundem ob reverentiam et honorem tante Principis committentis assumpserunt. Et secundum vim formam et effectum earundem ad omnem iuris effectum procedendum fore proque eorum iurisdictione iudicialiter decreverunt. **Deinde** personaliter constitutus quidam magister Robertus Cressye Officialis Archidiaconi Notyngham introduxit mandatum citatorium sibi alias ex parte prefate Domine Regine pro clero et populo decanatum de Notingham [. . .][4] movendum atque citandum visitacionem Regiam adtunc subituri unacum certificatorio de executione &c et nominibus et cognominibus omnium et singulorum in ea parte monitorum, ac desuper facta fide/de iure requisita omnes citatos et monitos nominatim publice preconizari fecerunt Commissarij antedicti. **Omnes** etiam monitos preconizatos et non comparentes pronunciaverunt contumaces &c. **Subinde** intimata habitaque ad populum docta quadam exhortatione per prelibatum magistrum Edwinum Sandis omnes laicos viz. parochianos et Iconomos cuiuslibet parochie tactis prius sacrosanctis Dei Evangelis monuerunt ut hora secunda a prandio detectiones et responsiones suas super Articulis inquisicionis eis unacum Iniunctionibus regijs adtunc lectis [et datis][5] in scriptis exhibeant &c.

f.4v.

Prefati quoque Domini Commissarij rectores vicarios capellanos curatos et non curatos presentes omnes et singulos firmiter iniungendo monuerunt quod ipsi hora et loco predictis personaliter compareant litteras ordinum dispensacionis et cetera instrumenta sua prout singula singulos concernant realiter exhibituri ulteriusque acturi quod iusticia et equitatis ratio suadebunt &c. **Hora** adveniente Iconomi et parochiani predicti billas detectionum unacum inventarijs bonorum ecclesiarum suarum exhibuerunt &c. **Deinde** clericorum et ecclesiasticorum personarum statu, doctrina et conversatione diligentem fecerunt examinationem unumquenque per se examinandum litteris ordinum et ceteris munimentis per illos exhibitis &c.

Adbolton

Eijsdem die et loco prefati Domini Commissarij super detectione quod ecclesia parochialis de Adbolton dicte Ebor' diocesis est curato destituta, fructus decimas et cetera emolumenta eiusdem ecclesie sequestranda fore decreverunt et sequestrandi potestatem Willelmo Lee et Thome Claye parochianis ibidem commiserunt &c.

f.5r.

In ecclesia collegiata de Sowthwell, Ebor' diocesis, die jovis viz.

xxiiij*to* die mensis Augusti Anno Domini Millesimo quingentesimo quinquagesimo nono.

Quibus die et loco Henricus Gates miles, Edwinus Sandis sacre Theologie doctor et Henricus Harvye legum doctor Commissarij antedicti iudicialiter sedentes clerum et populum decanatus de Newarke, [. . .]⁶ sub modo et forma prius descriptis actualiter visitaverunt &c.

Inter alia ubi detectum est quod ecclesia de Wynthorpe dicte Ebor' diocesis remansit et inpresenti remanet curato destituta &c.

Prefati Domini Commissarij fructus decimas et cetera emolumenta dicte ecclesie sequestranda fore decreverunt. Et vices suas ac potestatem sequestrandi dilectis Joanni Taverham⁷ clerico et Willelmo Parke commiserunt &c.

     Wynthorpe

Simili modo detectum est quod ecclesia vicarie de Edynglee Ebor' diocesis curato sit destituta. **Prefati** igitur Domini Commissarij fructus decimas et emolumenta dicte vicarie iuste sequestranda fore decernentes potestatem sequestrandi Joanni Sye et Ricardo Leeke de eadem &c commiserunt, prestita cautione de compoto habendo &c.

     Edinglee

     f.5v.

Eijsdem die et loco prefati Domini Commissarij fructus decimas et cetera emolumenta vicarie ecclesie parochialis de Westdrayton iam vacantis et curato destitute sequestraverunt, committentes sequestrationem Ricardo Sympson et Michaeli Swyfte de eadem, prestita cautione &c.

     Draiton

Detectum est quod Edwardus Baker de Wynthorpe husbondman dicte Ebor' diocesis vixit in adulterio cum quadam Margareta Brewer, **unde** vir evocatus in iudicium et obiecto sibi crimine fatebatur. Et predicti Domini Commissarij iniunxerunt sibi penitentiam publicam peragendam in foro de Newarke mercurij proximo nudis pedibus et capite lineis quoque sive laneis &c. Et simili modo in ecclesia parochiali de Newarke die dominica proxime sequente tempore Divinorum. Quodque plane et distincte, palam et publice, contenta in scedula sibi tradita ac continente factum predictum declarabit &c.⁸

     Baker

In domo capitulari Collegij Beate Marie de Sowthwell, Ebor' diocesis, die veneris viz. xxv*to* die mensis Augusti Anno Domini Millesimo quingentesimo quinquagesimo nono.

     f.6r.

Quibus die et loco prelibati Domini Commissarij dictum collegium tam in capite quam in membris, data prius exhortatione actualiter visitaverunt. Receptoque certificatorio de executione mandati per predictum magistrum Robertum Cressye exhibito prefati Domini Commissarij iudicialiter sedentes omnes prebendarios ceterosque dicti collegij ministros preconizari fecerunt &c. Omnesque citatos preconizatos et non comparentes pronunciaverunt contumaces, reservantes sibi penam &c.

6 THE ROYAL VISITATION OF 1559

Oxton **Robertus** Episcopus[9] suffraganeus Hullensis prebendarius de Oxton preconizatus non comparuit personaliter. Sed per Robertum Cressye exhibentem procuratorium litteratorium pro eodem &c.

Palice Hall **Galfridus** Downes prebendarius de Palyce Hall in Norwell comparuit per Robertum Salvyn clericum et non aliter.

Doneham **Joannes** Rokesbye legum doctor prebendarius de Doneham comparuit per magistrum Robertum Cressye et non aliter.

f.6v.
Northmuskham **Georgius** Palmes prebendarius de Northmuskham comparuit per Robertum Cressye.

Oxton **Henricus** Harvye[10] legum doctor prebendarius de Oxton personaliter.

Haluton **Willelmus** Mowse legum doctor prebendarius de Haluton nullo modo comparuit.

Norwell **Robertus** Cressye in legibus baccalaurius prebendarius tertie prebende in Norwell personaliter comparuit.

Normanton **Henricus** Bowell prebendarius de Normanton comparuit per Henricum Rabye litteratum et non aliter.

f.7r.
Woodborowe **Georgius** Dudeley clericus prebendarius de Woodborowe nullo modo comparuit.

Southmuskham **Willelmus** Taylor clericus prebendarius de Sowthmuskeham comparuit per Henricum Rabye litteratum et non aliter.

Rapton **Robertus** Drurye clericus prebendarius de Rapton comparuit personaliter.

Northleverton **Georgius** Lambe prebendarius de Northleverton nullo modo comparuit.

Eton **Robertus** Snell prebendarius de Eton[11]

Sacrist **Ricardus** Hopkynes prebendarius de Sacrist' comparuit personaliter.

f.7v.
Beckingham **Willelmus** Saxye clericus prebendarius prebende de Beckingham nullo modo comparuit.

Cristophorus Pennell ⎫
Franciscus Hall ⎬ chorales personaliter comparuerunt.
Ricardus Harryson ⎪
Edmundus Robinson ⎭

Overhall **Thomas** Wilson prebendarius de Overhall in Norwell comparuit per magistrum Robertum Cressye.

Visitacionis negocio solempniter peracto, idem Domini Commissarij preter communes, certas speciales Iniunctiones tradiderunt collegium predictum solum concernentes &c.

In ecclesia parochiali de Blythe, Ebor' diocesis, die Sabbati viz. vicesimo sexto die mensis Augusti Anno Domini Millesimo v^C quinquagesimo nono. f.8r.

Quibus die et loco Henricus Gates Miles, Edwinus Sandis sacre theologie doctor et Henricus Harvye legum doctor, Commissarij antedicti, finitis precibus et habita contionatione per magistrum Robertum Blunston[12] artium magistrum verbum Dei predicantem, iudicialiter sedentes et more solito procedentes, clerum et populum decanatuum de Retforde et Laneham actualiter visitaverunt.

Die et Loco predictis, coram prefatis Dominis Commissarijs personaliter comparuit quidam Dominus Hugo Wight clericus, et in presencia Alveredi Whitton et Joanne eius pretense uxoris conventorum in iudicio verbo allegavit quod ipse prefatus Hugo Wighte et dicta Joanna liberi et immunes ab omni contractu matrimoniali matrimonium verum purum et legitimum per verba de presenti mutuum eorum consensum exprimentia rite et legitime contraxerunt. Illudque postmodum erat in facie ecclesie solempnizatum, viz. in ecclesia parochiali de Estdrayton Ebor' diocesis/inter divinorum solempnia quodam Domino Edwardo Harlynge curato ibidem ad tunc ministrante circiter annos septem ultimos preteritos tempore recolendissime memorie Edwardi sexti Regis &c. Quodque post solempnizationem huiusmodi matrimonij tanquam vir et uxor simul cohabitaverunt iura coniugalia adinvicem exercentes. Quodque hoc sit notarium et manifestum ac desuper labore [famatum],[13] unde facta fide petit iusticiam &c. **Deinde** predicta Joanna publice per Dominos Commissarios interrogata fatebatur contenta allegationis predicte in presencia Alveredi Whitton mariti sui pretensi antedicti asserentis se nuptum prefate Joanne in ecclesia parochiali de Estdrayton predicte circiter tres annos preteritos et non antea, asserentis etiam quod ex eadem citra solempnizationem &c suscitabat duos proles &c. f.8v.

Postea prefatus Dominus Hugo Wighte ad probandum allegationem suam predictam in presenciam partium predictarum produxit in testes Dominum Edwardum Harlyng vicarium de Estdraiton et Thomam Mynnet de eadem parochia, quos Domini ad eius peticionem admiserunt et iurari fecerunt de dicendo veritatem &c, eorumque depositiones sequuntur, sub hijs verbis –

Edwardus Harling predictus, etatis lxx annorum, libere condicionis &c, et in vim sui iuramenti dicit allegationem predicti Hugonis Wighte esse veram. Et reddit causam scientie sue, dicendo quod ipsemet erat presens et ministravit in primis nuptijs ut in allegatione habetur, vigilia sancte Luce Evangeliste circiter tempus allegatum per prefatum Dominum Hugonem; et quod simili/modo presens erat et ministravit in secundis nuptijs inter dictam Joannam et Alveredum Whitton in f.9r.

ecclesia parochiali predicta quodam die dominica circiter tres annos elapsos &c.

Thomas Mynnete etatis xl annorum libere condicionis, testis ut supra suo iuramento dicit allegationem predicti Domini Hugonis Wight continere in se veritatem, et reddens causam scientie sue dicit, Quod presens erat in ecclesia parochiali de Estdraiton circiter septem annos preteritos quando matrimonium erat solempnizatum inter dictum Hugonem et prefatam Joannam, et quod post solempnizationem huiusmodi ipse novit eos simul cohabitare et pro veris coniungibus reputari palam publice et notarie. Et quod ipse postea erat presens in dicta ecclesia parochiali quodam die dominico circiter tres annos elapsos quando viderat secundas nuptias celebrari &c.

Unde prefati Domini Commissarij rimato integro processu predicto firmiter iniunxerunt prefato Alveredo Whitton necnon et predicte Johanne quod ipsi amplius non conversentur &c.

Detectum est per parochianos de Stokume Ebor' diocesis quod vicarius de Draiton tenetur suis impensis invenire curatum apud Stokum continue residentem; quodque incuria prefati vicarij sunt curato destituti. Unde prelibatus vicarius ad iudicium evocatus et respondendo detectioni huiusmodi fatebatur quod ipse tenetur ad sustentationem curati ibidem et quod propter lennitatem fructuum non est/habilis ad sustendandum curatum ibidem, et seipsum deserviturum cure proprie ecclesie, in presencia parochianorum. **Unde** prelibati Domini Commissarij de et cum consensu partium assignaverunt ut vicarius per seipsum deserviat tam cure de Drayton quam cure de Stokum alterius vicibus aut illis vijs et modis quibus hoc fieri possit magis aptius, usque in festum Pasche proximum. Et quod ab eodem festo sustentabit apud Stokum curatum suis sumptibus iuxta tenorem compositionis in ea parte, hoc est ut diebus dominicis et festo Divina celebret, et quod administrare sacra et sacramentalia quotiens opus fuerit &c.

f.9v.

Fledborowe

Detectum est quod ecclesia parochialis de Fledborowe Ebor' diocesis relinquitur inofficiata et curato destituta, **Unde** fructus decimas et cetera emolumenta dicte ecclesie sequestranda fore dicti Domini Commissarij iudicialiter decreverunt; et aucthoritatem sequestrandi iuxta tenorem commissionis in ea parte concesse, Edwardo Bassocke de eadem commiserunt quousque duxerint revocandam &c.

f.10r.

In ecclesia parochiali de Pontefracte, Ebor' diocesis, die lune, viz. xxviij° die mensis Augusti Anno Domini Millesimo quingentesimo quinquagesimo nono.

Quibus die et loco, Henricus Gates miles, Edwinus Sandis sacre theologie doctor, et Henricus Harvye legum doctor, finitis precibus, peracto etiam sermone, actualiter visitaverunt more solito clerum et populum decanatuum de Doncaster et Pontefracte. Receptoque certificatorio de executione mandati citatorij pronunciaverunt omnes absentes monitos et preconizatos contumaces reservantes penam &c.

In causa matrimoniali et divortij mota per Aliciam Alexander viduam contra Willelmum Smythe et Elizabetham Sudburye, partes viz. Alicia Alexander et Willelmus Smyth personaliter preconizate; dicta Elizabetha quamvis citata non comparuit; Domini Commissarij pronunciaverunt contumacem et in penam sue contumacie excommunicanda fore &c. Deinde ex consensu partium commiserunt causam ulterius tractandam substitutis infra Archidiaconatum Notingham &c.

Super detectione exhibita per parochianos de Thorne Ebor' diocesis quod ecclesia ibidem inofficiata et destituta sit curato, prelibati Domini Commissarij omnes et singulas decimas fructus et emolumenta eiusdem sequestranda fore decreverunt; et potestatem sequestrandi commiserunt Edwardo Stere et Ricardo Brodbente, Iconomis dicte ecclesie, &c.

f.10v.
Thorn

Super detectione exhibita per parochianos de Champsall, Ebor' diocesis quod ecclesia ibidem vacata et destituta sit curato, omnes fructus &c vicarie ibidem sequestraverunt, committentes potestatem colligendi et sequestrandi Thome Uscrofte et Roberto Briggis de eadem &c.

Campsall

Super detectione exhibita per Iconomos et parochianos de Maltbye quod ecclesia vacata et destituta sit curato, omnes fructus et decimas eiusdem sequestranda fore decreverunt, sequestracionem quoque eorundem fructuum Joanni Persleye et Willelmo Lynley ac Joanni Sheppard, dicte ecclesie Iconomis, commiserunt &c.

Maltby

Super presentatione exhibita per Iconomos et parochianos de Darfild, viz. quod vicaria ibidem inpresenti vacata et quod destituta sit curato, prefati Domini Commissarij fructus dicte vicarie sequestraverunt; et eorundem custodiam et sequestrationem Joanni Hogleye, Thome Hogley et Willelmo Rawson commiserunt &c.

f.11r.
Darfild

(*f. 11v. is blank.*)

In ecclesia parochiali de Hallyfax, Ebor' diocesis, die mercurij viz. ultimo die mensis Augusti Anno Domini Millesimo quingentesimo quinquagesimo nono.

f.12r.

Quibus die et loco Thomas Gargrave miles, Edwinus Sandis sacre theologie doctor et Henricus Harvye legum doctor, Commissarij antedicti, post preces finitas, verbo dei ad populum exposito per egregium virum magistrum [Jacobum][14] Pilkington sacre theologie Baccalaurium cunctis alacriter ascultantibus, clerum et populum prefate parochie necnon et aliarum parochiarum decanatus de Pontefracte illuc assignatarum sub modo et forma prius descriptis actualiter visitaverunt. Omnesque absentes citatos preconizatos et non comparentes pronunciaverunt contumaces reservantes penam &c.

Super detectione et informatione Dominis Commissarijs datis, viz. quod Laurentius Awood et Agnes eius uxor absque legitima causa separatim in aliorum perniciosum exemplum vivunt, prefatis Laurentio et Agneti evocatis et presentibus in iudicio nullamque causam rationabilem in hac parte allegantibus, Domini Commissarij iniunxerunt quod simul vivant secundum Christi leges &c sub pena iuris.

f.12v. **Super** detectione exhibita per Iconomos et parochianos de Huddersfild, viz. quod ecclesia ibidem sit destituta curato, Domini Commissarij fructus et decimas dicte ecclesie sequestraverunt committentes custodiam et sequestrationem fructuum Thome Walton et Percivallo Broke parochianis ibidem &c.

f.13r. **In ecclesia parochiali** de Otteley, Ebor' diocesis, die lune quarto die mensis Septembris, Anno Domini Millesimo quingentesimo quinquagesimo nono.

Quibus die et loco Thomas Gargrave miles, Edwinus Sandis sacre Theologie doctor et Henricus Harvye legum doctor, Commissarij antedicti solempniter adiverunt ecclesiam. Et postquam erant preces finite magister Christophorus Sugden predicavit. Ac deinde prefati Domini Commissarij modo et forma consuetis ad visitacionem cleri et populi adtunc interessentium et ad subeundum visitacionem huiusmodi monitorum actualiter processerunt eosdemque visitantes. Et recepto certificatorio de executione mandati citatorij &c, omnes absentes monitos preconizatos et nullo modo comparentes idem Domini Commissarij pronunciaverunt *omnes absentes* contumaces, reservantes sibi penam &c.

Boies **Deinde** Willelmus Boyes clericus rector de Giesleye, Ebor' diocesis, requisitus per Dominos Commissarios ut Suscepte Religioni subscribat expresse et obstinate recusavit. **Unde** prelibati Domini Commissarij primo omnes fructus decimas et f.13v. cetera emolumenta dicte rectorie de Giesley sequestranda fore/decreverunt. Ac deinde per eosdem Commissarios capta est recognitio[15] in qua unacum suis fideiussoribus in quingentis libris pro sua ulteriori comparicione quandocumque ad id monitus sive requisitus fuerat ut per eandem recognitionem certificatam in cancellariam Domine nostre Regine plenius liquet &c.

Predicitis die et loco coram prefatis Commissarijs personaliter comparuit quidam Robertus Woode clericus vicarius de Oteley.
Cristophorus Mygley vicarius de Kyldwicke etiam comparuit.
Alexander Jennynes clericus vicarius de Bingley simili modo comparuit &c.
Quos prefati Domini Commissarij iteratis vicibus requisiverunt Suscepte religioni subscribere. **Ipsi** tamen et eorum quilibet peremptorie et obstinate recusabant &c. Preterea supremitatem illustrissime Domine Regine denegaverunt. **Unde** prefati

Domini Commissarij primo omnes et singulos fructus decimas et emolumenta predictarum ecclesiarum sequestranda fore sub tutoque custodienda sequestro decreverunt. **Deinde** accersito constabulario prefate Domine Regine, prefatos Robertum Woode, Cristophorum Mygley/et Alexandrum Gennynes salve custodie dicti constabularij commiserunt, mandantes ei ex parte Domine nostre Regine ut eos adducat civitatem Ebor' ita ut personaliter compareant coram prefatis Dominis Commissarijs die jovis proximo in loco ubi infra dictam civitatem tunc fuerint &c.[16]

f.14r.

(f. 14v. is blank.)

f.15r.
Ecclesia Ebor'

> **In ecclesia metropolitica Eboracensi**[17] loco et domo capituli ibidem, die mercurij viz. sexto die mensis Septembris Anno Domini Millesimo quingentesimo quinquagesimo nono.

Quibus die et loco, permagna hominum multitudine congregata, sepedictus magister Edwinus Sandis sincere pariter et docte Iesu Christi verbum predicavit ad consolamen et gaudium Christi doctrinam vere amplectentem ac in terrorem omnium qui Christo pertinaciter adversantur.

Deinde Thomas Gargrave, Henricus Gates milites, Edwinus Sandis sacre Theologie doctor, et Henricus Harvye legum doctor, Commissarij antedicti locum in domo Capituli iudicialem adiverunt, ac Commissione Regia publice et solempniter lecta, introductoque certificatorio de executione mandati regij citatorij, ad visitationem huiusmodi expediendum processerunt. Omnesque absentes monitos preconizatos et nullo modo comparentes pronunciaverunt contumaces, reservantes sibi penam &c.

> Subinde continuata est per eos hec visitacio usque in horam secundam post meridiem hoc in loco, et sic de tempore in tempus prout eis visum fuerit necessarium &c.

Hora secunda predicta adveniente, dictis Dominis Commissarijs iudicialiter sedentibus, Magister Joannes Rokisbye legum doctor nomine totius Capituli exhibuit fundationem indotationem et Statuta prefate ecclesie. Quibus inspectis et examinatis, Domini Commissarij ad visitacionis negocium expediendum processerunt ut sequitur.

f.15v.

Primo preconizari fecerunt decanum et omnes ecclesie prebendarios &c. Deinde personaliter interessentibus prebendarijs Domini Commissarij Articulos suscepte Religionis per registrarium antedictum distincte legi mandaverunt. Eijsdemque ipsis audientibus sic lectis, Magistrum Joannem Rokeby predictum super eijsdem articulis examinaverunt. Et ipse bono spiritu ductus ut pauci arbitrantur voluntarie subscripsit &c. Articuli hunc habent tenorem:
We the clargie of the Cathedrall and Metropoliticall churche of Yorke whose

f.16r.

names ar subscribed, doo humblye confesse and acknowledge the restorynge
ageyne of the Auncyent iurisdiction over the State ecclesiasticall and spirituall to
the Crowne of this Realme. **And** thoblishing of all forreyn powre repugnaunte to
the same according to *an/therof* made in the late parlyament begon at Westminster the xxiij*th* day of Januarye in the first yere of the Reigne of our sover-
eigne Lady Quene Elizabeth, and ther contynued and kepte untill the viij*th* day
of Maye next after ensuynge. **We** confesse also and acknowledge thadmyny-
stracion of the sacramentis, the use and ordre of divyn sarvyce in manner and
forme as it is set forth in the boke commonly called the Boke of commen Prayer
&c established also by the same Acte, and thorders and Rules conteyned in the
Iniunctions geven by the Quenes Majestie and exhibited unto us in this present
visitacion to be according to the true worde of God and agreeable to the doc-
tryne and use of the prymative churche. **In** witnesse wherof and that the premisses
be trewe we have unfeynedly hereunto subscribed our names.

Downes

Galfridus Downes sacre theologie doctor, prebendarius dicte ecclesie requisitus
per Dominos Commissarios dictis Articulis subscribere expresse recusavit. **Postea**
iterum hoc est secundo requisitus etiam recusavit. **Et** Domini Commissarij
monuerunt ipsum ad comparendum hoc loco in crastino hora septima ante
meridiem. Qua adveniente hora, comparuit prefatus Galfridus coram Dominis

f.16v.

Commissarijs iudicialiter sedentibus,/et iterum hoc tertio monitus et requisitus ut
subscribat &c obstinate et peremptorie recusavit. Unde prefati Domini Commissarij monuerunt ipsum ad personaliter comparendum hoc in loco die Sabbati
proximo hora septima ante meridiem. Quibus die et hora advenientibus, prefati
Domini Commissarij ex habundanti gratia denuo prefatum Galfridum ad subscribendum monuerunt. Qui non consentiens posteriori parti articulorum[18]
recusavit ut prius. Unde prius per Dominos Commissarios ab eodem Galfrido et
suis fideiussoribus capta est recognitio[19] in qua ipse Galfridus obligatus in
centum libris et fideiussores in centum marcis cum condicione quod personaliter
comparebit &c quandocunque fuerit evocatus ut ex eadem recognitione certificata
in cancellariam liquebit. **Deinde** omnes et singulos fructus decimas et emolumenta
tam sue prebende quam dignitatum et ceterorum beneficiorum *iudicialiter
decreverunt.*[20]

Robertus Purseglove alias dictus Episcopus suffraganeus de Hull', prebendarius
antedictus, per Dominos Commissarios requisitus articulis predictis subscribere,
ipse expresse recusavit. **Postea** iterum hoc est secundo interrogatus monitus et
requisitus ut subscribat, ipse etiam denegavit. Tunc Domini Commissarij monuerunt ipsum ad comparendum hora septima mane, hoc in loco voluntatem eorum
auditurum. **Qua** hora adveniente prefati Domini Commissarij iudicialiter sedentes

f.17r.

prefatum Robertum iterum hoc tertio interrogaverunt et monuerunt/ut subscribat
articulis &c, ipse obstinate et peremptorie recusavit. **Unde** prefati Domini Commissarij monuerunt eum quod compareat personaliter coram ipsis hoc in loco
die Sabbati proximo hora septima mane. **Dictis** die hora et loco prefati Domini
Commissarij iudicialiter sedentes ex eorum habundanti gratia interrogaverunt prelibatum Robertum an tandem velit subscribere, ipse ut prius recusavit et precipue

posteriori parti &c. **Unde** Domini Commissarij primo accepta recognitione[21] in qua ipse prefatus Robertus recognovit se debere Domine nostre Regine ducentas libras et quilibet fideiussorum suorum recognovit se debere centum libras &c pro sua comparicione quandocunque evocatus fuerit &c, ut per eandem recognitionem certificatam in cancellariam plenius liquet &c. Deinde omnes fructus decimas et cetera emolumenta tam prebende quam dignitatum et beneficiorum suorum omnium et singulorum sequestranda fore decreverunt et sequestraverunt &c.

Georgius Palmes legum doctor prebendarius dicte ecclesie monitus et requisitus ut articulis suscepte religionis subscribat, ipse re et verbo recusavit. Deinde iterum hoc est secundo interrogatus monitus et requisitus ut supra ipse expresse denegavit. Tunc predicti Domini Commissarij monuerunt ipsum ad comparendum mane hora septima ad audiendum eorum voluntatem./**Dicta** septima hora adveniente Domini Commissarij loco predicto iudicialiter sedentes iterum hoc est tertio monuerunt et requisiverunt prefatum Georgium Palmes presentem in iudicio ad subscribendum articulis, ipse vero obstinate et peremptorie recusavit. **Unde** peremptorie monuerunt ipsum ad comparendum hoc in loco die Sabbati proximo hora septima mane. **Quibus** die et hora Domini Commissarij iudicialiter sedentes ex eorum habundanti gratia interrogaverunt dictum Georgium Palmes an tunc subscribere velit. Ipse vero ut prius obstinate recusavit, consentiens nulli parti articulorum. **Deinde** per eosdem Commissarios accepta recognitione[22] in qua prefatus Georgius Palmes recognovit se debere Domine Regine ducentas libras et quilibet fideiussorum recognovit se debere centum libras cum condicione quod ipse prefatus Georgius personaliter ulterius comparebit &c quandocunque ad id monitus et evocatus fuerit &c. **Subinde** prefati Domini Commissarij adhuc iudicialiter sedentes eundem Georgium Palmes obstinatum et recusantem tam a prebenda sua quam inpresenti obtinet in hac ecclesia cathedrali Ebor' quam ceteris suis dignitatibus prebendarijs rectorijs vicarijs et officijs suis ecclesiasticis quibuscunque per eorum Sententiam diffinitivam deprivaverunt et amoverunt in scriptis &c.

f.17v.

Rogerus Mershall clericus ac prebendarius dicte ecclesie monitus et requisitus ut Articulis suscepte Religionis subscribat, ipse vero peremptorie recusavit. **Postea** vero prefatus Rogerus iterum requisitus recusavit. **Unde** prefati Domini Commissarij monuerunt ipsum ad comparendum hora septima mane &c./Dicta hora septima adveniente predicti Domini Commissarij loco predicto iudicialiter sedentes prelibatum Rogerum Mershall presentem iterum hoc est tertio interrogaverunt et requisiverunt ut subscribat, ipse vero peremptorie et obstinate recusavit. **Unde** prefati Domini Commissarij monuerunt ipsum ad comparendum hoc in loco die Sabbati proximo hora septima &c. **Quibus** die et loco Domini Commissarij iudicialiter sedentes ex habundanti gratia iterum interrogaverunt ipsum Rogerum presentem an subscribere velit, ipse vero obstinate ut prius recusavit non consentiens alicui parti Articulorum &c. Tunc Domini Commissarij accepta prius recognitione[23] in qua ipse Rogerus recognovit se debere Domine nostre Regine centum marcas[24] et Thomas Clarke eius fideiussor recog-

f.18r.

novit se debere quadraginta libras &c, cum condicione quod ipse personaliter comparebit quandocunque ad id fuerat monitus seu requisitus ut per eandem recognitionem certificatam in cancellariam liquebit, contra prefatum Rogerum procedentes eundem tam a succentoria quam in ecclesia Ebor' inpresenti obtinet et possidet quam ceteris suis dignitatibus prebendis rectorijs vicarijs et officijs suis ecclesiasticis quibuscunque per Sententiam diffinitivam quam in scriptis tulerunt Christi nomine invocato deprivaverunt et amova*v*erunt, illa [etiam][25] vacari et pro vacantibus habenda fore decreverunt &c.

f.18v.

Robertus Babthorpe sacre Theologie doctor prebendarius dicte ecclesie requisitus per Dominos Commissarios ut subscribat articulis Religionis, ipse voluntarie ut apparuit consentiens supremitati &c, petijt sibi concedi tempus deliberandi super ceteris contentis in Articulis. **Et** Domini Commissarij assignaverunt sibi diem veneris proximum. Quo die advenienti voluntarie ut opinatur subscripsit.

Georgius Williamson artium magistrum prebendarius dicte ecclesie per Dominos Commissarios monitus et requisitus ut Articulis Religionis subscribat, ipse consentiens prime parti, viz. supremitati, humiliter petijt sibi tempus deliberandi concedi super ceteris contentis. Unde Domini Commissarij assignaverunt sibi diem veneris proximum sequentem. Quo die libenter subscripsit.

Ricardus Drewry clericus prebendarius dicte ecclesie personaliter voluntarie subscripsit &c.

Joannes Boxall prebendarius de Stillington in eadem ecclesia per procuratorem comparuit et non aliter.

f.19r.

Willelmus Taylor clericus prebendarius de Fenton comparuit per procuratorem et non aliter.

Mauritius Clennocke prebendarius dicte ecclesie comparuit per procuratorem.

Petrus Hedd clericus prebendarius dicte ecclesie comparuit per procuratorem.

Joannes Herde clericus prebendarius de Gevyndale per procuratorem. Sed antea in visitacione comparuit et subscripsit.

Willelmus Rokebye Archidiaconus de Estreding comparuit per procuratorem.

Joannes Grene prebendarius de Donnington comparuit per procuratorem &c.

f.19v.

Baudwinus Norton prebendarius de Langtofte comparuit per procuratorem.

Joannes Warren archidiaconus de Estredinge *archidiaconus Cleveland*[26] non comparuit.

Albanus Langdale prebendarius de Apleford non comparuit.

Arthurus Lowe prebendarius de Frydaythorpe non comparuit.

Ricardus Peter prebendarius de Knavesbrugh comparuit sufficienter per procuratorem.

Joannes Seaton prebendarius de Uskelfe nullo modo comparuit.

Joannes Hebden prebendarius de Bugthorpe comparuit per magistrum Edmundum Scambler.

Petrus Vannes prebendarius de Bole nullo modo comparuit.

Ricardus Norman prebendarius de Holme[27] archiepiscopi comparuit per Antonium Iveson.

Thomas Ardern prebendarius de Wighton nullo modo comparuit.
Galfridus Morlaye prebendarius de Strensall nullo modo comparuit.   f.20r.
Thomas Clement prebendarius de Apesthorpe[28] nullo modo comparuit.
Thomas Cheston prebendarius de Gryndall[29] nullo modo comparuit.
Willelmus Bell prebendarius de Bilton comparuit per Thomam Clarke[30] pro-
curatorem.
Georgius Blithe prebendarius de Tokerington nullo modo comparuit.

Predicto die Sabbati loco capitulari antedicto Domini Commissarij iudicialiter   f.20v.
sedentes Capitulo ibidem preter communes Iniunctiones regias certas peculiares
et speciales Iniunctiones[31] pro causarum et rerum necessitatibus conceptis a prebendarijs et ceteris dicte ecclesie ministris inviolabiliter observandas tradiderunt.

In ecclesia parochiali omnium sanctorum super pavimento, civi-   f.21r.
tatis Ebor', septimo die mensis Septembris Anno Domini
Millesimo quingentesimo quinquagesimo nono.

Quibus die et loco post preces dictas, egregius vir Magister [Jacobus] Pilkington
eleganter et publice ad populum predicavit. **Deinde** Thomas Gargrave, Henricus
Gates milites, Edwinus Sandis sacre Theologie doctor et Henricus Harvy legum
doctor iudicialiter in cancello dicte ecclesie sedentes more solito clerum et
populum eiusdem civitatis illuc monitos et citatos visitacionem huiusmodi subituros actualiter visitaverunt. **Et** introducto ac recepto certificatorio de executione
mandati, omnes absentes monitos citatos et non comparentes pronunciaverunt
contumaces, reservata pena &c.

In ecclesia parochiali divi Michaelis prope pontem de Owse die   f.21v.
veneris, viz. octavo die mensis Septembris Anno Domini Millesimo quingentesimo quinquagesimo nono.

Quibus die et loco post preces dictas, Magister Scambler concionator visitacionis
publice predicavit. **Deinde** Thomas Gargrave miles, Henricus Gates, miles,
Edwinus Sandis sacre theologie doctor et Henricus Harvye legum doctor Commissarij antedicti observatis in ea parte observandis clerum et populum decanatus
de Aynstye et partis decanatus sancte trinitatis Ebor' illuc monitos et citatos
visitacionem regiam subituros actualiter visitaverunt. **Et** introducto ac recepto
certificatorio dicti Domini Commissarij omnes absentes citatos preconizatos et
non comparentes pronunciaverunt contumaces pena contumaciarum reservanda,
&c.

In loco consistoriali ecclesie metropolitice Ebor', octavo et nono   f.22r.
respective diebus Anno Domini Millesimo quingentesimo quin-
quagesimo nono.

Ebor'   **Quibus die et loco**, viz. viij° die mensis Septembris coram Dominis Commissarijs iudicialiter sedentibus et per ipsos sic sedentes acta et gesta prout sequitur.

Petrus Coperthwaite de Pontefracte dicte Ebor' diocesis alias detectus de crimine incontinentie cum quadam Joanna Margetson de eadem personaliter comparuit, et obiecto crimine fatebatur. Unde per Dominos Commissarios imposita est ei penitentia canonica peragenda in ecclesia parochiali de Pontefracte predicta die dominica proxima ad septimanam inter divinorum solempnia dum maior fuerit populi multitudo &c. Et iniunxerunt eidem quod amplius cum eadem nullam habeat conversationem nisi locis publicis. Et quod certificet de executione &c decano rurali immediate post dictam diem dominicam &c.

Joannes Godfrey de Adingflete Ebor' diocesis alias detectus de crimine adulterij cum quadam Elizabetha Walkewood de eadem personaliter comparuit et obiecto crimine fatebatur. Unde Domini Commissarij iniunxerunt quod die exaltacionis

f.22v.   Crucis[32] proxime futuro tempore nundinarum apud Edingflete predicte more penitentis lineis sive laneis in publico foro recognitionem sui facinoris prout in scedula sibi tradita continetur penitenter agat &c. Quodque die dominica proxima sequente tempore divinorum post gracias in medio ecclesie dicendo contemplantibus parochianis tradat et imponat in cista pauperum dicte parochie decem solidos. Quodque nullo modo illicite conversetur cum muliere iuramentum prestitit, et sic dimissus facto certificatorio decano decanatus ibidem de peracta penitentia &c.[33]

Grene   **Thomas Grene** parochie de Gigiswicke dicte Ebor' diocesis alias detectus de crimine fornicationis cum quadam Margareta Parkinson de eadem etiam presens in iudicio, et obiecto crimine fatebantur. Unde Domini Commissarij primo iniunxerunt viro ut ebdomadatim det et contribuat mulieri pro sustentacione prolis fornicatorie: iiij^d. Deinde imposuerunt et viro et mulieri penitentiam publicam et canonicam et per ipsos peragendam in propria ecclesia die dominica proxima dum maior adfuerit populi multitudo. Et quod vir in publico foro ibidem die nundinarum penitentiam quoque peragat declarando facinoris substanciam prout in scedula sibi tradita continetur &c. Et certificandum de peracta penitentia decano decanatus ibidem. Et dimissi prestitis iuramentis quod amplius illicite adinvicem[34] conversentur &c.

f.23r.
Raynold   **Thomas** Raignold[35] de Whitgifte Ebor' diocesis detectus de crimine fornicationis cum quadam Margareta Heyton iam mortua personaliter comparuit et obiecto crimine fatebatur. Unde Domini Commissarij iniunxerunt ei penitentiam publicam peragendam in ecclesia parochiali ibidem die dominica proxima ad septimanam quo die inter alia declarabit publice causam sue penitentie prout in scedula sibi tradita continetur. Et ad certificandum de penitentia peracta decano decanatus &c.

Lunde   **Thomas** Lunde de Whitgifte predicto detectus quod incontinenter vixit cum famula sua personaliter comparuit et negavit crimen. Idcirco Domini Commissarij iniunxerunt ei ad purgandum se hoc in loco coram eorum substitutis quinta

manu[36] de vicinis dicte parochie de Whitgifte die martis proximo a festo sancti
Michaelis Archangeli &c.[37]

Isabella Pygus de Whitgifte predicto alias detecta quod communis sit meretrix
et quod peperit sepius extra matrimonium, parsonaliter comparuit et fatetur
detectionem dicendo quod incontinenter vixit et quod bis peperit non maritata.
Unde Domini Commissarij iniunxerunt ei publicam penitentiam in ecclesia parochiali predicta duabus successive dominicis proxime futuris nudis pedibus, lineis
sive laneis, et quod recitabit altero dierum confessionem publicam sibi traditam
&c. Et quod immediate certificabit decanum decanatus de penitentia peracta &c.[38]

Pygus

Elizabeth Smyth de Whitgifte predicto alias detecta quod incontinenter vixit et
quod peperit per quendam Joannem &c personaliter comparens fatebatur crimen
obiectum et allegavit matrimonium contractum fuisse et esse inter ipsam et dictum
Joannem &c. Idcirco Domini Commissarij iniunxerunt ei penitentiam publicam
ibidem peragendam die dominica proxima ad septimanam scedula sibi tradita
publice per ipsam declarata. Et ad certificandum decano rurali de executione, &c.

Smyth

Joanna Bolland et Alicia Waller de Whitby[39] Ebor' diocesis alias detecte quod
male et incontinenter cum nonnullis vixerunt, personaliter comparentes fatebantur
obiecta crimina. **Ideo** Domini Commissarij iniunxerunt eijsdem publicam penitentiam per easdem peragendam in ecclesia parochiali de Whitbye duabus diebus
dominicis proxime futuris post proximam dominicam ad septimanam. Et earum
primo dicta Johanna et secundo prefata Alicia publice declarabunt scedula publice
confessionis sibi tradita. Et ad certificandum decano rurali de executione &c.

Bolland
Waller

Ricardus Hudson de Rotherwell Ebor' diocesis alias detectus quod diu incontinenter vixit cum Alicia Smyth et quod ex eadem suscitavit quinque proles, personaliter comparens fatebatur crimen obiectum asserens se contentum coniungi in
matrimonio cum eadem Alicia. **Idcirco** sub spe matrimonij assignaverunt prefato
Ricardo ad comparendum hoc in loco coram substitutis generalibus martis a festo
Michaelis proximo, eorum voluntatem audituro, &c.[40]

Hudson

Predicto nono die Septembris coram prelibatis Dominis Commissarijs Henricus
More clericus rector Sancti Martini in Mydlegate civitatis Ebor' personaliter
comparuit, ac diversis vicibus interrogatus monitus atque requisitus ut articulis
suscepte Religionis subscribat ipse peremptorie recusavit. Unde prefati Domini
Commissarij capta prius recognitione[41] in qua ipse recognovit se debere Domine
nostre Regine quadraginta libras et quilibet fideiussorum per se recognovit debere
viginti libras cum condicione Quod ipse prefatus Henricus personaliter comparebit &c quandocunque ad id fuerit evocatus sive monitus, ut per eandem recognitionem certificatam in cancellariam plenius liquet, **deinde** omnes fructus decimas
et emolumenta rectorie sue predicte sequestraverunt &c.

More

Thomas Jeffrison clericus vicarius de Ledesham Ebor' diocesis sepius atque iteratis vicibus monitus et requisitus per Dominos Commissarios ad subscribendum

Jeffrison

Articulis Religionis &c ipse obstinate et peremptorie recusavit. **Idcirco** prefati Domini Commissarij omnes fructus decimas et emolumenta dicte vicarie sequestranda fore decreverunt, deinde ceperunt recognitionem[42] ab eodem in qua ipse recognovit se debere Domine nostre Regine quadraginta libras et quilibet fideiussorum viginti libras &c, cum condicione quod personaliter comparebit &c quandocunque monitus seu evocatus fuerit &c, ut per eandem recognitionem certificatam in cancellariam plenius liquet &c.

f.24v.
Pavier

Detectum est quod Georgius Pavyer de Spaworthe et Agnes Wayte de Thorpe male et suspiciose vixerunt. Idcirco Domini Commissarij evocatis partibus ipsi fide media promiserunt quod omni cum festinatione procurabunt solempnizacionem huiusmodi matrimonij initi confessati et contracti. **Unde** Domini Commissarij ut huiusmodi negocium citius expediatur curatis ecclesiarum de Spaworthe et Thorpe ad solempnizandum huiusmodi matrimonium bannis semel editis vices et aucthoritatem commiserunt &c et sic di[missi].[43]

f.25r.

In ecclesia parochiali de Hull, die lune viz. undecimo die mensis Septembris Anno Domini Millesimo quingentesimo quinquagesimo nono.

Quibus die et loco postquam preces erant solempniter et cum reverentia dicte, sepedictus magister Edwinus Sandis ad populum congregatum sempiternum dei verbum publice et predicavit et docuit, idque ab auditoribus gratialiter erat receptum. **Deinde** Henricus Gates miles, prefatus Edwinus Sandis sacre theologie doctor et Henricus Harvy legum doctor Commissarij antedicti more et solempnitate prerecitatis Chorum dicte ecclesie ad locum ibidem decentius ornatum simul adiverunt. **Et** lecta Commissione, recepto etiam et introducto certificatorio de executione mandati citatorij, ipsi Domini Commissarij decenti ordine clerum et populum monitos et citatos visitacionem hanc regiam subituros decenti ordine actualiter visitaverunt &c. Omnesque citatos, monitos et non comparentes pronunciaverunt contumaces pena sibi reservata &c.[44]

Dripole

Super detectione exhibita per Iconomos ecclesia parochialis de Drypole, viz. quod ecclesia ibidem sit destituta curato, Domini Commissarij omnes fructus et decimas que solebant converti ad sustentacionem curati ibidem sequestranda fore decreverunt. Et vices suas Henrico Cordiaxe, Georgio Amon, Briano Wetherall et Thome Wetherall de eadem parochia commiserunt &c.

f.25v.

In ecclesia parochiali de Baverlac, die martis viz. duodecimo die mensis Septembris Anno Domini Millesimo quingentesimo quinquagesimo nono.

Quibus die et loco, finitis precibus, magister Edmundus Scambler sincere verbum dei ad populum predicavit. **Deinde** Henricus Gates, miles, Edwinus Sandis sacre theologie doctor Henricus Harvye legum doctor et Cristophorus Estofte armiger, Commissarij in cancello dicte ecclesie iudicialiter sedentes more et solempnitate prerecitatis, clerum et populum huiusmodi visitacionem regiam subituros monitos et citatos actualiter visitaverunt. Et recepto ac introducto certificatorio de executione mandati citatorij, omnes absentes citatos preconizatos et nullo modo comparentes pronunciaverunt contumaces &c.

Super presentacione facta per Iconomos et parochianos de Keyingham Ebor'   **Keyingham**
diocesis, viz. quod vicaria vacata et destituta sit curato, Domini Commissarij fructus decimas et cetera emolumenta dicte vicarie sequestraverunt, committentes sequestrationem Willelmo Jonson, Olivero Griscrofte et Joanni Gawesman parochianis ibidem &c, prestita cautione &c.

In ecclesia parochiali de Malton, die jovis viz. decimo quarto   f.26r.
die mensis Septembris Anno Domini Millesimo quingentesimo quinquagesimo nono.

Quibus die et loco finitis precibus, habitoque sermone ad populum, Henricus Gates miles, Edwinus Sandis sacre theologie doctor et Henricus Harvye legum doctor in choro dicte parochie iudicialiter sedentes clerum et populum visitacionem hanc regiam debite subituros monitos et citatos actualiter more solito visitaverunt, ac recepto et introducto certificatorio de executione mandati citatorij &c, omnes absentes citatos monitos preconizatos et nullo modo comparentes pronunciaverunt contumaces &c.

Rogerus Thompson clericus vicarius de Apleford sepius ac iteratis vicibus inter-   **Tomson**
rogatus monitus et requisitus ut articulis suscepte religionis subscribat, ipse vero obstinate ac peremptorie recusavit. **Unde** Domini Commissarij capta prius recognitione ab eodem cum fideiussoribus pro sua ulteriori comparicione quandocuncue fuerat evocatus sive monitus, ut per eandem recognitionem[45] certificatam in cancellariam plenius apparebit;/**deinde** Domini Commissarij omnes   f.26v.
fructus decimas et cetera emolumenta prefate sue vicarie de Apleford sequestranda fore decreverunt &c.

Detectum est quod capella curata de Ellerkar diu remansit inofficiata et curato   **Ellerkar**
destituta. Unde Domini Commissarij fructus &c eiusdem capelle sequestranda fore decreverunt et sequestrandi aucthoritatem commiserunt Willelmo Yonge et Ricardo Clevynge de eadem parochia, prestita cautione &c.

Detectum est quod capella curata de Rascall relinquitur inofficiata et destituta   **Rascall**
curato. Unde prelibati Domini Commissarij fructus et decimas dicte capelle iuste sequestranda fore decreverunt, committentes sequestrationem Willelmo Lawson et Joanni Woodward, prestita cautione &c.

Detectum est quod vicaria de Folketon, Ebor' diocesis diu remansit inofficiata[46]   **Folketon**

curato/penitus destituta. **Unde** Commissarij antedicti fructus decimas et cetera emolumenta dicte vicarie sequestranda fore decreverunt, committentes custodiam sequestri et potestatem sequestrandi Briano Lacye generosus &c, prestita cautione &c.

Liethe

Detectum est quod vicaria de Lyethe, Ebor' diocesis vacua sit ac diu remansit curato destituta. **Unde** prefati Domini Commissarij fructus decimas et alia emolumenta eiusdem vicarie sequestrandi fore decreverunt. Ac custodiam sequestri et sequestrandi potestatem Rogero Atclif parochiano ibidem commiserunt, prestita cautione.

f.27v.

In ecclesia parochiali de Northallerton, Ebor' diocesis, die Sabbati, viz. xvj° die mensis Septembris Anno Domini Millesimo quingentesimo quinquagesimo nono.

Quibus die et loco, dictis precibus, expositoque sincere verbo dei ad populum per magistrum Edmundum Scambler contionatorem antedictum, Henricus Gates miles, Edwinus Sandis sacre theologie doctorem et Henricum Harvy legum doctor ordine et solempnitate visitacionis debite observatis clerum et populum decanatuum de Clevelond et Bulmere actualiter visitaverunt. Ac introducto et recepto certificatorio de executione mandati citatorij Domini Commissarij omnes absentes monitos preconizatos et non comparentes pronunciaverunt contumaces pena sibi reservata &c.

Wildom contra Wildom

In causa restitucionis iurium coniugalium mota per Joannem Wyldom contra et adversus Annam Wildom parochie de Cockolde Ebor' diocesis, mulier litteratorie citata per Cristophorum Foster &c. Et preconizata mulier comparuit et allegavit hanc causam pendentem apud Ebor' &c. Ideo Domini commiserunt causam ibidem finiendam &c.

f.28r.

Predictis die et loco coram prelibatis Dominis Commissarijs personaliter comparuit Ricardus Salvyn clericus rector de Hinderwell Ebor' diocesis et licet sepius fuerat monitus et requisitus articulis suscepte religionis subscribere hoc tamen facere obstinate recusavit. **Unde** Domini Commissarij capta prius recognitione[47] ab eodem cum suis fideiussoribus monuerunt ipsum ad personaliter comparendum coram eijsdem apud Dunelmiam in ecclesia cathedrali ibidem xxiij° instantis mensis Septembris eorum voluntatem in ea parte auditurum &c.

**f.28v.
Ridall**

Joannes Rydall detectus de crimine fornicationis cum quadam Alicia mendicante, comparuit et obiecto sibi crimine negavit. **Unde** Domini Commissarij iniunxerunt ei ad purgandum se sexta[48] de proximis vicinis coram decano rurali quandocunque precedenti monitione ad id evocatus fuerit. Et vocato decano Domini commiserunt ei potestatem ad id agendum &c.

In ecclesia parochiali de Aikeland, Dunelmensis diocesis, die jovis viz. vicesimo primo die mensis Septembris Anno Domini Millesimo quingentesimo quinquagesimo nono. Ad quem locum moniti sunt omnes visitacionem hanc regiam subituri. Et ex eo quod locus non sit satis aptus ad hoc negocium expediendum idcirco Domini Commissarij per Magistrum Edmundum Scambler prorogaverunt visitacionem ab dicta ecclesia ad magnam capellam infra palacium Domini Episcopi Dunelmensis apud villam de Aikeland illo presenti die expediendam et exercendam &c.

Quo die in magna capella antedicta, finitis precibus, Magister Robertus[49] Sewell, prebendarius ecclesie Carliolensis publice ad populum predicavit. Deinde Henricus Gates miles, Edwinus Sandis sacre theologie doctor et Henricus Harvye legum doctor, Commissarij antedicti in loco preperato iudicialiter sedentes, clerum et populum dimidij Archidiaconatus Dunelmensis solempnitatibus precedentibus actualiter visitaverunt. Introductoque et recepto certificatorio de executione mandati, Domini Commissarij omnes absentes monitos preconizatos et non comparentes pronunciaverunt contumaces, &c.

Eijsdem die et loco personaliter comparuit Thomas Sigiswicke sacre theologie professor[50] quem Domini Commissarij sepius monuerunt ut/Articulis suscepte religionis ex animo subscribat ipse vero obstinate recusavit. **Unde** Domini Commissarij, capta ab eodem unacum fideiussoribus recognitione &c, monuerunt ipsum ad personaliter comparendum in civitate Dunelmensi coram eijsdem Dominis Commissarijs inter horas octavam et decimam ante meridiem eiusdem diei eorum voluntatem tunc auditurum. **Dicto** vicesimo quinto die adveniente, in ecclesia cathedrali Dunelmensi coram Dominis Commissarijs personaliter comparuit predictus Thomas Sigiswicke et iterum atque iterum monitus et requisitus ut subscribat &c, obstinate et peremptorie recusavit. **Unde** Domini Commissarij cassantes priorem recognitionem &c ceperunt ab eodem recognitionem in qua ipse recognovit se debere Domine nostre Regine tricentas libras et quilibet fideiussorum recognovit centum libras, cum condicione quod personaliter comparebit quandocunque ad id monitus seu evocatus fuerit ut per eandem recognitionem certificatam ad cancellariam &c apparebit. **Deinde** Willelmus Dominus Evers, Henricus Gates, Edwinus Sandis et Henricus Harvy Commissarij Christi nomine primitus invocato eundem Thomam Sigiswicke a vicaria sua de Gaynesford quam tunc possidebat per eorum Sententiam diffinitivam in scriptis ad omnem iuris effectum deprivaverunt et amoverunt, dictamque vicariam et vacare pronunciaverunt. **Ac** etiam omnes fructus decimas et cetera emolumenta[51] omnium dignitatum beneficiorum et officiorum suorum ecclesiasticorum quorumcunque sequestranda fore decreverunt &c./

Predicto vicesimo primo die mensis Septembris capella predicta, personaliter comparuit Robertus Dalton sacre theologie baccalaurius vicarius ecclesie parochialis de Billingham quem Domini Commissarij sepius ac iteratis vicibus interrogaverunt atque monuerunt ut articulis suscepte religionis subscribat ipse peremptorie recusavit. **Unde** Domini Commissarij prestita prius cautione obligatoria pro sua ulteriori comparicione monuerunt ipsum ad personaliter comparendum coram eijsdem apud civitatem Dunelmie die lune xxv^{to} die instantis mensis Septembris infra precinctum ecclesie Cathedralis ibidem ubi tunc sedere contigerint eorum voluntatem auditurum &c. **Deinde**, viz. Sabbato xxiij^o die mensis predicti, coram Willelmo Domino Evers, Henrico Gates, Edwino Sandis et Henrico Harvy, Commissarijs ac in domo Capitulari ecclesie cathedralis Dunelmensis iudicialiter sedentibus inter canonicos et prebendarios eiusdem ecclesie dictus Robertus Dalton personaliter comparuit et requisitus iterum ut articulis subscribat peremptorie recusavit, allegans quoad primam partem Articulorum: *That he belevith that he who sittithe in the seate of Rome hath and oughte to have the iurisdiction ecclesiasticall over all Christian Realmes.*[52] **Deinde** predicto xxv^{to} die mensis antedicti loco capitulari antedicto coram eijsdem Dominis Commissarijs personaliter comparuit prelibatus Robertus Dalton et iterum hoc est tertio requisitus &c, obstinate et peremptorie recusavit. **Idcirco** per eosdem Commissarios capta est recognitio in qua prefatus Robertus recognovit se debere Domine nostre Regine tricentas libras et quilibet fideiussorum centum libras, cum condicione quod personaliter comparebit quandocunque fuerit evocatus &c, ut per eandem recognitionem[53] ad cancellariam certificatam liquebit &c, omnesque fructus tam prebende quam dignitatum et beneficiorum suorum sequestranda fore decreverunt.

f.30v.
Bennet

Predicto xxj^{mo} die mensis Septembris in capella antedicta personaliter comparuit Willelmus Bennet sacre theologie doctor vicarius ecclesie parochialis de Ayclif Dunelmensis diocesis, et sepius interrogatus per Dominos Commissarios antedictos ut suscepte Religionis articulis subscribat ipse hoc facere peremptorie recusavit. **Unde** prefati Domini Commissarij recepta prius fideiussoria et obligatoria cautione pro sua personali et ulteriori comparicione monuerunt ipsum ad personaliter comparendum apud Dunelmiam in loco ubi tunc fuerint die Lune proximo inter horas octavam et decimam ante meridiem eiusdem diei eorum voluntatem ulterius auditurum. **Deinde** prelibatus Willelmus Bennet in domo Capitulari ecclesie cathedralis Dunelmensis inter alios prebendarios dicte ecclesie personaliter coram Dominis Commissariis comparens ac iterum hoc est secundo monitus et requisitus ut subscribat, peremptorie recusavit. **Predicto** die lune adveniente Domini Commissarij loco Capitulari antedicto iudicialiter sedentes prefatum Willelmum Bennete monuerunt et interrogaverunt an subscribere velit, ipse vero peremptorie et obstinate recusavit. **Unde** Domini Commissarij primo fructus decimas et cetera emolumenta tam prebende quam omnium beneficiorum suorum sequestranda fore decreverunt. Deinde ceperunt quandam recognitionem in qua ipse recognovit se debere Domine nostre Regine tricentas libras, et quilibet fideiussorum centum libras cum condicione quod ipse parsonaliter comparebit quandocunque fuerit evocatus &c, ut per eandem recognitionem[54] certificatam in Cancellariam Domine Regine plenius liquet &c.

Predicto xxj*mo* die Septembris in capella antedicta personaliter comparuit f.31r.
Whithede
Willelmus Whithede clericus, vicarius de Highington, Dunelmensis diocesis, et
monitus atque requisitus per Dominos Commissarios antedictos ad subscribendum articulis Religionis, ipse expresse recusavit. **Unde** Domini Commissarij
monuerunt ipsum ad personaliter comparendum coram ipsis apud civitatem
Dunelmie xxv*to* die instantis mensis Septembris eorum voluntatem in hac parte
auditurum, capta cautione fideiussoria et obligatoria pro sua comparicione &c.
Dicto xxv*to* die adveniente coram Dominis Commissarijs personaliter comparens,
et iterum hoc est secundo monitus ut subscribat peremptorie id facere recusavit.
Tunc monitus est ad comparendum die crastino inter horas octavam et undeci-
mam ante meridiem &c. Dictoque adveniente die prefatus Willelmus iterum, hoc
est tertio monitus et iudicialiter requisitus subscribere obstinate et peremptorie
recusavit. **Unde** Domini Commissarij, capta prius recognitione[55] in qua ipse
Willelmus recognovit se debere Domine nostre Regine centum libras et quilibet
suorum fideiussorum centum marcas levandas &c, cum condicione quod ipse
personaliter comparebit coram commissarij Londini residentibus &c, quandocunque fuerit ad id monitus seu requisitus &c. Deinde fructus decimas et emolumenta
vicarie sue de Highington predicte sequestraverunt.

(fol. 31v. is blank.)

Ecclesia cathedralis Dunelmensis f.32r.

In domo capitulari ecclesie Cathedralis Dunelmensis, die Sabbati viz.
vicesimo tertio die mensis Septembris Anno Domini Millesimo quingentesimo quinquagesimo nono.

Quibus die et loco Willelmus Dominus Evers, Henricus Percy, Henricus Gates,
milites; Edwinus Sandis sacre theologie doctor et Henricus Harvy legum doctor,
Commissarij illustrissime Domine nostre Regine antedicti, postquam preces erant
in choro solempniter dicte, dictum domum Capitularem more decentiori adiverunt. Et in loco iudiciali ibidem preperato sedentes ad visitacionis negocium
expediendum processerunt et procedebant, habita prius in ecclesia verbi Dei
predicatione per prelibatum Edwinum Sandis &c. **Ac recepto** certificatorio de
executione mandati, omnibusque citatis preconizatis, Domini Commissarij pronunciaverunt omnes absentes citatos preconizatos et nullo modo comparentes
contumaces, &c. **Deinde**, lecta publice Commissione, tam prebendarios quam
dicte ecclesie omnes ministros ad tacta dei evangelia iurari fecerunt de inquisitione et presentacione facienda de et super articulis visitacionis generalibus eis
adtunc etiam lectis et traditis &c. Deinde continuaverunt hanc visitacionem usque
in horam secundam a meridie, et sic de tempore in tempus prout eis visum
fuerit necessarium.

Dicta secunda hora adveniente in loco predicto Domini Commissarij iudicialiter f.32v.
sedentes prebendarios et ceteros ministros examinando processum est ut sequitur:

Thomas Robertson sacre theologie doctor decanus pretensus[56] eiusdem ecclesie **Robertson**

monitus et requisitus oblatis et lectis articulis suscepte religionis subscribere, ipse vero peremptorie recusavit, totaliter denegando eosdem articulos et dicendo, *That the Bisshope of Rome owghte to have the iurisdiction ecclesiasticall of this Realme.* Tunc Domini Commissarij monuerunt ipsum ad comparendum die Lune proximo hoc in loco eorum voluntatem ulterius auditurum; dictoque adveniente die prelibatus Thomas Robertson iterum monitus et requisitus ut subscribat, obstinate recusavit. **Unde** Domini Commissarij ceperunt ab eodem recognitionem[57] ad usum Domine Regine in qua ipse recognovit se debere prefate Domine Regine quingentas libras et quilibet fideiussorum centum libras cum condicione &c, quod personaliter comparebit coram commissarijs generalibus Londini residentibus quandocunque ad id monitus seu requisitus fuerat &c.

Watson

Rogerus Watson sacre theologie professor prebendarius dicte ecclesie monitus et requisitus subscribere, ipse, inspectis articulis, voluntarie et ex animo ceteris aspectantibus, subscripsit &c.

f.33r.
Crauforthe

Joannes Crauforthe sacre theologie baccalaurius, prebendarius dicte ecclesie per Dominos Commissarios monitus ut articulis suscepte religionis subscribat; ipse vero peremptorie recusavit. Deinde humiliter petijt deliberandi tempus sibi concedi, viz. usque in diem Lune extunc proxime futurum, et Domini concesserunt, monentes ipsum ad comparendum eodem die hora septima hoc in loco. **Die** hora advenientibus comparuit dictus Joannes coram Commissarijs iudicialiter sedentibus et primo recognovit supremitatem Domine Regine et deinde religioni subscribere recusavit. **Unde** Domini Commissarij primo ceperunt ab eodem recognitionem in qua ipse recognovit se debere Domine nostre Regine ducentas libras, et quilibet fideiussorum centum libras &c, cum condicione quod personaliter comparebit coram Commissarijs generalibus Londini residentibus &c quandocunque ad id evocatus et requisitus fuerat ut per eandem recognitionem certificatam[58] ad cancellariam plenius apparet. Deinde fructus et proventus dicte sue prebende fore sequestranda decreverunt &c.

Marley

f.33v.

Stephanus Marley sacre theologie baccalaurius prebendarius dicte ecclesie sepius requisitus subscribere Articulis Religionis &c, peremptorie recusavit. Tunc Domini Commissarij monuerunt ipsum ad personaliter comparendum die lune proximo hora septima ante meridiem eiusdem diei. **Dicto** die lune adveniente, Commissarijs iudicialiter sedentibus, comparuit dictus Stephanus Marleye, monitusque et requisitus ut supra, obstinate et peremptorie recusavit. **Unde** Domini Commissarij primo ceperunt recognitionem[59] in qua ipse Stephanus recognovit se debere Domine nostre Regine ducentas libras et quilibet fideiussorum centum libras &c, cum condicione &c, quod ipse personaliter comparebit coram Commissarijs generalibus Londini residentibus &c quandocunque ad id monitus seu requisitus fuerit &c. Deinde fructus et emolumenta dicte sue prebende sequestraverunt &c.

Tuttyn

Joannes Tuttyn sacre theologie baccalaurius prebendarius dicte ecclesie sepius monitus et requisitus suscepte religionis articulis subscribere, peremptorie recusavit dicendo, *that he belevith that the bisshope of Rome oughte to have the iurisdiction ecclesiasticall within this Realme.* Tunc Domini Commissarij monuerunt ipsum ad comparendum lune proximo hora septima. **Dictis** die et hora, coram Dominis Commissarijs iudicialiter sedentibus comparuit dictus Joannes qui monitus ut supra magis peremptorie et obstinate recusavit. **Unde** dicti Domini Commissarij primo ceperunt recognitionem[60] in qua ipse recognovit se debere Domine Regine tricentas libras/et quilibet fideiussorum suorum centum libras &c, cum condicione &c, quod parsonaliter comparebit coram Commissarijs Domine Regine generalibus Londini residentibus quandocunque ad id monitus seu requisitus fuerit &c. **Deinde** fructus et emolumenta dicte sue prebende sequestranda fore decreverunt.

f.34r.

Nicolaus Marley sacre theologie baccalaurius prebendarius dicte ecclesie sepius per Dominos Commissarios monitus et requisitus subscribere suscepte religionis articulis peremptorie recusavit et publice dixit, *that he woll not aunswer directlye to tharticle of supreamycy, but said that the Bisshope of Rome had som iurisdiction in this Realme.* Deinde monitus per Commissarios ad personaliter comparendum coram ipsis die lune proximo hora septima eorum voluntatem ulterius auditurus. **Dicto** die lune adveniente ac loco predicto prefatus Nicolaus Marley iterum monitus et requisitus ut supra obstinate et peremptorie recusavit. **Unde** Domini Commissarij primo ceperunt recognitionem in qua ipse recognovit se debere domine nostre Regine ducentas libras et quilibet fideiussorum centum libras &c, cum condicione &c quod personaliter comparebit coram commissarijs generalibus Londini &c quando ad id monitus seu requisitus fuerit &c, ut per eandem recognitionem[61] certificatam in cancellariam apparet &c. Deinde tam prebendam suam in dicta ecclesia quam alia beneficia et dignitates sequestranda fore decreverunt, &c.

Marley

f.34v.
Bullocke

Georgius Bullocke sacre theologie doctor prebendarius dicte ecclesie pretensus[62] monitus et requisitus subscribere articulis suscepte religionis obstinate et peremptorie recusavit, dicendo, *That he belevith that the bisshope of Rome hath and ought to have the iurisdiction ecclesiasticall within this realme, and by playne and flate wordis he affirmed that the sea of that bisshope was the sea Apostolicke.* **Tunc** monitus est per Dominos Commissarios ad comparendum ulterius die lune proximo hora septima mane &c. Quo die adveniente comparuit dictus Georgius et iterum requisitus ut supra obstinate recusavit. **Unde** Domini Commisarij[63] ceperunt recognitionem[64] in qua ipse Georgius recognovit se debere Domine nostre Regine tricentas libras et quilibet fideiussorum centum libras &c, cum condicione quod ipse personaliter comparebit coram Commissarijs generalibus Londini residentibus quandocunque ad id fuerit monitus seu requisitus &c.

Antonius Salvyn sacre theologie Baccalaurius prebendarius dicte ecclesie per Dominos Commissarios iudicialiter sedentes sepius monitus et interrogatus subscribere suscepte religionis articulis peremptorie recusavit. *And to tharticle of Supreamycy he will not directly aunswer; but after longe communication he sayde that he belevith rather that the Bisshope of Rome hath iurisdiction within this*

Salvyn

Realme[65] *then otherwise &c.* **Tunc** monitus est ad comparendum personaliter hoc in loco die lune proximo inter horas septimam et nonam ante meridiem voluntatem eorum in hac parte ulterius auditurus./**Dicto** die lune adveniente in loco predicto comparuit personaliter prefatus Anthonius qui iterum monitus et requisitus ut supra obstinate et peremptorie recusavit. **Unde** Domini Commissarij primo ceperunt recognitionem[66] in qua ipse recognovit se debere Domine nostre Regine tricentas libras et quilibet fideiussorum centum libras &c, cum condicione &c, quod personaliter comparebit coram Commissarijs generalibus Londini residentibus quandocunque ad id fuerat monitus seu requisitus. **Deinde** dicti Domini Commissarij matura deliberatione prehabita, ac Christi nomine primitus invocato eundem Anthonium Salvyn a prebenda sua quam in dicta ecclesia cathedrali Dunelmensi inpresenti possidet per eorum Sententiam diffinitivam in scriptis deprivaverunt et amoverunt &c. Aliasque suas dignitates beneficia et officia ecclesiastica sequestranda fore decreverunt &c.

Clife

Georgius Cliffe sacre theologie Baccalaurius prebendarius dicte ecclesie sepius per Dominos Commissarios iudicialiter sedentes monitus et requisitus articulis suscepte religionis subscribere, obstinate et peremptorie recusavit, et dixit, *That he dothe beleve that the pope hath and ought to have the iurisdiction ecclesiasticall and not the Quene.* Tunc monitus est per Dominos Commissarios quod personaliter compareat coram eijsdem die lune proximo eorum voluntatem super premissis auditurus facturusque quod iusticia suadebit. Dictoque die lune adveniente prelibati Domini Commissarij/prefatum Anthonium presentem iterum monuerunt et requisiverunt ut dictis articulis subscribat, ipse vero ut prius obstinate et peremptorie recusavit. **Unde** Domini Commissarij primo ceperunt recognitionem in qua ipse Georgius Clif recognovit se debere Domine nostre Regine ducentas libras et quilibet fideiussorum centum libras &c, cum condicione quod ipse personalem faciat comparicionem coram generalibus Commissarijs Domine Regine Londini residentibus quandocunque ad id monitus vel requisitus fuerit &c ut per eandem recognitionem[67] certificatam apparet in cancellariam. **Deinde** fructus decimas et cetera emolumenta dicte prebende quam ceterorum dignitatum et beneficiorum suorum ecclesiasticorum iuste sequestranda fore decreverunt.

Sparke

Thomas Sparke sacre theologie baccalaurius prebendarius dicte ecclesie preconizatus comparuit per Magistrum Chaitor eius procuratorem, allegantem ipsum adversa valetudine detineri &c.

Tode

Willelmus Todde sacre theologie professor prebendarius dicte ecclesie preconizatus non comparuit attamen omnes prebendarij asserebant ipsum ex fractura tibie iacere ita quod extra eius domum iusta precinctum dicte ecclesie existentem venire non potuit sine periculo. Deinde Domini Commissarij/substituerunt magistros [Bernardum][68] Gilpyn et Edmundum Scambler, comnittentes eis vices eorum ad examinandum dictum Willelmum Todde super articulis suscepte religionis. **Et** predicti substituti in presencia Thome Percy notarij publici dictum Willelmum Todde in proprio hospitio ex parte Domine nostre Regine instanter et monuerunt et requisiverunt ut dictis articulis sibi perlectis subscribat; ipse vero peremptorie

f.35r.

f.35v.

f.36r.

recusavit. **Unde** Domini Commissarij omnes fructus decimas et cetera emolumenta tam prebende quam vicarie de Northallerton sequestranda fore decreverunt.

Canonici minores

Willelmus Smythe canonicus eiusdem ecclesie requisitus articulis suscepte religionis subscribere recusavit.

Joannes Browne canonicus ibidem simili modo requisitus recusat.

Joannes Byndley clericus canonicus predicte ecclesie requisitus ut supra recusat.

Thomas Pentland clericus canonicus predicte ecclesie sic ut superius requisitus subscribere peremptorie recusat.

Robertus Bekinsope clericus canonicus dicte ecclesie ad subscribendos articulos predictos sic ut premittitur requisitus peremptorie recusat attamen fatetur supremitatem.

Joannes Peerson clericus canonicus dicte ecclesie requisitus subscribere articulis suscepte religionis peremptorie recusavit attamen fatetur supremitatem &c.

Willelmus Smyth clericus canonicus euisdem ecclesie requisitus subscribere recusat.

Willelmus Ball canonicus dicte ecclesie ad subscribendum articulos requisitus recusat.

(f. 36v. blank)
f.37r.

> **Idcirco Domini** Commissarij antedicti monuerunt ipsos eorumque quemlibet ad personaliter comparendum coram eijsdem die lune proximo hora septima mane eorum voluntatem ulterius audituros.

Die et hora advenientibus, predicti Domini Commissarij iudicialiter sedentes, predictos Willelmum Smythe, Joannem Browne, Joannem Byndley, Thomam Pentland, Robertum Blekinsoppe, Joannem Peerson, Willelmum Smyth, et Willelmum Ball antedictos et eorum quemlibet separatim requisiverunt ut articulis subscribant. Ipsi vero, eorumque quilibet peremptorie et obstinate recusaverunt et recusavit. **Idcirco** Domini Commissarij ceperunt ab eorundem quolibet separatim recognitionem in qua unusquisque per se recognovit debere Domine Regine quadraginta libras et quilibet fideiussorum viginti libras &c, cum condicione quod personaliter comparebit eorum quilibet coram Commissarijs generalibus Domine Regine Londini residentibus aut alijs quandocunque ad id fuerint [evocati][69] seu requisiti, ut per eorum recognitiones[70] sic captas et certificatas ad cancellariam latius apparet.

f.37v.
Thewles

Willelmus Thewles, ludimagister scole grammatice monitus et requisitus ut subscribat Articulis Religionis, ipse nullis persuasionibus ad id faciendum inductus, obstinate et peremptorie recusavit. **Unde** Domini Commissarij ceperunt recognitionem[71] in qua ipse recognovit se debere Domine nostre Regine quadraginta libras et quilibet fideiussorum viginti libras &c, cum condicione quod ipse personaliter comparebit coram Commissarijs generalibus Londini residentibus aut alijs quandocunque evocatus seu requisitus fuerit.

Predicto xxv*to* die mensis Septembris, recepto Inventario bonorum dicte ecclesie, unacum billis presentacionis factis per quemlibet predictorum, viz., prebendariorum et ministrorum ecclesie; exhibitisque fundatione statutis et indotatione dicte ecclesie, eisque inspectis et diligenter examinatis, Domini Commissarij iudicialiter sedentes monuerunt omnes prebendarios et ceteros ecclesie ministros ad comparendum eodem loco die crastino hora septima tunc audituros et recepturos quod iusticia et equitatis ratio persuadebunt. **Dictis** die et hora advenientibus, Domini Commissarij iudicialiter sedentes prefatis prebendarijs alijsque ecclesie ministris inter[e]ssentibus exhortatione quadam celica et deo grata per prelibatum magistrum Edwinum Sandis docte proposita et revelata in qua precipue persuasum erat inter alia ut rationem habeant de fide et obedientia erga Christum

f.38r.

salvatorem et Illustrissimam Dominam nostram Reginam &c, certas/Speciales iniunctiones ac preter communes impressatos specialiter secundum rerum neccessitatem, [a]⁷² prefatis prebendarijs et ministris inviolabiliter observandas tradiderunt⁷³ et deliberaverunt sub sigillo Regie Majestatis ad causas ecclesiasticas dicta visitacione usitato &c.

f.38v.

In ecclesia parochiali divi Nicolai civitatis Dunelmensis, die lune viz. xxv*to* die mensis Septembris Anno Domini Millesimo quingentesimo quinquagesimo nono.

Quibus die et loco, finitis precibus, ac predicatione habita ad populum more et solempnitate prerecitatis, ad visitacionis negocium procedebant Domini Commissarij antedicti, in loco iudiciali sedentes. Omnes absentes citatos preconizatos et non comparentes pronunciaverunt contumaces, et in penam contumaciarum suarum contra ipsos procedendum fore prout iusticia suadebit.

Carter

Dictis die et loco personaliter comparuit Willelmus Carther sacre theologie professor, Archidiaconus Northumbr', qui per Dominos Commissarios monitus et requisitus ad subscribendum articulis suscepte Religionis peremptorie recusavit. Tunc Domini Commissarij monuerunt ipsum ad comparendum in domo

f.39r.

capitulari ecclesie Dunelmensis crastino hora septima &c./**Dictis** die et hora advenientibus, in domo capitulari antedicto coram Dominis Commissarijs iudicialiter sedentibus, comparuit personaliter dictus Willelmus Carther qui iterum atque iterum monitus et requisitus ad subscribendum articulis ut supra ipse peremptorie et obstinate recusavit. **Unde** ipsi Domini Commissarij primo ceperunt recognitionem in qua ipse recognovit se debere Domine nostre Regine tricentas libras et quilibet suorum fideiussorum centum libras &c, cum condicione quod ipse personaliter comparebit coram Commissarijs generalibus Londini residentibus vel alijs quandocunque ad id fuerit evocatus seu requisitus ut per eandem recognitionem⁷⁴ certificatam in cancellariam latius apparet. Deinde matura deliberatione precedenti ac Christi nomine primitus invocato ac ipsum deum oculis suis preponentes, ipsum Willelmum Carther a dignitate sui archidiaconatus Northumbrorum predicti per eorum Sententiam diffinitivam in scriptis in ipsius presencia latam deprivaverunt et amoverunt proque deprivato habendo et censendo fore decreverunt, dictumque archidiaconatum Northumbr' vacari et vacuam esse &c. Et insuper decimas fructus et emolumenta ceterorum dignitatum et beneficiorum suorum quorumcunque sequestranda fore decreverunt.

In ecclesia divi Nicholai ville Novi Castri, die mercurij viz. xxvij° die mensis Septembris Anno Domini Millesimo quingentesimo [quinquagesimo nono].[75]

f.39v.

Quibus die et loco, finitis precibus, verboque omnipotentis Dei ad populum syncere predicato per sepedictum magistrum Edwinum Sandis in cancello dicte ecclesie iudicialiter in loco ibidem preperato, Willelmus Dominus Evers, Henricus Percy, Henricus Gates, milites; Edwinus Sandis sacre theologie doctor, et Henricus Harvy legum doctor, Commissarij antedicti ad visitacionis negocium expediendum processerunt more et solempnitate solitis. Ac recepto certificatorio de executione mandati citatorij omnes absentes monitos preconizatos et nullo modo comparentes pronunciaverunt contumaces et in penam suarum contumaciarum contra eos procedendum iuxta iuris et equitatis rationem &c.

Eijsdem die et loco super detectione quod vicaria de Heighington curato sit destituta[76] omnes fructus decimas et emolumenta dicte vicarie sequestranda fore decreverunt. Et potestatem colligendi et sequestrandi fructus Willelmo Sherwood et Willelmo Carr generosis commiserunt, quousque duxerint revocandam &c.

Heighington

f.40r.
Turnor

Detectum est[77] quod Cuthbertus Turnor de Morpeth fornicatorie vixit cum Elisabetha Ambrye de eadem. Vir evocatus ad iudicium personaliter comparuit et obiecto sibi crimine fatebatur. Unde Domini Commissarij iniunxerunt ei quod se peniteat in foro de Morpeth proximo nundinarum die nudis pedibus et capite, lineis sive laneis quo tempore declarabit scedulam facti substanciam continentem sibi adtunc traditam; et quod deinceps nullo modo cum eadem conversetur sub pena iuris &c. Et preterea per curatum ibidem iniungatur mulieri quod ipsa die dominica proxima ad septimanam in ecclesia parochiali ibidem se peniteat more publice penitentis, cum declaracione scedule publice confessionis &c. Et monitus est vir ad certificandum de utraque penitentia magistro Willelmo Sherwood[78] infra mensem &c.

Detectum est quod Robertus Marton de Gateshede incontinenter vixit et vivit cum Joanna Atkinson de eadem. Unde partes evocate et presentes in iudicio, ac obiecto crimine, fatebantur, et submiserunt se. Tunc viro assignatur ad penitendum se more penitentis die Sabbati proximo in publico foro apud novum castrum ubi scedulam publice confessionis declarabit, et mulieri assignatur ad penitendam se in ecclesia sua parochiali de Gateshed duobus dominicis diebus proximis futuris, lineis sive laneis ac cum declaratione publice confessionis &c. Et habent ad certificandum infra mensem magistro Willelmo Sherwood. Et preterea moniti sunt quod ab omni illicita conversatione abstineant.

Marton

Detectum est quod Joannes Lore et Katherina Foxe ville Novi Castri,[79] partes presentes in iudicio et obiecto crimine fatebantur. Unde Domini Commissarij viro iniunx*it* quod ipse more penitentis nudis pedibus et capite die Sabbati proximo in publico foro ibidem[80] et quod declarationem faciat sui facinoris secundum scedulam sibi traditam. Et ad certificandum magistro Willelmo Sherwood de peracta penitentia infra mensem. Et quia mulier sit gravida et prope puerperium ideo penitentiam differtur quousque peperit &c. Deinde onerati sunt iuramentis quod posthac ab omni illicita conversatione penitus abstineant et quod non conversentur nisi in locis publicis aut saltem duobus presentibus &c.

Detectum est quod Joannes Davyson et Margareta Sterke ville Novi Castri fornicatorie vixerunt. Unde Domini Commissarij mulieri presenti in iudicio sibique obiecto crimine fatenti iniunxerunt quod ipsa die dominica proxima in propria ecclesia penitentiam agat publicam nudis pedibus &c, cum declaratione scedule sibi tradite &c. Et ad certificandum magistro Willelmo Sherwood de peracta penitentia infra mensem sequentem, et prestito iuramento quod deinceps ab illicita conversatione cum dicto Joanne refrenabit, dimittitur &c.

Detectum est quod Thomas Jakeson de Gateshede et Helena May de eadem suspitiose vi[v]unt. Unde partes evocati ad iudicium negaverunt crimen, attamen fatebantur quod adinvicem contraxerunt; et ad collendam omnem suspitionem in ea parte voluntarie assumpserunt in se sub iuramenti vinculo ad procedendum in solempnizatione huiusmodi matrimonij citra diem Lune proximum ad quindenam &c.

Detectum est quod Katherina Forman de Gateshed incontinenter vixit cum multis; et predicta Katherina monita per apparitorem ibidem ad personaliter comparendum ad hos diem et locum venire recusavit, ut certificatum est per eundem apparitorem; et preconizata non comparuit, unde Domini Commissarij pronunciaverunt ipsam contumacem, et in penam sue contumacie excommunicandam fore decreverunt et [emanavit][81]

Detectum est quod Jana Hodeson ville Novi Castri incontinenter vixit et quod sit gravida; unde mulier evocata et fatebatur crimen cum quodam Georgio Myll. Domini iniunxerunt mulieri ad penitendam se die Sabbati proximo in publico foro et quod declarabit scedulam publice confessionis &c, et ad certificandum magistro Willelmo Sherwood immediate post peractam penitentiam.

Detectum est quod Agnes Jobeson ville Novi Castri incontinenter vivit cum Thome Weddarhaulte, pretenso marito ex eo quod habet alium virum maritum superstitem. Unde prefata Agnes evocata ad iudicium comparuit et obiecta sibi detectione negavit se unquam matrimonio coniunctam esse nisi prefato Thome Weddarhaulte; attamen confessa est se carnaliter et fornicatorie vixisse cum quodam Ricardo Hyecope ante matrimonium inter ipsam et Wedderhaulte. **Unde** Domini Commissarij super confessione sua iniunxerunt ei ad penitendam se die Sabbati proximo in publico foro quo tempore declarabit scedulam sui facinoris sibi adtunc traditam &c, et ad certificandum de penitentia magistro Sherwood infra quindenam. Deinde Domini Commissarij stricte monuerunt et predicto Thome Wedderhaulte etiam presenti et prefate Agneti quod non cohabitent nec conversationem aliquam habeant nisi in locis publicis &c, quousque doceatur an matrimonium ut pretenditur erat solempnizatum inter dictam Agnetam et Ricardo Hyecope predicto, sub pena iuris &c.

Detectum est quod navis ecclesie parochialis omnium sanctorum ville predicte magnam patitur ruinam. **Unde** iniunxtio data est precipue gardianis dicte parochie quod debite reparetur citra festum omnium sanctorum proxime futurum &c, sub pena iuris &c.

Super billa presentacionis exhibita per Iconomos et parochianos de Gosforthe   f.42r.
contra et adversus vicarium divi Nicholai ville Novi Castri predicte pro sustentacione curati celebraturi apud Gosforthe, accersitis partibus Domini Commissarij in dicta ecclesia parochiali divi Nicholai iudicialiter sedentes inter dictas partes ac de eorum consensu decretum imposuerunt, viz.: **That** *the vicar aforsaid by Sonday forthnighte nexte shall provyde an hable curate contynually to sarve the cure at Gosforthe, and to have and receive in consideration therof of the parishners of Gosforthe fortye shillinges by the yere quarterly to be payd by even portions over and besides the hole tithes of the sayd parishe.* **Also** *itt ys ordered and decreed that yf the sayd vycar fayle and not provyde a curat accordingly, That then and from thensforthe the churchwardens and parishners of the sayd parishe of Gosforthe shall provide themselfes of a curate, and so from tyme to tyme as nede shall require. And in consideration therof they to have and enjoye all the tithes and other proffittes belonging to the vycarege payenge yerely to the said vycar of Newcastell and his successors yerelye foure poundes quarterly to be payde by evyn portiones &c.*
                              et sic dimissi &c.

                                                                                    f.42v.
Robertus Atkin et Joanna Hunter parochie de Tynmowthe detecti per parochianos   **Atkyn**
ibidem quod fornicatorie vixerunt. Unde Domini Commissarij partibus agnoscentibus crimen et personaliter interessentibus, iniunxerunt ad penitendas se in ecclesia parochiali de Tynmowthe [duobus][82] diebus dominicis proximis, et quod penitenter declarabunt scedulam publice confessionis eis traditam et ad certificandum infra mensem de peracta penitentia sub pena iuris &c.

Georgius Otwaye et Joanna Horswell de Tynmowthe predicto detecti quod   **Otway**
suspiciose vi[v]unt et quod contraxerunt matrimonium anno preterito non curantes illud solempnizari. Unde Domini Commissarij, evocatis partibus ac confitentibus contractum, iniunxerunt quod procedant ad huiusmodi matrimonij solempnisationem citra finem proximi mensis, et illud facturas fide media promiserunt, &c.

Alnewicke

Et quamvis prelibati Domini Commissarij priusquam Novum Castrum advenerunt, sessionem pro regia visitacione in ecclesia parochiali de Alnewicke ultimo die instantis mensis Septembris per eos exercendam assignaverunt, Attamen ex certis rationabilibus causis ipsos specialiter moventibus dictam sessionem per surrogatos suos potius quam seipsos fore expediendam tutius putaverint. **Vicesque** suas et aucthoritatem ac potestatem sufficientas ad illius visitacionis negocium expediendum Joanni Foster militi, Barnardo Gilpin sacre theologie baccalaurio et Willelmo Harrison clerico, assumpto Joanne Stace deputato Thome Percy in actorum scribam concesserunt et commiserunt &c.

Quibus die et loco prenominati Joannes Foster miles, Barnardus Gilpin et Willelmus Harrison virtute litterarum commissionalium substitucionis predicto ultimo die mensis Septembris in ecclesia parochiali de Alnewicke visitacionem regiam actualiter exercebant, finitis prius precibus et habito sermone ad populum per prefatum magistrum Barnardum Gilpin. **Et** recepto certificatorio de executione mandati citatorij pronunciaverunt contumaces absentes &c, et in penam contumacie contra eos et eorum quemlibet procedendum fore iuxta iuris exigenciam &c.

Deinde lectis articulis ac traditis Iniunctionibus, receperunt billas presentacionis &c. Et prefatus magister Barnardus Gilpyn examinavit clerum eorumque subscriptiones ad articulos religionis suscepit &c.

Super detectione quod Georgius Yedding de Alnewicke incontinenter vixit cum quadam Margareta quondam famula sua, prefatus Georgius personaliter fatebatur crimen allegans matrimonium inter ipsum et prefatam Margaretam &c. Et *in se* assumpsit *in se* sub iuramenti vinculo quod infra spacium unius mensis sequentis procurabit huiusmodi matrimonij solempnizacionem Domini Substituti predicti sub ea condicione dimiserunt eum usque in tempus prerecitatum &c.

Carliolensis Diocesis

In domo capitulari ecclesie cathedralis Carliolensis die martis, viz. tertio die mensis Octobris Anno Domini Millesimo quingentesimo quinquagesimo nono.

Quibus die et loco postquam preces erant dicte, verboque Domini ad populum sincere predicato per sepedictum magistrum Edwinum Sandis, ipse prefatus Edwinus, Henricus Harvye legum doctor et Georgius Browne armiger iudicialiter sedentes visitationem regiam tunc et ibidem solempniter exercebant. Ac introducto certificatorio Domini pronunciaverunt omnes absentes contumaces &c.

Lancelotus Salkeld clericus, Decanus dicte ecclesie personaliter comparuit. Et perlectis sibi suscepte religionis Articulis, voluntarie et bono animo subscripsit.[83] Deinde Domini Commissarij oneraverunt eum iuramento de presentacione facienda ad communes articulos visitacionis sibi traditos, et ad exhibendum crastino hora secunda a meridie &c.

Edwardus Micchell in legibus baccalaurius prebendarius dicte ecclesie persona- liter comparuit.
Hugo Sewell sacre theologie baccalaurius prebendarius dicte ecclesie personaliter comparuit.
Barnabas Kyrkebreade clericus prebendarius dicte ecclesie personaliter comparuit.
Ricardus Brandlynge clericus prebendarius dicte ecclesie personaliter comparuit.

Quibus sic comparentibus Domini Commissarij fecerunt legi articulos suscepte religionis, et ipsi prima fronte voluntarie et libenter subscripserunt. **Deinde** sub iuramenti vinculo onerati erant de fideliter inquirendo et presentando de et super articulis visitacionis generalibus. Et moniti ad exhibendum billas in crastino &c.

Canonici minores

Joannes Thompson clericus, preconizatus non comparuit. Et ceteri interrogati dixerunt ipsum rure adversa detineri valetudine.

Joannes Austyne
Henricus Monke
Joannes Ricardson
C*hro*phorus Lowther
Thomas Watson
Willelmus Hayre
Antonius Duglas

Preconizati parsonaliter comparuerunt omnes.

33

Et moniti per Dominos Commissarios suscepte Religionis articulis subscribere, ipsi omnes sic comparentes subscripserunt. **Deinde** de fideliter inquirendo super Articulis inquisitionis iurati per Dominos Commissarios moniti fuerunt hoc in loco ad comparendum crastino hora secunda a meridie billas detectionum exhibituri. **Dicta** hora adveniente, Dominis Commissarijs iudicialiter sedentibus, preconizati fuerunt tam prebendarij quam canonici minores antedicti. Et per eos exhibitis billis et receptis, Domini Commissarij monuerunt ipsos ad comparendum ibidem hora septima in aurora. **Quinto** die mensis Octobris antedicti ac loco predicto super inspectione detectionum litterarum fundacionis indotacionis ac Statutorum eiusdem ecclesie prelibati, Domini Commissarij iudicialiter sedentes ipsis decano et canonicis ceterisque ecclesie ministris quasdam Iniunctiones speciales preter communes impressatos ab eijsdemque inviolabiliter observandos tradiderunt &c.

f.45r.

f.45v.

In ecclesia cathedrali Carliolensi, quarto die mensis Octobris Anno Domini Millesimo quingentesimo quinquagesimo nono.

Quibus die et loco predicti Domini Commissarij finitis precibus Verboque Domini ad populum publice et sincere per sepedictum magistrum Edwinum Sandis predicato in choro eiusdem ecclesie iudicialiter sedentes, clerum et populum decanatuum de Carlill et Allerdale actualiter visitaverunt &c. **Ac recepto** certificatorio de executione mandati citatorij &c, omnibusque monitis preconizatis omnes absentes citatos preconizatos et nullo modo comparentes pronunciaverunt contumaces. Et in penam suarum contumaciarum contra eos procedendum prout iura velint &c.

f.46r.

In ecclesia parochiali de Perithe, Carliolensis diocesis die veneris, viz. sexto die mensis Octobris Anno Domini Millesimo quingentesimo lix^{no} &c.

Quibus die et loco, postquam preces erant dicte, et verbum Domini publice predicatum per magistrum Hugonem Sewell, predicti Domini Commissarij visitationem Regiam more solempniori observatisque observandis actualiter exercebant, visitantes clerum et populum decanatuum de Cumberlonde et Westmurlande &c.

Ac recepto certificatorio de executione mandati citatorij preconizatisque omnibus citatis, Domini Commissarij pronunciaverunt omnes absentes contumaces, et in penam contumaciarum contra eos procedendum prout iusticia suadebit &c.

Marton

Et Domini Commissarij ex certis rationabilibus causis ipsos moventibus, fructus decimas et cetera emolumenta rectorie de Marton quam Willelmus Burye[84] clericus inpresenti possidet sequestranda fore decreverunt. Et sequestrandi potestatem Joanni Dudeley generoso commiserunt.

(fol. 46v. is blank.)

Visitatio regia in et per civitatem et diocesim Cestrenses.

In ecclesia parochiali de Rychemonde, die mercurij xviij° die Mensis Septembris Anno Domini Millesimo quingentesimo lix^{no}.

Cestrensis
Diocesis

Quibus die et loco, Henricus Gates miles, Edwinus Sandis sacre theologie doctor et Henricus Harvye legum doctor Commissarij antedicti locum eis preperatum adeuntes, primo omnipotenti Deo preces publicas effunderunt. Deinde postquam prelibatus magister Edwinus Sandis publice ad populum salvationis verbum predicaverat loco iudiciali sedentes ac lecta Commissione ad visitacionem regiam actualiter exercendam more et solempnitate debitis processerunt visit*ates* clerum et populum decanatuum de Richemond Catericke et Borowbrige. **Receptoque** certificatorio de executione mandati citatorij &c, omnes citatos preconizari fecerunt, citatosque et preconizatos ac non comparentes pronunciaverunt contumaces &c. **Ac** illis comparentibus, publice per Thomam Percy registrarium antedictum/Articulis inquisitionis perlectis unacum regijs iniunctionibus, Iconomos et gardianos cuiuslibet parochie tactis sacrosanctis evangelijs de fideliter inquirendo et detegendo &c, Domini Commissarij monuerunt quod personaliter compareant eodem [loco][85] hora secunda post meridiem billas presentacionis exhibituri; monuerunt etiam clericos interessentes ad tunc comparendum litteras ordinum, institutiones dispensationes ac alia sua munimenta secundum tenorem mandati citatorij &c exhibituros ac visitationem regiam ulterius tunc subituros. **Hijs** expeditis Domini Commissarij continuaverunt hanc visitacionem usque in dictam horam secundam cum continuatione et prorogatione ulteriori prout eis visum fuerit neccessarium. **Dicta secunda** hora adveniente Domini Commissarij in loco predicto iudicialiter sedentes visitacionis negocium in omnibus expediverunt.

Super detectione quod vicaria de Myton inpresenti sit vacua et curato destituta, Domini Commissarij fructus decimas et cetera emolumenta dicte vicarie sequestranda fore decreverunt. Et emanavit sequestracio Ricardo Crawford de eadem.

In ecclesia parochiali de Kendall, die lune nono die mensis Octobris Anno Domini Millesimo quingentesimo quinquagesimo nono.

Dictis die et loco Magistri Edwinus Sandis sacre theologie Doctor et Henricus Harvye legum doctor Commissarij antedicti, finitis precibus, ac sempiterno Dei verbo ad populum honorifice predicato et evangelizato per magistrum Edwinum Sandis[86] antedictum ad locum iudicialem in cancello dicte ecclesie ornatum, unacum Georgio Browne armigero Commissario antedicto decentius adeuntes, ibidemque iudicialiter sedentes visitacionem hanc regiam pro clero et populo Decanatuum de Kendall, Copeland et Furnes omnibus via et modo melioribus actualiter exercebant. **Et** recepto certificatorio de executione mandati omnibusque citatis preconizatis, Domini Commissarij pronunciaverunt omnes absentes contumaces &c. Perlectisque Articulis ac traditis iniunctionibus regijs, receptisque ab Iconomis et parochianis iuramentis de inquisitione facienda super articulis &c, monuerunt clerum interessentem ad ulterius comparendum hora secunda a meridie tunc visitacionem ulterius subiturum &c, iuxta mandati tenorem. In quam horam continuata est visitacio et sic de tempore in tempus prout eis visum fuerit neccessarium &c. **Dicta** secunda hora adveniente Domini Commissarij iudicialiter sedentes visitacionis negocium in omnibus debite expediverunt &c.

f.48v.
Cockermouth

Predictis die et loco super contentione habita inter parochianos ecclesie parochialis de Cokermouth et Iconomos et parochianos de Embylton Capelle annexe ad Cockermouthe de et cum consensu partium Domini Commissarij gravaminibus ex utraque parte propositis debite examinatis, decretum imposuerunt sub hoc tenore, viz.: **That** *that*[87] *the parishners of Embilton shalbe contributors and pay to the reparations of the churche of Cockermowthe and all other chargies of the churche, suche deuties as they have byn accustomed to paye at auny tyme within this xxxᵗⁱ yeres last paste* &c.

Eversham

Super contraversia orta et habita inter Iconomos et parochianos de Crostlewayte capelle annexe de et cum consensu utriusque partis predicti Domini Commissarij inter eos decretum imposuerunt habens hunc tenorem, viz.: **That** *of all corses and burialles within the chapell of Crostlewayte halfe the monneye recevyd for the same shalbe contributed and geven to Eversham churche.* **Also** *that the parishners of the chapell of Crostlewayte shall contribute and give quarterly: ijˢ, towardes the clarkes wagis at Eversham*

f.49r.

In ecclesia parochiali de Lancaster, Cestrensis diocesis, die jovis viz. duodecimo die mensis Octobris Anno Domini millesimo quingentesimo quinquagesimo nono.

Predictis die et loco, dictis precibus ac verbo Dei ad populum sincere predicato per Magistrum Barnardum Gilpin sacre theologie baccalaurium, sepedicti magistri Edwini Sandis sacre theologie doctor et Henricus Harvy legum doctor ac Georgius Browne armiger, Commissarij antedicti visitationem Regiam solempniter et more consueto celebrantes et exercentes preconizari fecerunt omnes citatos visitacionem hanc subituros &c. Omnesque absentes citatos pronunciaverunt contumaces &c. **Deinde** lectis articulis et Iniunctionibus generalibus omnes Iconomos et gardianos iuraverunt de fideliter inquirendo et presentando super articulis predictis, monueruntque et eos et clericos omnes comparentes ad personaliter comparendum hoc in loco hora secunda a meridie ulterius visitacionem subituros iuxta tenorem mandati citatorij. In quam horam visitacionem continuaverunt et sic de tempore in tempus quotiens et quando eis videbitur oportunum &c. **Dicta** hora adveniente Domini Commissarij iudicialiter sedentes visitacionem debite expediverunt et terminaverunt &c.

> **In ecclesia parochiali** de Wiggan, Cestrensis diocesis, die lune, viz. decimo sexto die mensis Octobris Anno Domini Millesimo quingentesimo lix^{no}.   f.49v.

Dictis die et loco, finitis precibus, ac Salvationis verbo ad populum publice predicato per Jacobum Pilkington sacre theologie baccalaureum Edwinus Sandis sacre Theologie doctor, Henricus Harvye legum doctor et Georgius Browne armiger Commissarij antedicti ad locum in choro preperatum adeuntes visitacionem Regiam reverenter exercebant. Et preconizatis omnibus ad hanc visitacionem monitis prout in certificatorio introducto et recepto continetur, omnes absentes monitos preconizatos et non comparentes pronunciaverunt contumaces, et in penam contumaciarum suarum contra eos procedendum iuxta equitatis rationem &c. **Deinde** Iconomos et parochianos cuiuslibet parochie lectis prius articulis et Iniunctionibus generalibus, iuraverunt de fideliter inquirendo et presentando super eijsdem. Et predicti Domini Commissarij tam prefatos gardianos quam clericos omnes monitos et presentes ad comparendum hoc in loco die presenti hora secunda a meridie tunc ulterius facturos et recepturos quod huiusmodi visitacionis negocium de se exigit ac iuxta tenorem mandati citatorij &c. Dicta hora adveniente per Dominos Commissarios iudicialiter sedentes debite huiusmodi visitacionis negocium erat expeditum &c.

> **In ecclesia parochiali** de Manchester, Cestrensis diocesis, die mercurij viz. decimo octavo die mensis Octobris Anno Domini millesimo quingentesimo lix^{no}.   f.50r.

Dictis die et loco postquam preces erant solempniter dicte, sepedictus magister Edwinus Sandis publice ad populum Jesu Christi verbum evangelisavit &c, quo finito ad locum preperatum prefatus Edwinus Sandis, Henricus Harvye legum doctor et Georgius Browne armiger Commissarij antedicti adeuntes, lecta Commissione ad visitacionis negocium expediendum processerunt. Omnibusque monitis et citatis hanc visitacionem subituris debite preconizatis iuxta tenorem certificatorij introducti, omnes absentes pronunciaverunt contumaces. Et in penam contumacie procedendum iuxta equitatis rationem &c. **Deinde** Domini Commissarij proposita exhortatione per sepedictum magistrum Edwinum Sandis ac lectis articulis et Iniunctionibus generalibus traditis omnes ecclesiarum gardianos et parochianos iurari fecerunt de fideliter inquirendo et presentando de et super Articulis predictis, eosdemque gardianos et parochianos et clericos presbiteratos presentes monuerunt ad comparendum hoc in loco hora secunda a meridie tunc ulterius exhibituros facturos et recepturos quod visitacionis negocium exigit et requirit, iuxta tenorem mandati originalis citatorij./**Dicta** secunda hora adveni-   f.50v.

ente per Dominos Commissarios iudicialiter sedentes debite in omnibus expeditum erat visitacionis negocium &c.

Holme

Super detectione quod Georgius Holmes de Manchester et Elizabetha Robinson de eadem fornicationem commiserunt, Domini Commissarij viro personaliter comparenti obijcierunt crimen, qui fetebatur. Unde iniuncta est ei penitentia peragenda in ecclesia parochiali de tribus diebus dominicis a festo divi Andree proxime futuro, nudis pedibus et capite, et quod decenter manifestabit scedulam publice confessionis sibi traditam. Et ad certificandum de peracta penitentia decano rurali ibidem. Et monitus est ultro quod illicite amplius eam non cognoscet. Et ad id prestitit iuramentum ad tacta Dei evangelia &c.

f.51r.

In domo capitulari ecclesie collegiate de Manchester, xix^{no} die mensis Octobris Anno Domini Millesimo quingentesimo lix^{no}.

Manchestor Collegium

Dictis die et loco predicti Domini Commissarij iudicialiter sedentes dictum collegium actualiter visitaverunt. Et preconizatis tam magistro quam socijs et ceteris collegij ministris, pronunciaverunt contumaces et in penam contumacie contra eos et eorum quemlibet procedendum iuxta equitatis rationem &c.

Laurentius Vawce clericus gardianus sive magister dicti collegij preconizatus comparuit per quendam Stephanus Beche exhibentem procuratorium pro eodem qui allegavit se profectum fuisse Londinum.
Dominus Joannes Copage socius dicti collegij preconizatus non comparuit.
Robertus Erlond socius personaliter comparuit et subscripsit.
Robertus Prestwiche stipendiarius personaliter comparuit et subscripsit, quem Domini Commissarij stricte monuerunt quod deinceps non frequentabit tabernas ut solitus, sub pena suspensionis ab officio.

Harte
f.51v.

Ricardus Harte clericus socius dicte collegij personaliter comparens obstinate et peremptorie Religionis Articulis subscribere [recusavit],[88] unde/prefati Domini Commissarij ceperunt ab eodem et suis fideiussoribus recognitionem ad usum Domine nostre Regine, in qua ipse Ricardus recognovit se debere tricentas libras et quilibet fideiussorum centum libras &c, cum condicione quod ipse personaliter compareat coram generalibus Commissarijs Londini residentibus vicesimo die mensis Novembris proximi &c, quod tunc recognitio vacua sit ut per eandem recognitionem[89] ad cancellariam certificatam plenius apparebit, &c.

Predicti vero socij iterum atque iterum moniti et requisiti ut fundationem et alia dicti collegij munimenta exhiberi faciant seu exhibeant, ipsi vero respondendo asserebant quod gardianus sua custodia habet omnia, ipsis non consentientibus &c.

f.52r.

In ecclesia parochiali de Northwiche, Cestrensis diocesis, vicesimo die mensis Octobris Anno Domini Millesimo quingentesimo lix^{no}.

Dictis die et loco, finitis precibus verboque Dei per magistrum[90] Johannem Beste concionatorem antedictum publice predicato, Edwinus Sandis sacre theologie doctor, Henricus Harvye legum doctor et Georgius Browne armiger, Commissarij antedicti ea qua usi sunt solempnitate visitacionem regiam actualiter exercentes omnes citatos preconizari fecerunt, omnesque absentes pronunciaverunt contumaces, &c. **Deinde** perlectis publice Articulis et Iniunctionibus generalibus, omnes ecclesiarum gardianos et parochianos Domini iurari fecerunt de fideliter inquirendo et presentando super articulis predictis, et monuerunt eos ad comparendum hora secunda a meridie billas exhibituros secundum originale mandatum. Monuerunt etiam et clerum eadem hora ad comparendum tunc facturum exhibiturum et recepturum quod huiusmodi visitacionis negocium exigit et requirit. **Dicta** hora secunda adveniente per dominos commissarios iudicialiter sedentes debite sit visitacionis negocium expeditum &c.

Deinde Domini Commissarij antedicti ob certas rationabiles causas et precipue ob   f.52v.
pestem sementem tam in civitate Cestrensi quam in locis circumvicinis et adiacentibus illos moventes, ad exercendum et expediendum Visitacionis Regie negocium tam in prefata civitate Cestrensi, quam apud Tarwin secundum monitionem in ea parte prius emanatam, dilectos sibi in Christo Edwardum Fyton militem, Edmundum Scambler sacre Theologie baccalaurium, Willelmum Morton armigerum et Thomam Percy generosum surrogatos suos nominaverunt et substituerunt &c, eijsque et eorum duobus vices suas et aucthoritatem committentes &c.
Assumpto Joanne Stace in Registrarium et Scribam.

Sessio apud Tarwyn   f.53r.

Die martis viz. vicesimo quarto die mensis Octobris Anno Domini Millesimo quingentesimo quinquagesimo nono, in ecclesia parochiali de Tarwyn,[91] Edwardus Fyton miles, Edmundus Scambler sacre theologie baccalaurius, et Willelmus Morton armiger Surrogati et substituti per egregios viros Edwinum Sandis sacre theologie *baccalaurium* et Henricum Harvye legum doctorem Commissarios antedictos regia auctoritate suprema sufficienter et legitime aucthorizati in loco ibidem preperato sedentes, lectis prius litteris Commissionalibus eis directis onus executionis earundem litterarum in se assumpserunt. Et secundum vim formam et effectum earundem procedendum fore decreverunt in presencia Thome Percy registrarij antedicti.

Deinde, finitis precibus, verboque Dei ad populum predicato per prelibatum magistrum Scambler &c, idem Domini surrogati ad visitationem regiam ibidem actualiter exercendum solempniter processerunt, et procedebant. Receptoque certificatorio de executione originalis mandati citatorij omnes absentes citatos preconizatos et nullo modo comparentes pronunciaverunt contumaces, et in penam suarum contumaciarum procedendum fore iuxta equitatis rationem &c. Ac postea publice perlectis et traditis articulis et Iniunctionibus idem Domini Surrogati omnes ecclesiarum gardianos et parochianos iuramento oneraverunt de fideliter inquirendo detegendo et presentando de et super articulis predictis, et

f.53v.

exhibendo billas hora secunda/a meridie. Monuerunt etiam clericos omnes et singulos eadem hora ad comparendum tunc et ibidem facturos exhibituros et recepturos quod huiusmodi visitacionis negocium exigit et requirit. **Dicta** hora adveniente Domini Surrogati debito modo visitacionis negocium peregerunt.

Et Iconomis predicte ecclesie parochialis de Tarwyn per Dominos Surrogatos precipitur quod ipsi indilate omnes fornicatores in dicta parochia moneant quod ipsi personaliter compareant coram eijsdem substitutis in ecclesia cathedrali Cestrensi die jovis proximo detecta visitacionis responsuri &c.

f.54r.

In ecclesia cathedrali Cestrensi, xxvj^{to} die mensis Octobris Anno Domini Millesimo quingentesimo quinquagesimo nono.

Dictis die[92] et loco postquam preces erant dicte, Magister Edmundus Scambler sacre theologie baccalaurius publice ad populum evangelium Domini predicavit. Quo finito prefatus Edmundus et Thomas Percye generosus in choro dicte ecclesie adiverunt ibidemque litteras commissionales surrogacionis a prenominatis Dominis Commissarijs eis directas publice legi fecerunt &c. Ac recepto executionis onere ad visitacionis negocium pro clero et populo prefate civitatis Cestrensis procedebant, omnibusque citatis debite preconizatis omnes absentes pronunciaverunt contumaces &c. Deinde Iconomos et parochianos cuiuslibet parochie, tactis evangelijs, iuraverunt de fideliter inquirendo detegendo et present-ando de et super Articulis generalibus et Iniunctionibus sibi adtunc traditis. Deinde dicti surrogati monuerunt eos ad exhibendum billas suas iuxta monitionem eis datam citra horam secundam crastino a meridie. Et illico clericis examinatis omnes voluntarie suscepte Religionis Articulis subscripserunt &c.

Memorandum quod sedes episcopalis ibidem diu[98] vacavit, quodque decani dignitas per duos annos[94] vacavit. Et in eadem ecclesia solummodo duo sint prebendarij residentes. Dictaque ecclesia cathedralis tanta est inopia suppressa ut pauperibus et ecclesie ministris salaria sua satisfacere et persolvere non possint &c.

f.54v.

Radulphus Haselherst de Waverton detectus de crimine fornicationis cum quadam Margeria Moncke de eadem. Quibus evocatis et presentibus Domini Surrogati obijcerunt crimen. Et ipsi negantes fatebantur matrimonii contractum sub hijs verbis: *I am contente to marye with you when so ever I have auny lyvynge, and therapon the sayd Ralphe kissed the sayd Margerye consenting therunto.* Et propterea quod vir interrogatus nullam potuit allegare causam quare ad solempnizationem huiusmodi matrimonij compelli non debeat, idcirco prefati Surrogati precipiendo monuerunt virum ad procurandum matrimonium solemp-nizari citra festum Annunciationis Beate Marie Virginis proximum sub pena iuris, in presencia mulieris consentientis &c.

(fols. 55r.–56v. are blank.)

Acta et processus habita et facta coram Commissarijs
antedictis tempore visitacionis Regie in et per totam
provinciam Ebor' in causis beneficialibus et restitucionis beneficij[1] &c, prout sequitur:

Apud Nottyngham, xxij*do* die mensis Augusti Anno Domini millesimo
quingentesimo quinquagesimo nono, coram Commissarijs visitacionem
exercentibus.

In causa sive negocio beneficiali sive restitucionis beneficij mota per Oliverum
Columben clericum, rectorem se asserentem ecclesie parochialis de Stanford
Ebor' diocesis, contra et adversus Dominum Elizeum Umfrye cler*i* recto*ris*
ibidem pretens*i* &c, partes presentes in iudicio. Et prefatus Oliverus Columben
viva voce apud acta allegavit quod ipse in plena et pacifica possessione dicte
rectorie de Stanford existens, in eademque rite et legitime institutus et inductus
inter parochianos aliosque vicinos et circumvicinos pro rectore dicte ecclesie
nominatus dictus et reputatus fuit et est palam publice et notarie. Quodque dicta
sua ecclesia et rectoria solum propter matrimonij causam contra ius et fas
spoliatus amotus seu deprivatus per iudicem omnino incompetentem &c, fuit et
est. Unde facta fide de iure requisita/prefatus Dominus Oliverus petijt instanter se
ad dictam suam ecclesiam unacum suis iuribus et pertinentijs universis restitui,
prefatumque Dominum Elizeum ab eadem amoveri &c. Deinde Domini Commissarij ad peticionem prefati actoris interrogaverunt predictum Elizeum an dicta
allegacio sit vera*m*. Ipse vero respondendo fatebatur continere in se veritatem in
presencia dicti actoris acceptantis eius confessionem. Et Domini Commissarij ad
peticionem dicti Domini Oliveri ulterius interrogaverunt dictum Elizeum si
causam aliquam rationabilem pro se dicere sciat quare dictus Dominus Oliverus
ad prefatam ecclesiam de Stanford restitui non debet. Et dictus Elizeus respondendo asseruit se nullam habere causam. Ideoque voluntarie tunc et ibidem dicte
ecclesie cessit ac ab eadem recessit unacum suis iuribus et pertinentijs universis,
asserendo etiam se contentem ut dictus Oliverus ad prefatam ecclesiam de Stanford restituatur. **Unde** Domini Commissarij matura prius deliberatione habita de
et cum consensu predicti Domini Elizei eundem Oliverum Columben ad dictam
ecclesiam de Stanford unacum suis iuribus et pertinentijs universis restituendum
fore decreverunt.

In ecclesia collegiata de Sowthwell coram Commissarijs visitacionem
regiam actualiter exercentibus, xxv*to* die mensis Augusti Anno Domini
Millesimo quingentesimo lix*no*:
In causa beneficiali sive restitucionis negocio mota per Magistrum Christoferum Cristophorus
Sugden
vicarius de
Newarke
contra
Joannem
Taverham
vicarium
pretensum
ibidem
Sugden sacre theologie baccalaureum vicarium ecclesie parochialis de Newarke
Ebor' diocesis, contra et adversus Joannem Taverham vicarium ibidem pretensum. Prefatus Cristophorus tunc et ibidem coram Dominis Commissarijs
iudicialiter sedentibus introduxit monitionem originalem sive mandatum
citatorium executum per Robertum Tonge litteratum, viz. per publicam
citacionem in valvis ecclesie ibidem affixam iuxta tenorem eiusdem mandati &c.
Et preconizatus dictus Joannes Taverham personaliter comparuit, quem Domini
41

Commissarij ad peticionem dicti actoris iuramento oneraverunt de fideliter respondendo contentis dicte monitionis quam quidem dictus actor loco summarie peticionis exhibuit, petijtque ut in hoc negocio procedatur summarie et de plano. Et Domini Commissarij ita procedendum decreverunt. Deinde pars rea respondendo articulis in monitione deductis, ad primum articulum dicit continere in se veritatem;

f.58v.   Ad secundum articulum fatetur deprivationem dicti Sugden attamen iuste ut credit;

Ad tertium articulum fatetur quod sciens erat deprivationis et possessionis dicti Sugden fatetur propriam suam possessionem esse iuste &c.

Ad quartum et quintum articulos fatetur.

Ad sextum credit credita et negat negata.

Deinde Sugden in supplementum probacionis exhibuit litteras institucionis dicte vicarie necnon processum deprivationis in registro Ebor'[2] remanentes quatenus sibi expedit et non aliter. Et predictus Taverham ulterius interrogatus an credit dictum Sugden deprivatum esse matrimonij causa solum respondit eum deprivatum ob eam causam. Et Domini Commissarij monuerunt partes ad comparendum in consistorio Ebor' die Sabbati proximo ad quindenam ulteriorem processum fieri visuras, et ad probandum hincinde eodem die. Dicto die Sabbati adveniente in loco Consistoriali Ebor' Domini Commissarij iudicialiter sedentes de et cum consensu partium ad ferendum decretum in hac causa procedendum fore ad statim decreverunt. Et postea tunc et ibidem parte dicti Sugden petente sententiam ferri, dictoque Taverham iusticiam sibi fieri Domini Commissarij sententiam diffinitivam sive finale decretum pro et ex parte dicti partis actricis tulerunt in scriptis per quam inter alia prefatum Christophorum Sugden ad dictam vicariam de Newarke ac possessionem eiusdem restituerunt &c.

f.59r.   **Apud Blithe die Sabbati** xxvj[to] die mensis Augusti Anno Domini Millesimo quingentesimo lix[no] coram Commissarijs antedictis visitacionem Regiam exercentibus.

Georgius
Monsume
clericus
rector de
Claworthe
contra
Magistrum
Rogerum
Dallyson
rectorem
ibidem
pretensum

In causa beneficiali sive negocio restitucionis mota per Georgium Monsum clericum rectorem de Claworth Ebor' diocesis, partem actricem, et magistrum Rogerum Dallison rectorem ibidem pretensum partem ream. Comparuit quidem Cuthbertus Cornford litteratus et introduxit monitionem originalem sive mandatum citatorium continentem in se peticionem et materiam interesse dicte partis actricis, et quod ipse prefatus Cuthbertus eandem monitionem sive mandatum debite fuisse executum per publicationem et affixationem eiusdem in valvis ecclesie de Claworth &c. Deinde preconizatus Rogerus Dallison comparuit per Robertum Pullyn suum procuratorem litteratorie constitutum, quod exhibuit et fecit se partem pro domino suo &c. Deinde actor constituit iudicialiter in hac causa Joannem Stace suum procuratorem, et prefatus Stace exhibens suum procuratorium fecit se partem &c, exhibuitque contenta deducta in monitione originali

f.59v.   pro/summaria peticione et petijt eandem admitti et procedendum fore summarie et de plano. Et Domini Commissarij admiserunt et sic procedendum fore decreverunt in presencia Pullyn procuratoris antedicti fatentis dominum suum habere copiam monitionis &c. Deinde dictus Pullyn responsum dedit articulis deductis in monitione prout sequitur:

Ad primum articulum fatetur.

Ad secundum respondit et dicit *that Monsume was deprived*[3] *and as tocching the cawse therof he referrithe himself to the processe of deprivation, how be it he doth beleve that he was iustlye deprived.*

Ad tertium articulum respondit et dicit *that Mr Doctor Dallison dyd not entire immediatly after the deprivation of the said Monsume but afterwardes apon the resignacion of one Thurlond, and therfor he belevythe that Mr Dallyson possessith the benefice iustlye* et aliter negat.

Ad quartum fatetur.

Ad ultimum credit credita et negat negata.

Deinde Domini Commissarij monuerunt partes ad comparendum loco consistoriali Ebor', nono die mensis Septembris proximo ad videndum ulteriorem processum fieri. Quo die adveniente Dominis Commissarijs iudicialiter sedentibus Stace *exhibuit exhibuit* sententiam et acta deprivationis domini sui &c, necnon et litteras institucionis &c, in supplementum probacionis, et petijt terminum assignari ad ferendum decretum in dicta causa in presencia Pullyn procuratoris antedicti, exhibentis materiam exceptoriam/quam Domini ad eius peticionem admiserunt   f.60r.
quatenus de iure. Repetitaque materia Domini Commissarij assignaverunt Monsume ad personaliter respondendum eidem proxima sessione apud civitatem Cestrensem, monuerunt etiam utranque partem ad tunc comparendum ulteriorem processum fieri. **Vicesimo** sexto die mensis Novembris[4] in ecclesia cathedrali Cestrensi coram surrogatis Dominorum Commissariorum presentes erant partes in iudicio ubi Monsome ad materiam exceptoriam respondebat negative. Deinde ad peticionem Monsume dicti surrogati assignaverunt ad ferendum decretum in ecclesia parochiali de Doncaster die Sabbati proximo ad quindenam inter horas primam et tertiam a meridie eiusdem diei, monueruntque Pullyn ad tunc interessendum &c. Et ulterius non est processum in causa &c, quia Monsume moritur sententia non lata.

Apud Pontefracte, xxviij° die mensis Augusti Anno Domini Millesimo   f.60v.
quingentesimo quinquagesimo nono coram Commissarijs visitationem regiam actualiter exercentibus.

In causa beneficiali sive negocio restitucionis beneficij mota per Antonium Blake sacre theologie baccalaureum vicarium de Doncaster partem actricem, et Joannem Hudson clericum vicarium ibidem pretensum partem ream, partes presentes in iudicio. Domini Commissarij ex eorum consensu continuaverunt causam expediendam hoc loco crastino hora octava. **Dicta** hora adveniente Blake exhibuit edictum citatorium sive mandatum originale remanens penes acta loco summarie peticionis in presencia partis ree. Qua repetita et admissa primo Domini Commissarij procedendum fore summarie et de plano decreverunt. Deinde prefatum Hudson presentem in iudicio iuramento ad tacta dei evangelia iuraverunt de fideliter respondendo articulis deductis in monitione. Et examinatus respondit ut sequitur:

Ad primum articulum fatetur.

Antonius
Blake
clericus
vicarius de
Doncaster
Ebor' diocesis,
contra
Johannem
Hudson
clericum
vicarium
ibidem
pretensum
&c.

Ad secundum respondit et dicit *that he dothe beleve that he was depryved for that he was maryed, and to the rest*[5] *article viz. that he shold be iniustly depryved he doth/referr hymselfe to the lawe.* **Ad** quartum negative respondit.

Ad quintum fatetur.

Ad sextum credit credita et negat negata.

Deinde Blake in supplementum probacionis exhibuit litteras institucionis in presencia Hudson exhibentis materiam quandam exceptoriam quam Domini admiserunt quatenus de iure. **Ad** eiusque peticionem Domini oneraverunt iuramento dictum Blake de fideliter respondendo dicte materie. Et in partem probacionis Hudson exhibuit litteras suas institucionis &c. Deinde Blake constituit Stace iudicialiter, quod procuratorium Stace exhibuit et fecit se partem &c. Deinde Blake super dicta materia examinatus respondit ut sequitur:

Ad primum articulum refert se ad iura.

Ad secundum negative respondit.

Ad tertium fatetur *that he kepte his wif by all the tyme deduced but he dothe denye auny suche statute to be made.*

Ad quartum negative respondit.

Ad quintum fatetur *that he was called bifore the iudges*[6] *for his mariage, and that he did always dissente from them.*

Ad vj et vij articulos negative respondit.

Ad octavam negative respondit, dicendo *that he did dissente from the iudges, and assone as ther was tyme and place he soughte his remedy as the lawe wold permytte,* et aliter negat.

Ad nonum articulum credit famam laboratam super per eum confessatis et aliter negat.

Ad decimum credit credita et negat negata.

Deinde ex consensu Domini assignaverunt ad probandum hincinde die jovis proximo ad septimanam in ecclesia metropolitica Ebor'. **Dicto** die adveniente Domini Commissarij iudicialiter sedentes preconizari fecerunt dictum Hudson, et preconizatus non comparuit, unde ad peticionem partis actricis accusantis eius contumaciam pronunciaverunt contumacem et in penam sue contumacie assignaverunt ad ferendum decretum die crastino in ecclesia sancti Michaelis super pontem hora causarum &c. Quibus die et loco Domini continuaverunt causam expediendam in loco consistoriali Ebor' hora secunda a meridie istius diei in contumacia Hudson. Quo tempore Domini assignaverunt ad id in crastino eodem loco hora causarum in contumacia Hudson &c. **Nono** die mensis[7] Septembris Domini Commissarij loco consistoriali Ebor' iudicialiter sedentes ad peticionem partis dicti Antonii Blake in contumacia Hudson preconizati et non comparentis pronunciaverunt et tulerunt sententiam diffinitivam pro et ex parte eiusdem Antonij per quam eundem ad dictam vicariam restituendum et dictum Hudson amovendum fore decreverunt, &c.

Apud Pontefracte, xxviij° die mensis Augusti predicto.

In causa beneficiali sive negocio restitucionis mota per Antonium Blake sacre theologie baccalaureum partem actricem contra Johannem Atkinson rectorem ibidem pretensum partem ream. Et prefatus Antonius Blake introduxit mandatum citatorium executum per Franciscum Metcalfe litteratum qui virtute sui iuramenti certificavit se executum fuisse illud mandatum secundum tenorem eiusdem per affixationem in valvis ecclesie. Et preconizatus dictus *Franciscus*[8] non comparuit, unde Dominus[9] ad peticionem Blake accusantis eius contumaciam pronunciavit ipsum contumacem et assignaverit causam expediendam crastino hora octava ante meridiem. Dicta hora adveniente comparuit personaliter dictus Atkinson, in cuius presencia Domini Commissarij ad peticionem Blake procedendum fore summarie et de plano decreverunt et postmodum exhibuit deducta in monitione originali pro summaria peticione et partem adversam eidem respondere compelli. Et Dominus Commissarius ad eius peticionem oneravit eundem de fideliter respondendo dicte materie, et examinatus respondit ut sequitur &c.:

Ad primum articulum credit eundem continere veritatem.

Ad secundum articulum respondit et fatetur *that he was depryved as he belevithe for that he was maryed, notwithstanding he saiethe that itt was not uniustlye, nether ageynst the lawes and statutes of this Realme as he belevithe.*

Ad tertium articulum *he saiethe and belevith that he had knowledge that Blake was depryved for mariage and that he entered and possessed the sayde parsonage from the sayd deprivation, and as he belevithe iustlye, by presentacion, institucion and induction.*

Ad quartum articulum non credit continere veritatem.

Ad quintum fatetur.

Ad sextum credit credita et negat negata.

Deinde Blake in supplementum probacionis exhibuit litteras institucionis &c, in presencia Atkin simili exhibentis suas litteras institucionis &c, et ex consensu partium Domini assignaverunt ad ferendum decretum in loco consistoriali Ebor' die Sabbati nono die mensis Septembris proximo, monueruntque partes adtunc comparendas. **Quo** die adveniente in loco consistoriali predicto, Domini Commissarij iudicialiter sedentes pro et ex parte dicti Antonij Blake sententiam ferri petentis decretum suum finale sive sententiam diffinitivam in scriptis tulerunt in contumacia Atkyn moniti preconizati et non comparentis, &c, per quam quidem sententiam prefatum Antonium ad dictam ecclesiam unacum suis iuribus et pertinentiis universis restituerunt eundemque Joannem Atkyn ab eadem amovendum decreverunt, &c.

Apud Ottley die lune quarto die mensis Septembris Anno Domini Millesimo quingentesimo lix*no*, coram Commissarijs visitationem regiam ibidem actualiter exercentibus &c.

In causa beneficiali sive restitucionis beneficij mota per Dominum Milonem Walker rectorem ecclesie parochialis de Latheleye partem actricem, et Thomam Helme clericum rectorem ibidem pretensum, Domini Commissarij iudicialiter procedentes, tandem, viz. nono die mensis Septembris antedicto in loco consis-

Marginal notes:

f.62r.
Antonius Blake clericus rector de Whyston Ebor' diocesis contra Johannem Atkynson rectorem ibidem pretensum

f.62v.

f.63r.
Dominus Milo Walker rector ecclesie

parochialis
de Latheley
Ebor' diocesis
contra
Dominum
Thomam
Helme
rectorem
ibidem
pretensum
f.63v.

toriali Ebor' iudicialiter sedentes ad peticionem partis actricis sententiam ferri petentis in presencia *partis* assignaverunt ad ferendum decretum in proxima sessione apud Lancaster data interim responsione ad materiam exceptoriam per partem ream oblatam; xij^{mo} die mensis Octobris Domini Commissarij in ecclesia parochiali de Lancaster iudicialiter sedentes ad peticionem Stace procuratoris partis actricis assignaverunt ad id in proxima sessione apud civitatem Cestrensem in contumacia partis ree non comparentis &c. Et ulterius non est processum in causa &c.

Antonius
Holgate
clericus
rector
unius
medietatis
ecclesie
parochialis de
Burnsall
Ebor' diocesis
contra
Ricardum
Summerscall
clericum
rectorem
pretensum
ibidem

In causa beneficiali sive restitucionis beneficij mota per eundem Antonium Holgate rectorem unius medietatis ecclesie parochialis de Burnsall predicto partem actricem contra et adversus Ricardum Summerscall clericum rectorem ibidem pretensum partem ream, Domini Commissarij iudicialiter procedentes inter nonnullos actus iudiciales tandem terminum ad ferendum decretum in dicta causa assignaverunt ad peticionem partis actricis in presencia partis ree in ecclesia parochiali de Lancaster xij^{mo} die mensis Octobris proxime futuro. Quo die adveniente Domini Commissarij iudicialiter sedentes in dicta ecclesia parochiali de Lancaster ad peticionem dicte partis actricis in presencia partis ree sententiam diffinitivam sive finale decretum pro et ex parte dicti Antonij Holgate tulerunt in scriptis, per quam prefatum Antonium Holgate ad dictam medietatem ecclesie parochialis de Burnsall unacum suis iuribus et pertinentiis universis restituerunt, et eundem Ricardum Summerscall ab eadem amovendum fore decreverunt &c.

f.64r.

Apud civitatem Ebor' loco consistoriali ibidem, nono die mensis Septembris Anno Domini Millesimo quingentesimo lix^{no}, coram commissarijs visitacionem regiam exercentibus.

Willelmum
Denman
rector
de Ordsall
Ebor' diocesis
contra
Robertum
Blunston
rectorem
pretensum
ibidem

In causa beneficiali sive restitucionis beneficij mota per Willelmum Denman artium magistrum contra Robertum Blunston clericum, predicti Domini Commissarij iudicialiter sedentes inter nonnullos actus iudiciales per ipsos in hoc negocio gestos, tandem ad peticionem dicti Willelmi Denman partis actricis ac de et cum consensu prefati Roberti Blunston ad id consentientis et ut dictus actor restituatur, terminum ad ferendum decretum in hoc negocio assignaverunt, viz. decimum nonum diem instantis mensis Septembris in ecclesia parochiali de Richemond. **Dicto** decimo nono die adveniente in ecclesia parochiali de Richemond iudicialiter sedentes ex consensu partium decreverunt dictum Willelmum Denman ad possessionem rectorie de Ordesall dictumque Robertum ab eadem amovendum fore[10] &c.

f.64v.
Yokesall
contra
Mershall

In consistoriali loco Ebor', nono die mensis Septembris antedicto
In causa beneficiali sive restitucionis beneficij mota per Dominum Willelmum Yokesall vicarium de Sowth Kyrbye Ebor' diocesis contra Johannem Mershall vicarium pretensum ibidem partes presentes in iudicio ac de eorum consensu Domini Commissarij assignaverunt causam tractandam et expediendam fore proxima sessione apud Lancaster, monueruntque partes adtunc comparendas.
Memorandum quod ulterius non est processum[11] in causa.

Apud Rychemond in ecclesia parochiali ibidem coram Commissarijs predictis visitacionem regiam actualiter exercentibus, xviij° die mensis Septembris Anno Domini Millesimo quingentesimo lix*no*.

In causa sive negocio restitucionis beneficij mota per Ricardum Baldwyn magistrum hospitalis divi Nicolai prope Richemond Cestrensis diocesis partem actricem et Willelmum Burye clericum magistrum pretensum dicti hospitalis partem ream, actor per Stace exhibentem procuratorium et facientem se partem pro eodem &c qui introduxit mandatum citatorium executum per Thomam Tylston litteratum &c in presencia Joannis Jonson litterati procuratoris dicti Willelmi Burye litteratorie constituti &c. **Deinde** inter nonnullos actus iudiciales in dicto negocio gestos et factos Domini Commissarij ad peticionem Stace assignaverunt ad ferendum decretum dicto loco in crastino hora octava ante meridiem &c. **Qua** hora adveniente Domini Commissarij iudicialiter sedentes rimato primitus toto processu ac matura deliberatione prehabita ad peticionem dicti Stace &c sententiam diffinitivam sive finale decretum pro et ex parte dicti Ricardi Baldwyn in presencia Joannis Jonson procuratoris predicti Willelmi Burye in scriptis tulerunt per quam inter cetera prefatum Ricardum Baldwyn ad dictam hospitalem cum suis iuribus et pertinentijs universis restituendum et Willelmum Burye ab eodem amovendum decreverunt &c.

In ecclesia parochiali de Richemond, xviij° die mensis Septembris antedicto.

In causa beneficiali sive negocio restitucionis beneficij mota per Robertum Pates clericum rectorem de Spennythorn Cestrensis diocesis contra et adversus Dominum Thomam Plewes rectorem ibidem pretensum. Partes personaliter in iudicio, et Domini Commissarij assignaverunt parti actrici ad proponendum in debita iuris forma quod habet &c, crastino hora octava hoc in loco, et pars rea ad tunc comparendum et recipiendum. **Hora** octava adveniente Pates exhibuit summariam peticionem quam Domini Commissarij admiserunt quatenus de iure in presencia Plewes moniti ad comparendum dicteque peticioni respondendum die lune proximo hora octava ante meridiem loco consistoriali ecclesie cathedralis Dunelmensis.

Memorandum quod ulterius non est processus in hoc negocio.

In magna capella infra Palacium Reverendi Patris Dunelmensis episcopi apud Aykelond, vicesimo primo die mensis Septembris Anno Domini Millesimo quingentesimo lix*no*, coram Commissarijs visitacionem regiam exercentibus.

In causa beneficiali sive negocio restitucionis beneficij mota per Magistrum Robertum Wisedom rectorem ecclesie parochialis de Settrington Ebor' diocesis partem actricem contra et adversus Joannem Thornton rectorem pretensum ibidem, actor per Johannem Stace apud acta constitutum, qui quidem exhibens suum procuratorium ac faciens se partem pro eodem introduxit monitionem originalem sive mandatum citatorium executum per Leonardum Sawle apparitorem iuratum per affixationem eiusdem mandati publice in valvis ecclesie ibidem die dominica ultima inter divinorum solempnia in presencia partis ree personaliter comparentis. Et ad peticionem Stace Domini Commissarij decreverunt procedendum fore summarie et de plano Et illico dictus Stace exhibuit contenta et deducta in monitione pro summaria peticione, qua repetita et admissa, pars rea virtute sui iuramenti dedit responsum eidem ut sequitur:

Ad primum articulum respondit affirmative.

Ad secundum fatetur ipsum esse deprivatum ob matrimonij causam et cetera negat.

Ad tertium respondit et dicit *that he entir' & possessith benefice, and as he belevith iustlye.*

f.66v.   **Ad** quintum[12] respondit negative.

Ad sextum fatetur.

Ad septimum credit credita et negat negata.

Deinde Stace acceptanti confessionem partis, Domini Commissarij ex consensu assignaverunt causam ulterius tractandam et expediendam proxima sessione in ecclesia cathedrali Cestrensi. Et monite sunt partes adtunc comparendum. Deinde Thornton constituit Magistrum Harte iudicialiter in hoc negocio &c. **Vicesimo** primo die mensis Octobris Anno Domini predicto apud villam de North Wiche, Cestrensis diocesis, coram Dominis Commissarijs iudicialiter sedentibus comparuit predictus magister Herte et exhibens suum procuratorium remanens apud acta pro dicto Thornton, fecit se partem pro eodem in presencia Stace. Deinde dicti procuratores consentientes tam in locum quam in tempus petierunt ut Domini Commissarij in huiusmodi negocio procedant &c. Et dictus Harte exhibuit quandam materiam exceptoriam quam Domini Commissarij admiserunt quatenus de iure &c. Et Stace incontinenti respondendo eidem responsionem dedit negativam &c, prefatusque Stace in supplementum probacionis ex parte sua exhibuit litteras institucionis dicti Magistri Wisedom remanentes penes acta, deinde Domini Commissarij ex consensu procuratorum assignaverunt ad ferendum decretum ad statim, &c. **Et** incontinenti Domini Commissarij ad peticionem Stace sententiam ferri pro parte sua instanter petentis ac in presencia

f.67r.   dicti Harte iusticiam/sibi et parti sue ministrari, rimato primitus toto et integro processu, maturaque deliberatione prehabita, sententiam diffinitivam sive finale decretum pro et ex parte predicti Roberti Wisedom tulerunt in scriptis, per quam quidem sententiam prefatum Robertum Wisedom ad dictam ecclesiam parochialem de Settrington unacum suis iuribus et pertinentijs universis restituendum predictumque Joannem Thornton ab eadem amovendum decreverunt, &c. **A qua** quidem sententiam Herte procuratorio nomine appellavit &c, ad illustrissimam Dominam Reginam et eius cancellarium[13] &c.

f.67v.   **In domo capitulari** ecclesie cathedralis Dunelmensis, xxiiij[to][14] die mensis Septembris Anno Domini Millesimo quingentesimo quinquagesimo nono coram Commissarijs visitacionem regiam ibidem exercentibus.

Atkinson   **In causa** beneficiali sive negocio restitucionis beneficij mota per Thomam Atkin-
contra   son clericum rectorem de Elwicke Ebor' diocesis partem actricem et Georgium
Clife   Clife rectorem ibidem pretensum partem ream. Actor per Stace apud acta *quod*

exhibuit[15] et fecit se partem &c, exhibuitque mandatum originale citatorium executum per Rogerum Atkinson litteratum &c in presencia Cliffe personaliter interessentis, deinde Domini Commissarij inter nonnullos actus iudiciales per eos in dicto negocio habitos et factos, tandem ad peticionem Stace procuratoris antedicti terminum ad ferendum decretum viz. diem jovis proximum in ecclesia divi Nicolai apud Novum Castrum hora causarum assignaverunt in presencia dicti Clif moniti ad tunc comparendum et audiendum. **Dictoque** die jovis adveniente predicti Domini iudicialiter sedentes ad peticionem Stace procuratoris antedicti in presencia Cliff sententiam diffinitivam sive finale decretum pro et ex parte dicti Thome Atkinson tulerunt, per quam inter alia eundem Thomam ad dictam ecclesiam de Elwicke cum suis iuribus et pertinentiis universis restituendum eundemque Georgium Clif ab eadem amovendum decreverunt &c.

In domo capitulari ecclesie cathedralis Dunelmensis predicto, xxv*to* die mensis Septembris.

f.68r.

In causa beneficiali sive negocio restitucionis beneficij mota per Joannem Rudde clericum prebendarium decime prebende in cathedrali Dunelmensi predicta partem actricem et Georgium Bullocke prebendarium dicte prebende pretensum partem ream Domini Commissarij rite et legitime procedentes tandem ad peticionem partis actricis inter nonnullos alios actus iudiciales per eos in dicto negocio habitos et factos ad ferendum decretum hoc in loco die crastino hora septima ante meridiem assignaverunt in presencia Bullocke[16] moniti ad tunc interessendum et audiendum. **Dicta hora** adveniente ad peticionem partis actricis sententiam diffinitivam sive finale decretum pro et ex parte sua in presencia Bullocke tulerunt in scriptis per quam dictum Joannem Rudd ad dictam decimam prebendam unacum suis iuribus et pertinentiis universis restituendum prefatumque Georgium Bullocke ab eadem amovendum decreverunt Domini Commissarij antedicti &c.

Rudd
contra
Bullock

Apud Dunelmiam in domo Capitulari ecclesie cathedralis ibidem, xxvj*to* die Mensis Septembris coram Dominis Commissarijs antedictis.

f.68v.

In causa beneficiali sive negocio restitucionis beneficij mota per magistrum Willelmum Latymer rectorem de Kyrkebye in Clevelonde partem actricem contra et adversus Willelmum Burye rectorem ibidem pretensum. Actor per Joannem Stace apud acta quod exhibuit et fecit se partem pro eodem exhibuitque mandatum originale citatorium executum per Laurentium Sutton litteratum, in presencia Joannis Jonson procuratoris dicti Willelmi Burye litteratorie constituti quod exhibuit et fecit se partem pro eodem deinde Stace exhibuit deducta et contenta in monitione pro summaria peticione qua admissa et repetita Jonson monitus est ad personaliter respondendum dicte materie hora prima a meridie. Et Domini Commissarij procedendum fore summarie et de plano ad peticionem Stace in presencia dicti Jonson iudicialiter decreverunt. **Hora** prima adveniente coram Dominis Commissarijs iudicialiter sedentibus comparuit Jonson et

Latymer
contra
Burye

exhibuit in scriptis responsum ad summariam peticionem &c quam Stace procuratorio nomine quo supra acceptavit, dictusque Jonson monitus est ad comparendum in ecclesia divi Nicolai apud Novum Castrum hora causarum ulteriorem processum fieri in causa visurus. **Dicto die** jovis adveniente in ecclesia divi

Nicolai Novicastri/comparuit Jonson et exhibuit quandam materiam sive allegationem in scriptis quam Domini ad eius peticionem admiserunt quatenus de iure. Et in probacione eiusdem exhibuit quoddam scriptum testimoniale sic incipiens, **Elizabeth** &c, et finiens sic: Regni nostri primo, sigillo prefate Domine Regine in curia Scaccarij sigillatum. Instanterque petijt illud registrari et originale sibi retradi, in presencia Stace procuratoris antedicti ac exhibens in supplementum probacionis summarie peticionis Institucionis Litteras dicti Latymer remanentes penes acta necnon sententiam et originalia acta deprivationis[17] dicti Latymer inactitata et remanentia inscripta in libro exhibito et transmisso a decano et Capitulo ecclesie cathedralis Ebor' &c deinde ad peticionem Stace Domini Commissarij assignaverunt ad ferendum decretum in tertia sessione apud Westchester, viz. xxv^{to} die mensis Octobris, monueruntque Jonson ad tunc comparendum et audiendum. **Dicto** xxv^{to} die adveniente Domini Surrogati &c ad peticionem Stace assignaverunt ad id in crastino hora octava ante meridiem. **Vicesimo** sexto die mensis Octobris in domo capitulari Ecclesie cathedralis Cestrensis Domini Surrogati ex certis causis se moventes remiserunt causam Commissarijs generalibus Londini residentibus coram eis finiendam &c.

In domo capitulari ecclesie cathedralis Dunelmensis, xxv^{to} die mensis Septembris Anno Domini predicto &c.

In causa beneficiali sive negocio restitucionis beneficij mota per Magistrum Joannem Rudde vicarium de Norton Dunelmensis diocesis partem actricem et querelantem, contra et adversus Robertum Dalton vicarium ibidem pretensum. Actor per Stace iudicialiter apud acta &c quod exhibuit et fecit se, exhibuitque mandatum citatorium executum per apparitorem &c. Et preconizatus Dalton non comparuit. Ideo ad peticionem Stace Domini pronunciaverunt contumacem reservantes penam in proximam sessionem apud civitatem Cestrensem &c.
Memorandum quod ulterius non est processum in hoc negocio.

In domo capitulari ecclesie cathedralis Carliolensis, tertio die mensis Octobris Anno Domini Millesimo quingentesimo lix^{no}, coram Dominis Commissarijs antedictis visitacionem regiam actualiter exercentibus.

In causa beneficiali sive negocio restitucionis beneficij de Ormysyde mota per Thomam Atkinson rectorem dicte ecclesie parochialis de Ormysyde Carliolensis diocesis partem actricem et querelantem, contra et adversus tam Joannem Yates clericum quam alios quoscumque interesse in hac parte pretendentes. Actor per Stace apud acta quod exhibuit et fecit se partem pro eodem in presencia Yates comparentis pro interesse suo &c. Deinde inter nonnullos actus et assignationes iudiciales Domini Commissarij tandem ad ferendum decretum in dicto negocio proxima sessione apud Perith, viz. sexto die instantis Octobris, ad peticionem

Stace in presencia Yates assignaverunt, monueruntque partes adtunc comparendum. **Dicto** sexto die Octobris adveniente in ecclesia parochiali de Perithe Domini Commissarij iudicialiter sedentes sententiam diffinitivam pro et ex parte dicti Thome Atkinson ad peticionem Stace ac in presencia Yates tulerunt in scriptis per quam quidem sententiam inter alia prefatum Thomam Atkinson ad dictam ecclesiam de Ormysyde unacum suis iuribus et pertinentijs universis restituendum eundemque Joannem Yates ab eadem amovendum fore decreverunt &c.

Domo Capitulari et die antedictis &c.

f.70v.

In causa beneficiali sive restitucionis beneficij *mota dominum* Willelmum Harrison rectorem de Bottell Dunelmensis diocesis partem actricem et querelantem, contra et adversus Robertum Pace rectorem ibidem pretensum. Actor per Stace apud acta quod exhibuit et fecit se partem &c, exhibuitque mandatum originale citatorium executum per Ricardum Kyrkelar litteratum per personalem citacionem dicti Pace cui tradidit copiam &c. Deinde inter nonnullos alios actus et assignationes iudiciales in ista causa habitos et factos tandem Domini Commissarij rimato primitus toto processu ac matura deliberatione prehabita in domo capitulari antedicto quarto die mensis predicti Octobris iudicialiter sedentes ad peticionem partis actricis sententiam diffinitivam sive finale decretum in dicta causa pro et ex parte dicti Willelmi Harison in presencia Pates tulerunt in scriptis per quam Domini Commissarij eundem Harrison ad dictam ecclesiam de Bottell unacum suis iuribus et pertinentijs universis restituendum eundemque Robertum Pace ab eadem removendum fore decreverunt.

Haryson
contra
Pates

Domo Capitulari Carliolensi coram Dominis Commissarijs antedictis, quinto die mensis Octobris predicto.

f.71r.

In causa beneficiali sive negocio beneficij restitucionis mota per Percivallum Wharton clericum vicarium de Brydkirke Carliolensis diocesis partem actricem et querelantem, contra et adversus Willelmum Graye vicarium pretensum ibidem partem ream presentem in iudicio, quem Domini Commissarij ad peticionem partis actricis monuerunt ad comparendum in ecclesia parochiali de Kendall decimo die Octobris proximo ad recipiendum libellum sive summariam peticionem &c. **Dicto** decimo die adveniente actor constituit Stace iudicialiter, qui exhibuit et fecit se partem &c, deditque in presencia partis ree summariam peticionem qua repetita et admissa predictus Graye respondendo eidem fatebatur et dixit: *That the sayde Percyvall Wharton was instituted and inducted in the sayd benefice and beynge in possession was depryved for that he was maryed; And as to the statutes he doth refer himself to the same.* Et fatetur iurisdictionem, creditque credita et negat negata. Quam confessionem Stace acceptavit, et [ad][18] eius peticionem Domini assignaverunt ad ferendum decretum hora prima a meridie. **Dicta** hora adveniente ad peticionem partis actricis Domini iudicialiter sedentes pro et ex parte eiusdem sententiam diffinitivam tulerunt in scriptis in presencia partis ree iusticiam petentis &c.

Wharton
contra
Graye

f.71v.

In ecclesia parochiali de Kendall, nono die mensis Octobris Anno Domini Millesimo quingentesimo lix*no*, coram Henrico Harvye legum doctore et Georgio Browne armigero Commissarijs antedictis &c.

Sandis
contra
Redman

In causa beneficiali sive negocio restitucionis beneficij mota per egregium virum Magistrum Edwinum Sandis sacre theologie doctorem vicarium ecclesie parochialis de Eversham Cestrensis diocesis partem actricem et querelantem contra et adversus Thomam Redman vicarium pretensum ibidem partem ream litteratorie monitum per Joannem Holme qui certificavit. Actor per Harte iudicialiter qui exhibens suum procuratorium fecit se partem &c. Et pars rea preconizata non comparuit; contumax. In cuius contumacia Harte exhibuit materiam deductam in citacione qua admissa Domini decreverunt procedendum fore summarie et de plano &c. Deinde personaliter comparuit Dominus Joannes Fawcet clericus et exhibens procuratorium pro dicto Thoma Redman fecit se partem pro eodem. Deinde habita ab eodem responsione ad summariam peticionem[19] quam Harte acceptavit quatenus &c, Domini Commissarij assignaverunt ad ferendum decretum hora prima a meridie, et monitus est Fawcett ad tunc comparendum. Qua hora adveniente Domini assignaverunt ad id in proximam sessionem apud civitatem Cestrensem et reum ad tunc interessendum &c. Deinde inter alios actus iudiciales in domo capitulari ecclesie cathedralis Cestrensis surrogati Commissariorum iudicialiter sedentes ad peticionem partis actricis in contumacia partis

f.72r.

ree preconizate et non comparentis pro parte dicti Edwini Sandis tulerunt sententiam/diffinitivam sive eorum finale decretum in scriptis per quam ipsum prefatum Edwinum ad dictam vicariam de Eversham unacum suis iuribus et pertinentijs universis restituendum eundemque Thomam Redman ab eadem et possessione eiusdem amovendum fore decreverunt &c.

In ecclesia parochiali de Kendall, die et anno predictis, coram Dominis Commissarijs visitacionem regiam ibidem actualiter exercentibus.

Soorye
contra
Atkinson

In causa beneficiali sive negocio restitucionis beneficij mota per Willelmum Soorye clericum vicarium ecclesie parochialis de Sedbar, Cestrensis diocesis partem actricem contra et adversus Thomam Atkinson vicarium pretensum ibidem partem ream. Actor per Stace, quod exhibuit et fecit se &c, exhibuitque mandatum citatorium executum fuisse per Ricardum Bland litteratum certificans &c. Decimo Octobris in ecclesia predicta comparuit Robertus Atkynson exhibens procuratorium per Thomam Atkinson predicto fecit se partem &c. In cuius presencia Stace exhibuit contenta et deducta in citatione pro summaria peticione,

f.72v.

qua repetita et admissa, dictus/Robertus Atkinson procurator antedictus ad dictam summariam petitionem responsum dedit quod Stace acceptavit quatenus sibi expedit exhibuitque institucionem dicti Soorye in supplementum probacionis. Et Domini Commissarij ad eius peticionem assignaverunt ad ferendum decretum hora prima a meridie, monueruntque reum ad tunc interessendum. Deinde dictus Soorye exhibuit dispensacionem sibi concessam per Thomam Cantuariensem archiepiscopum auctoritate parliamenti[20] datam anno xxxviij° Henrici octavi &c ad probandum se sufficienter munitum ad recipiendum duo beneficia. Dicta hora prima adveniente Domini Commissarij iudicialiter sedentes ad peticionem partis actricis sententiam diffinitivam sive finale decretum pro et ex parte dicti Willelmi Soorye in scriptis tulerunt in presencia procuratoris partis ree iusticiam petentis &c.

Die et loco predictis

In causa beneficiali sive negocio restitucionis mota per Dominum Willemum Soorye clericum vicarium ecclesie parochialis de Orswicke Cestrensis diocesis contra et adversus Thomam Dobeson vicarium pretensum ibidem personaliter comparentem. In cuius presencia Stace exhibuit procuratorium suum remanens penes acta et fecit se &c./exhibuitque summariam peticionem deductam in mandato originali citatorio &c, qua repetita et admissa Domini Commissarij monuerunt Dobeson ad comparendum crastino hora septima dicte peticioni responsurum et ulteriorem processum visurum. **Dicta** hora adveniente Domini Commissarij iudicialiter sedentes loco predicto, habita responsione per ream summarie peticioni quam Stace acceptavit, exhibitisque litteris institucionis et inductionis in supplementum probacionis &c, assignaverunt ad ferendum decretum hora prima a meridie, monueruntque Dobeson ad tunc comparendum et audiendum ad peticionem Stace. **Dicta** hora prima adveniente in ecclesia predicta Domini Commissarij iudicialiter sedentes sententiam diffinitivam sive finale decretum pro et ex parte dicti Willelmi Soorye in presencia partis ree petentis iusticiam tulerunt in scriptis per quam inter alia prefatum Willelmum Soorye ad dictam ecclesiam sive vicariam de Orswicke unacum suis iuribus et pertinentijs universis restituendum eundemque Thomam Dobeson ab eadem amovendum decreverunt &c.

Soorye
contra
Dobeson

f.73r.

In ecclesia parochiali de Kendall, coram Dominis Commissarijs antedictis, nono die mensis Octobris Anno Domini predicto &c.

In causa beneficiali sive negocio restitucionis mota per Dominum Georgium Taylor rectorem ecclesie parochialis de Bolmer Ebor' diocesis partem actricem et querelantem, contra et adversus Johannem Jakeson rectorem ibidem pretensum partem ream. Actor per Stace apud acta quod exhibuit &c, introduxitque mandatum citatorium executum per Christophorum Harison certificantem se personaliter citasse dictum Jakeson qui preconizatus non comparuit et ideo Domini Commissarij pronunciaverunt contumacem pena reservata usque in horam septimam crastino in aurora hoc in loco. **Dicta** hora septima adveniente Stace exhibuit deducta et contenta in citacione pro summaria peticione in contumacia partis ree preconizate et non comparentis et Domini Commissarij admiserunt ad eius peticionem et decreverunt procedendum fore summarie et de plano. Deinde Stace exhibuit litteras institucionis et inductionis dicti Tailor unacum sententia et processu deprivacionis[21] remanentibus penes acta ad probandum dictam peticionem suam, adque eius peticionem Domini assignaverunt ad ferendum decretum hora prima a meridie in contumacia partis.[22] **Hora** prima adveniente Domini iudicialiter sedentes ad peticionem Stace in contumacia partis ree sententiam tulerunt diffinitivam in scriptis pro parte dicti Taylor &c.

f.73v.

Tailor
contra
Jakeson

f.74r.

In **ecclesia de** Manchester coram Edwino Sandis sacre theologie doctore, Henrico Harvye, legum doctore, et Georgio Browne armigero, Commissarijs &c, decimo octavo die mensis Octobris Anno Domini Millesimo quingentesimo lix^{no}.

Johannes
Horleston
contra
Johannem
Hanson

In causa beneficiali sive negocio restitucionis mota per magistrum Joannem Horleston archidiaconum Richemond contra et adversus Joannem Hanson archidiaconum pretensum ibidem, comparuit quidam Robertus Barker clericus qui certificavit se executum fuisse mandatum originale citatorium per publicam citationem ita quod citacio de veresimili ad noticiam dicti Hanso*m* si infra Regnum Anglie extiterat pervenire potuisset. Et preconizatus reus non comparuit; contumax, pena reservata usque in horam septimam crastino hoc in loco. **Dicta** hora adveniente Domini Commissarij ad peticionem partis actricis pronunciaverunt dictum Hansom contumacem et in penam sue contumacie procedendum fore summarie et de plano. Dictusque actor exhibuit deducta et contenta in mandato originali pro summaria peticione, et in probacione eiusdem exhibuit litteras institucionis sive collacionis dicti Archidiaconatus sub sigillo reverendi patris Joannis nuper Cestrensis Episcopi, et ad probandum ulteriora deducta in summaria peticione dictus actor produxit Edwardum Planckney, Ricardum Horleston,/Alexandrum Turner et Joannem Shawe in testes quos Domini Commissarij ad eius peticionem iurare fecerunt &c. Deinde ad peticionem actoris Domini assignaverunt ad ferendum decretum apud ecclesiam parochialem de Northwiche die Sabbati proximo. Dicto die Sabbati advenienti in loco predicto ad id in hora prima a meridie ad peticionem partis ac in contumacia ree in hospitio Commissariorum.[23] **Dicta** hora prima adveniente ad peticionem Horleston actoris ac in contumacia partis ree sententiam diffinitivam sive finale decretum pro et ex parte dicti Horleston tulerunt in scriptis per quam inter alia prefatum Joannem Horlston ad dictum archidiaconatum Richemond unacum suis iuribus et pertinentijs universis restituendum eundemque Joannem Hansom ab eadem amovendum sententialiter decreverunt &c.

f.74v.

f.75r.

In **ecclesia** de Manchester die anno et coram Dominis Commissarijs antedictis.

Hyde
contra
Ethell

In causa beneficiali sive negocio restitucionis beneficij mota per Nicolaum Hyde vicarium de Motram Cestrensis diocesis partem actricem contra et adversus Dominum Davidem Ethell vicarium ibidem pretensum partem ream. Actor per Stace iudicialiter qui exhibuit procuratorium &c, et fecit se partem &c, exhibuitque deducta in mandato originali loco summarie peticionis, et procedendum fore summarie et de plano petijt, et Domini Commissarij sic assignaverunt, in presencia Ethell partis ree personaliter comparentis, qui respondendo dicte summarie peticioni fatebatur et dixit, *That Hyde was leafully instituted and inducted in the sayd vicarege, and further that he was depryved for that he was maryed as he belevith, and that this respondent enteryd immediatly after, beyng instituted and inducted as he belevithe leafullye.* Fatetur etiam iurisdictionem, creditque credita et negat negata, quam quidem confessionem Stace acceptavit quatenus sibi expedit. Et in supplementum probacionis exhibuit litteras institucionis dicti Nicolai Hyde, adque eius peticionem Domini Commissarij assignaverunt ad ferendum decretum crastino hora septima ante meridiem hoc in loco, et pars rea monita ad tunc comparendum et audiendum. **Dicta** hora adveniente Domini Commissarij iudicialiter sedentes pro parte dicti actoris tulerunt sententiam diffinitivam in scriptis in presencia partis ree &c.

In ecclesia de Manchester coram prefatis Dominis Commissarijs die et anno predictis.

In causa beneficiali sive negocio restitucionis beneficij mota per Marmaducum Pulleyn rectorem de Ripleye partem actricem, et querelantem, contra et adversus Robertum Percivall rectorem ibidem pretensum partem ream. Et introducto certificatorio de executione mandati citatorij, Pulleyn exhibuit summariam peticionem in presencia Stace procuratoris Percivall et exhibuit &c. Et Domini decreverunt procedendum fore summarie et de plano. Deinde repetita et admissa materia, Stace oneratus iuramento summariam peticionem responsum dedit ut sequitur:

Ad primum credit continere veritatem.

Ad secundum refert se ad statuta.

Ad tertium credit non continere veritatem.

Ad quartum negative respondit.

Ad quintum credit non continere veritatem.

Ad sextum fatetur.

Ad septimum fatetur confessata et negat negata.

Deinde Stace exhibuit materiam exceptoriam quam Domini admiserunt quatenus de iure, eademque repetita, Domini assignaverunt Pulleyn ad personaliter respondendum crastino hora septima. **Dictaque** hora adveniente, ac habita responsione dicti Pulleyn ad materiam exceptoriam, Domini Commissarij de et ex consensu partium assignarunt causam et negocium finienda coram commissarijs generalibus Londini &c.

Apud Northwiche in ecclesia parochiali ibidem coram Commissarijs visitacionem regiam exercentibus, xx^{mo} die mensis Octobris Anno Domini Millesimo quingentesimo lix^{no}.

In causa beneficiali sive restitucionis beneficij mota per Joannem Adams clericum rectorem de Hockerton Ebor' diocesis partem actricem contra et adversus Thomam Huddleston rectorem ibidem pretensum, actor per Henricum Yonge &c. Domini Commissarij assignaverunt causam expediendam apud Cestriam prima sessione; $xxiij^o$ Octobris Yong exhibuit edictum citatorium executum per Joannem Sharpe litteratum &c, et preconizatus Hudleston non comparuit, et ad peticionem Yong accusantis eius contumaciam Domini surrogati decreverunt procedendum fore summarie et de plano, exhibuitque dictus Yong summariam peticionem in contumacia partis &c. Deinde inter nonnullos actus et assignationes iudiciales tandem Domini Surrogati ad peticionem actoris ac in presencia Joannis Sharpe facientis fidem dictum Hudleston voluntarie renunciasse interesse in dicta rectoria ac contentum esse ut actor restituatur, sententiam sive finale decretum pro et ex parte dicte partis actricis tulerunt in scriptis per quam ipsum Joannem Adams ad dictam ecclesiam inter alia unacum suis iuribus et pertinentijs universis restituendum fore decreverunt &c.

f.76v.

Whytbye
contra
Ellys

Loco consistoriali Ebor' coram surrogatis Dominorum Commissariorum apud Ebor' 1559.

In causa beneficiali sive negocio restitucionis mota per Dominum Thomam Whytbee vicarium de Hutton in Craneswycke partem actricem contra et adversus Willelmum Ellys vicarium ibidem pretensum partem ream, comparuit magister Johannes Farley et introduxit mandatum citatorium &c, exhibuitque procuratorium *per* actor*e* et fecit se partem &c, in presencia Ellys personaliter comparentis. Dictusque Farley exhibit summariam peticionem quam domini admiserunt quatenus de iure et procedendum fore summarie et de plano &c. Repetitaque materia Domini Surrogati monuerunt partem ream ad personaliter respondendum dicte peticioni hora quarta post meridiem &c. **Dicta** hora adveniente dictus Ellys iuramento oneratus ad peticionem Farley responsum dedit ad summariam peticionem ut sequitur:

Ad primum et secundum credit continere veritatem.

Ad tertium credit dictum Whitbye deprivatum esse ob matrimonij causam.

Ad quartum dicit *that he did succede one Thomas Monckton dyenge vicar ther, and so by his deth the vicarege beyng voyde he entered, and was not ymmediat successor to Whitbye.*

Ad quintum refert se ad statutum.

Ad sextum credit continere veritatem.

Ad septimum credit credita et negat negata.

Quam quidam confessionem et responsionem Farleye acceptavit quatenus facit pro domino suo, ad eiusque peticionem Domini surrogati assignaverunt ad ferendum decretum die martis proximo post conceptionis &c, casu quo Domini Commissarij ad id consentient, et monitus est Ellys dissentiens, ad tunc comparendum &c.

Ulterius non est processum in causa.

(fols. 77r.–78v. are blank.)

Sequntur nomina eorum qui per Dominos Commissarios antedictos tempore visitacionis regie infra provinciam Eboracensem
admissi et instituti fuer*i*nt ad et in beneficijs vacantibus.

Apud Nottingham, vicesimo secundo die mensis Augusti Anno Domini
predicto.
Henricus Nicolson clericus admissus est ad rectoriam ecclesie parochialis de
Tiriswell Ebor' diocesis, et in eadem rectoria institutus, ad presentationem Joannis
Hercye militis &c.

Tiriswell

Alexander Fasett clericus admissus et institutus in vicaria de Ledes Ebor' diocesis,
ad presentacionem Rolandi Cowycke generosi &c.

Ledes

Keyworth

Edmundus Stubbes clericus admissus fuit ad ecclesiam parochialem de Key-
worthe Ebor' diocesis, ac in eadem canonice institutus cum suis iuribus et pertinentiis universis, ad presentacionem Ricardi Pendocke et Matilde eius uxoris
patronorum &c, prestito iuramento &c.

Joannes Drurye clericus admissus est ad ecclesiam parochialem de Lowdam Ebor'
diocesis, et in eadem prestito iuramento fidelitatis institutus, ad presentationem
Domine Regine &c.

Lowdam

Willelmus Undern clericus admissus est ad ecclesiam parochialem de Wollaton
Ebor' diocesis, ac prestito iuramento fidelitatis canonice in eadem institutus cum
suis iuribus et pertinentiis universis, ad presentationem Gabrielis Harwycke et
Joannis Hall, executorum testamenti Henrici Willobye defuncti &c.

Wollaton

Apud Sowthwell, xxiiij*to* die mensis Augusti Anno Domini 1559.
Thomas Marsee clericus admissus fuit ad vicariam de Estmarkeham in eademque
prestito primitus iuramento fidelitatis, institutus ad presentationem per Edmundum London unacum suis iuribus et pertinentiis universis.

Estmarkham

Willelmus Abbote clericus admissus erat ad rectoriam de Buryethorpe Ebor'
diocesis, ac prestito iuramento fidelitatis in eadem institutus, ad presentationem
Domine nostre Regine &c.

Burythorpe

Apud Blithe, xxvj*to* Augusti &c.
Jacobus Raworthe clericus admissus fuit ad vicariam de Cropishill Bisshop, ac
prestito iuramento fidelitatis in eadem institutus, ad presentacionem Henrici
Harvye patroni eiusdem.

Grove

Robertus Rothwood clericus admissus est ad ecclesiam parochialem de Grove Ebor' diocesis, ac prestito iuramento in eadem institutus cum suis iuribus et pertinentiis universis, ad presentacionem Joannis Hercye militis.

Walton

Willelmus Walton clericus admissus erat ad ecclesiam sive vicariam ecclesie parochialis de Wheatley Ebor' diocesis, ac prestito iuramento fidelitatis in eadem institutus cum suis iuribus et pertinentiis universis, ad presentationem Galfridi Foliampe.

f.81r.

Apud Pontefracte, xxviij^o die mensis Augusti Anno Domini Millesimo quingentesimo lix^{no}.

Churchesandall

Hamletus Taylor clericus admissus est ad rectoriam ecclesie parochialis de Churchesandall Ebor' diocesis, ac prestito fidelitatis iuramento in eadem institutus unacum suis iuribus et pertinentiis universis.

Armethorpe

Joannes Dodworthe clericus admissus erat ad ecclesia, parochialem de Armethorpe Ebor' diocesis, ac prestito fidelitatis iuramento in eadem canonice institutus unacum suis iuribus et pertinentiis universis.

Wathe

Ricardus Byrde clericus admissus ad vicariam de Wathe Ebor diocesis, ac prestito iuramento fidelitatis in eadem canonice institutus unacum suis iuribus et pertinentiis universis ad presentacionem decani et capituli ecclesie Christi Oxon'.

f.81v.
Kellington

Willelmus Oglethorpe clericus admissus fuit ad vicariam de Kellington Ebor' diocesis, ac prestito iuramento fidelitatis in eadem institutus cum suis iuribus et pertinentiis universis, ad presentationem Magistri et sociorum collegij Sancte Trinitatis Cantabrigie.

f.82r.

Apud Ottley, quarto die mensis Septembris Anno Domini Millesimo quingentesimo lix^{no}.

Romaldkirke

Joannes Beste artium magister admissus erat ad ecclesiam parochialem de Romaldkirke Cestrensis diocesis, ac prestito iuramento fidelitatis in persona Ricardi Beste sui procuratoris canonice in eadem institutus cum suis iuribus et pertinentiis universis, per presentationem illustrissime Domine nostre Regine.

f.82v.

Apud civitatem Ebor', sexto die mensis Septembris Anno Domini Millesimo quingentesimo quinquagesimo nono.

Dalbye

Robertus Rome clericus admissus erat ad rectoriam ecclesie parochialis de Dalbye Ebor' diocesis, ac prestito iuramento fidelitatis in eadem canonice institutus cum suis iuribus et pertinentiis universis per presentationem Rogeri Raisinge, Thome Sothebye et Thome Dowman ratione advocationis facte per abbatem et conventum nuper monasterij Beate Marie Ebor'.

Thomas Britton admissus erat ad vicariam de Thorneye Ebor' diocesis, ac pres- | Thorney
tito iuramento fidelitatis in eadem canonice institutus unacum suis iuribus et
pertinentiis universis, per presentationem Rogeri Phrappe.

f.83r.
Robertus Morres clericus admissus est ad rectoriam beate Marie de Bisshophill | Bisshopehill
veteris Ebor' diocesis, ac prestito iuramento fidelitatis in eadem institutus cum
suis iuribus et pertinentiis universis, per presentacionem Jacobi Philips patroni
ratione advocationis &c.

Willelmus Davyson clericus admissus fuit ad ecclesiam parochialem de Patrington | Patrington
Ebor' diocesis, ac prestito iuramento fidelitatis in eadem canonice institutus una-
cum suis iuribus et pertinentiis universis, per presentationem Radulphi Crake de
Hawtonprice &c.

Nicolaus Pettinger clericus admissus fuit ad rectoriam ecclesie parochialis de | Westretford
Westretford Ebor' diocesis, ac prestito iuramento fidelitatis in eadem canonice
institutus unacum suis iuribus et pertinentiis universis, per presentacionem
Johannis Hercye militis patroni eiusdem &c.

f.83v.
Robertus Morres clericus admissus erat ad rectoriam ecclesie parochialis de | Brignall
Brignall Eboracensis diocesis, ac prestito iuramento fidelitatis in eadem institutus
unacum suis iuribus et pertinentiis universis, per presentationem Jacobi Philipe
ratione advocationis presentacioni annexe.

Apud Hull, undecimo die mensis Septembris Anno Domini Millesimo | f.84r.
quingentesimo quinquagesimo nono.
Robertus Robinson clericus rector de Halsham ad eandem admissus est, ac pres- | Halsham
tito fidelitatis iuramento &c in eadem institutus et investitus unacum suis iuribus
et pertinentiis universis, per presentacionem Johannis Constable militis patroni
eiusdem.

Oswaldus Emerson clericus admissus est ad rectoriam de Kyrkeby Underdale, ac | Kyrkebye
prestito fidelitatis iuramento &c in eadem institutus et investitus unacum suis iuribus
et pertinentiis universis, per presentationem illustrissime Domine nostre Regine.

Apud Malton, xiij^{to} die mensis Septembris Anno Domini Millesimo | f.84v.
quingentesimo lix^{no}.
Carolus Clarkeson clericus admissus fuit ad vicariam ecclesie parochialis de Yed- | Yeddingham
dingham Eboracensis diocesis, et prestito fidelitatis iuramento in eadem institutus
et investitus cum suis iuribus et pertinentiis universis, per presentacionem Thome
Spencer generosi.

Apud Northallerton, decimo sexto die mensis Septembris Anno Domini | f.85r.
Millesimo quingentesimo lix^{no}.

Bossall

Cristophorus Morland clericus admissus erat ad vicariam ecclesie parochialis de Bossall Ebor' diocesis, ac prestito iuramento fidelitatis in eadem institutus cum suis iuribus et pertinentiis universis, per presentationem Willelmi Mershall.

Langton

Thomas Tailor diaconus admissus erat ad rectoriam ecclesie parochialis de Langton Cestrensis diocesis, ac prestito iuramento fidelitatis in eadem canonice institutus cum suis iuribus et pertinentiis universis, per presentationem Nicolai Girlington, &c.

Cosmoderlay

Joannes Peerson clericus admissus erat ad vicariam ecclesie parochialis de Cosmoderleye,[1] ac prestito per eum iuramento fidelitatis canonice in eadem institutus &c, cum suis iuribus et pertinentiis universis, per presentacionem Cuthberti Episcopi Dunelmensis &c.

f.85v.

Apud Richemonde, xxj^{mo} die mensis Septembris Anno Domini Millesimo quingentesimo quinquagesimo nono.

Eddiston

Thomas Benson clericus admissus erat ad vicariam ecclesie parochialis de Ediston Ebor' diocesis, et prestito fidelitatis iuramento in eadem canonice institutus et investitus cum suis iuribus et pertinentiis universis, per presentationem Willelmi Domini Evers.

Righton

Ricardus Ledbetter clericus admissus erat ad capellam de Righton Ebor' diocesis, ac prestito iuramento fidelitatis in eadem institutus et investitus cum suis iuribus et pertinentiis universis, per presentationem Willelmi Lutton generosi ratione advocationis presentacioni annexe.

f.86r.

Apud Novum Castrum, xxvij^{mo} Septembris Anno Domini Millesimo quingentesimo lix^{no}.

Mancefild

Cristophorus Parker clericus admissus erat ad vicariam de Mauncefyld in comitatu Nottingham, Ebor' diocesis, ac prestito iuramento fidelitatis in eadem canonice institutus et investitus cum suis iuribus et pertinentiis universis, per presentationem Francisci Mallett.

f.86v.

Apud Wiggan, xvj^{to} die mensis Octobris Anno Domini Millesimo quingentesimo quinquagesimo nono.

Babworth

Robertus Lylly artium magister admissus erat ad rectoriam ecclesie parochialis de Babworthe Ebor' diocesis, ac prestito fidelitatis iuramento in eadem canonice fuit institutus cum suis iuribus et pertinentiis universis, per presentationem Ioannis Hercye militis patroni eiusdem.

f.87r.

Apud Northwiche, vicesimo die mensis Octobris Anno Domini Millesimo quingentesimo lix^{no}.

Henricus Mershall clericus admissus erat ad vicariam de Warmfild Ebor' diocesis, ac prestito iuramento fidelitatis canonice in eadem institutus cum suis iuribus et pertinentiis universis, ad presentationem Ricardi Bynney armigeri.

Warmfilde

Willelmus Pyke clericus admissus fuit ad vicariam ecclesie parochialis de Frodisham Cestrensis diocesis, ac prestito fidelitatis iuramento canonice in eadem fuit institutus et investitus cum suis iuribus et pertinentiis universis, per presentationem Joannis Pyke ratione advocationis presentacioni affixate.

Frodisham

(fols. 87v.–89v. are blank.)

Detectiones et comperta Visitacionis Regie infra diocesim Ebor', Anno Domini millesimo quingentesimo
lix^{no}

Notingham

In the parishe of our Lady it is presented that no registor boke hath byn kept ther
by all *qwenes* Mary reigne. The chauncell is in gret decaye and the wyndowes
unglased.

Orston

The vicar of Orston dothe present that ther is no communion boke. The parishners kepe no scilence in the churche.

Anslay

The parishners present that they have no curate, and that their vicarege ys not
worthe above fyve markes by the yere, and yet ar they in numbre viij^{xx} *poe*ple.

Notingham

The parishners of Sayncte Peters doo present that they have no registor boke
kepte. The chauncell ys in sore decaye. Their parsonage ys and hathe byn vacante
from February laste. The curate apon Sondaies and hollydaies after the Gospell
dothe not use the Lordes prayer the beleif and the tene commaundmentes.
The parishners of Sayncte Nycolas doo present that they have no registor boke
kepte. The personage and chauncell is far owt of reparations. The personage hath
byn voyde thies vj yeres.

Adbolton

The parishners doo presente that they have had no service ther thies too yeres.

Bonyne

The parishners doo presente that they have no curate. They delyvered a communion boke, the homelies & other small bokes to Wm Orton to be burned.

Lowdham

The parishners and wardens doo present that their chauncell is unrepayred. The
churche is in greate decaye. They delyvered to Mr Cressye a paraphrases and too
communion bokes to be burned.

Hoveringham

The wardens and parishners doo presente that they have byn long without a
curate, the benefice being impropriated to trinity colledge in Cambridge.

Kirkeby

The churchwardens and parishners doo present that their parson is not resident with them nether dothe distribute to the poor.

Aponborowe

The wardens and parishners present that the cure is unserved. They lake a communion boke and other bokes.

Colson Basset

The wardens and parishners doo presente that they have no registor boke kepte this three yeres.

Watton

The wardens and parishners doo presente that the communion boke and other bokes of service was burnned in quene Maries tyme. Their churche hath byn vacante sithen candelmas laste.

Nuthall

The parishners and wardens doo presente that William Budbye and Margarete Whitworthe doo lyve suspiciouslye.

Estwaite

The wardens and parishners doo presente that Sir Richard Barlowe their curate toke awaye their bokes of the communion and the paraphrases.

Stapleforth

The churche is vacante and they have no curate. Their bokes wer burned in Quene Maris tyme.

Lenton

The churchwardens and parishners doo presente that they have nether vicar nor curate.

Scarington

The churchwardens and parishners doo presente that their benefice is voyde and that they have no curate. Their bokes wer burnte by thofficiall.

Sowthwell

It is presented that all the prebendaries howsies be in decaye.

Wynthorpe

The churchwardens and parishners doo presente that their chauncell is un-coveryde. That Edward Baker a maryed man begat Margaret Brewer being a crepill with childe, and the child was deade borne and he gave her counsell to take too pennyworthe of savyn to distroye itt.

Edingley

The churchwardens and parishners doo present that they have no curate. The bokes wer delyvered to the bayly of Sowthwell to be burnned.

Calverton

The wardens and parishners doo presente that their chauncell is almost fallen down for lacke of reparations.

North Clyfton

The churchwardens and parishners doo presente that they have had no curate this too yeres.

Stanton

The churche is muche in decaye for lacke of reparations.

Cropwell Bisshope

They presente that their vicarege is farr in decaye.

Howton

The wardens and parishners doo present that the Bible the communion boke and other bokes wer burnned.

Stoke

The wardens and parishners doo present that the vicarege is farr in decaye. The vicar is not resydent nether hathe sayd anny sarvice sithen mydsomer.

Eyton

The church and the vicarege be in decaye for lacke of reparations.

Balderton

The church wardens and parishners doo presente that their parson ys not resident. The churche is in decaye for lacke of reparationes.

West Draiton

The churchwardens and parishners doo presente that they have no curate this xij monethe. The chauncell is moche in decaye. The benefice vacante this xij monethe.

Claworthe

The wardens and parishners doo present that the chauncell is moche in decaye for lacke of reparationes.

Carlenton

The wardens and parishners doo presente that their Bible the communion boke and the Paraphrases wer delyvered to thofficiall to be burnned as he sayd.

Bevercotes

The wardens and parishners doo presente that their chauncell is moche in decaye.

Tuxeforthe

The wardens and parishners doo presente that their vicarege is vacante, and they without a curate.

Bawtry

They have no curate this xij moneth.

Estredforthe

They be unserved and have no curat to serve the cure ther.

Whetley

The churchwardens and parishners doo presente that their vicarege is vacante. The chauncell ys moche in decaye.

Stokewith

The wardens and parishners doo presente that they have nether parson vicar or curate to serve the cure this xij monethe.

Sturton

The wardens and parishners do presente that they have nether vicar nor curate. They present that Mr Mawen and mistres Thorneye wer maryed withowt askynge.

Bodamsall

The wardens and parishners do presente that their chauncell is far in decaye.

Hemysworthe

The wardens and parishners doo presente that their parson is not resident. The chauncell ys unrepayred.

Fyslake

The wardens and parishners do presente that William Hall and Margaret Rydall doo lyve in fornication. Jane Shatter doth use inchauntment and wychecrafte. Lawrence Padleye troblethe the curate in tyme of the commen Praier.

John Wilkinson
William Auleye } doo dispise the commen service
George Tailor

The parson dothe not kepe a convenyent tyme for the commen prayer.

Oston

The chauncell *is decaye* by the defaulte of Leonard Wraye farmer.

Adingflete

The churchwardens and parishners doo presente that John Godfrey beyng a maried man dothe kepe in his howse a woman by whom he had a childe. George Wetherall dothe likewise kepe in his howse a woman by whom he hath had too children. Elisabeth Walker beyng unmaryed hath had a child but by whom it is not knowen.

Whitgifte

The wardens and parishners presente that Roger Bogson hath had a child by

Elisabeth Savage. The same Roger hath had a chylde by Elisabeth Ashton. The said Elisabeth Asheton hath had a nother childe by one Wygilford. Robert Raignold hath had a child bye Margaret Heyton. Richard Estofte hath had a child withe Alice Waller. Agnes Ducke hathe had a child bye Antony Beanbye./The said parishners of Whitgifte doo presente that Thomas Lune hathe had too children by Isabell Pygus. Elisabeth Smythe hath had a child by one Martyn. Jennett Bolland hath had a child.

Rothewell
The wardens and parishners do present that Mistres Wombewell hathe byn from her husbond this iij yeres. Willam Tabyer hath byn from his wyf this vij yeres. Richard Hudson ys a commen fornycator and hathe kept one as his wif this xvij yeres and nowe asked to a nother. William Hobson of Stanleye owieth xls yerelye to the mending of the hie waies whiche was bequethed by Mr Robarte Challenor, and that they be behynd for iij yeres.

Kyrkesandall
They have no parson nor curate.

Felkirke
The wardens and parishners doo present that their chauncell is unrepayred. Their churche bokes wer delyvered to the dean of Doncaster, Mr Hudson.

Warmesworth
The wardens and parishners doo presente that their chauncell is in decaye. That the churche also lackithe reparations.

Arkesey
The wardens and parishners doo presente that Lyonell Portington had tene shillingis owt of the poor mens boxe, and not restored. Raphe Bradford thelder deteyneth from the poor mens boxe and the churche xxxiij s. George Wyntworthe and Edwarde Aykelande doo wilfully absent themselfs from the churche and from the dyvyne Servyce to the yvill example of *all parishe.*

Sprotborough
The wardens and parishners doo presente that William Asheley hathe maryed the wif of James Gibson, he being lyvynge.

Woulley
The wardens and parishners doo presente that they ar without vicar and curate.

Melton
The wardens and parishners doo presente that the chauncell is in greate ruyn and decaye and the wyndowes unglased. Isabell Forster hath a child unlefullye.

Hicketon

The wardens and parishners doo presente that they have had no curate this twelve monthes. The Bible and other bokes wer delyvered to the dean to be burnned.

Snathe

The wardens and parishners doo presente that Agnes the wif of Richard Adam dothe absente herself from her husbond. Alice Grene hath had a child unlefullye.

Edlington

The Churchwardens and parishners doo present that Sir Christophor Colson parson hathe not byn resident this xx^{ti} yeres. Ther hathe byn no curate this xij moneth and more. Ther is no registor boke kept.

Doncaster

The wardens and parishners doo presente that the parsonage is in decaye. And certen glasse wyndowes in the churche to be amended. The imagies be in the vestrye not distroyed.

Hothersfilde

They present that certin legacies geven by Dam Agnes Broke to the churche be not performed accordinglye.

Oteley

The wardens and parishners doo presente that James Ynglond hathe conveyde awaye the Bible owt of the churche. George Pykard the yongar lyveth in fornication with Isabell Bayleton.

Fuiston

The chauncell wyndowes be in greate ruyne and decaye.

Kyrkeby Overblus

The wardens and parishners doo present that William Sowtheron hathe had a child by Jennet Higgon. Roberte Bramleye hathe had a childe by Jane Armysted widoo. The churche is in grete decaye.

Arnclife

They presente that the churche *is grete decaye for reparations*. They have no communion boke.

Kyrkeby Mallondale

The wardens and parishners doo presente that Thomas Atkinson had a child by Isabell Smythe unlefully. Thomas Den had a child by Jennette Seriauntson &c. Thomas Althan had a child unlefullye by his woman.

St Olives in Yorke

The wardens and parishners doo present that they lacke a curate.

Belbroughe

The wardens and parishners presente that they have no curate.

Sherborn

They present and say that Henry Lethom kepithe a woman in his howse, beynge commaunded to putt her away. And was adiudged at Yorke to marye with a nother woman whom he hath procured to be maryed to Dionysse Rawdon of Pontefracte.

f.99r.

Stillingflete

The wardens and parishners doo presente that the vycarege is moche in decaye.

Byrkyn

The wardens and parishners doo presente that thexecutors of Leonard Horsman owieth to the poor . . . . . xls. Raphe Driffild owiethe, by the will of John Goldyng . . . . xls. Robert Selbye executor of George Good owiethe . . . . xls. George Gawthorpe owieth by the will of Raphe Levett . . . . xls. John Pynckney owith lykewise . . . . xiijs iiijd.

Hull

They doo present that Hawkeswelles wif the potycarye is a skold. That Jane Gray is likewise a scolde. That Sir Nycolas Alexander Newman and John Appelyn be vehemently suspected to use calculation, coniuration and other unlefull scyence.

f.99v.

Catwicke

The wardens and parishners do presente that the parson is suspected of incontynency with a woman whiche he kepith in his house.

Keyingham

The wardens and parishners do presente that the chauncell is in decaye. That the vicarege is also in ruyn & decay.

Skawby

The wardens and parishners do presente that James Radleff kepithe in his howse a woman that hathe had too children, and no man knowen to be father. Margaret Symones is axed iij tymes to one Robert Redman and now will mary a nother.[1]

Westowe

The wardens and parishners do present that the churche lackithe reparations. That one Helen Gerrard hathe & dothe lyve in fornycation.

f.100r.

Lestingham

The wardens and parishners doo present that their churche is in ruyn & decay.

Hovingham

The wardens and parishners doo presente that the chauncell is in ruyn and decaye.

Estralsey

The wardens and parishners doo presente that they have no curate. They have no registor boke in the churche.

Wharlton

The wardens and parishners doo presente that Thomas Thomson hath lived with one Ellys Wiggan incontynentlye and hath her with chylde. Richard Joolye hathe in his howse his wifes suster whoo hathe lyved in adulterye with a maryed man whiche man hath had a chyld by her. The chauncell lackithe reparations.

Osmoderley

f.100v.

The wardens and parishners doo presente that their ymagies be convayed awaye, but by whom they knowe not. The chauncell at Northallerton is in decaye.

Beynton

The wardens and parishners doo presente that the ymage of our Ladye hathe byn used for pilgrymage. They have no pulpitte ther.

Bridlington

The wardens and parishners doo present that the ymages be secretly kepte. That Robert Copeland hathe of the churche goodes in his handes . . . . . xxxvj s, Gawen Boynton . . . . ixs, Raphe Osteler . . . . ijs. That Raphe Cowlynge[2] a bacheler hathe commytted fornycation with Margaret Brown. That Jennett Sawston hath had a childe as it is sayd by George Kyrkewicke.

Foston

f.101r.

The wardens and parishners do presente that John Shaes wif hath in her handes of the churche goodes . . . . xs. Robert Usher . . . . xs. Hughe Kyrkebye . . . . xiiijs.

Kylnewycke

The wardens and parishners doo presente that Ellyn Ewell hath had a chylde and fatherithe it apon John Brown.

Benton

The wardens and parishners doo presente that Esabell Wilson hathe had a chylde unlefully by John the sone of Hughe Wrightes wif of Kyrkeborn.

Rewle

The wardens and parishners doo say that the chauncell is unrepayred. That the Rode still remeynethe.

Thornton

f.101v.

The wardens and parishners doo presente that the parson kepith no residence nether relevithe the poure.

Whenbye

The wardens and parishners doo presente that John Wyldon gent. lyeth ther suspiciously and will not resorte to his wif.

Wynteringham

The wardens and parishners doo presente that Margaret Symones beyng three tymes asked with Robert Redman long tyme sithen and yet not maryed, and now wold marye with one Koltos of Knapton[3]

Westowe[4]

The wardens and parishners doo presente that Helen Jegarde of the same parishe hath & doth lyve in fornycation.

f.102r.

Bridlington

The churchwardens and parishners do presente that Robert Collynge hathe commytted fornycation with Margery Browne. That Jennete Skrowson hath had a child by George Kyrkewicke.

Ellyn Dickeson, Ellyn Twysell, Agnes Tailor, Margaret Scale, Elizabeth Mychelson, Agnes Hill and Belaes wife presented for scoldes and unquyet wemen.

Burton Agnes

The wardens and parishners doo presente that William Mesle and Margaret Smyth doo lyve incontynentlye. That William Menson and Margaret Tathwell doo lyve incontynentlye.

f.102v.

Ecclesia Cathedralis Metropolitica Ebor'

It is detected that their alters stand still all saving the hie alter.

Item, that the gospell and epistle is so redd that no man can well understand, and likewise the homylyes.

Item ther is no cheste for the poor.

Item, they have no sermones preached nor Lector of dyvynytye redd.

Item, the churche is moche defyled with pigions.

Item, the prebendaries house of Rycall ys in muche ruyn and decaye.

Item, ther be but iij or iiij prebendaries abiding at Yorke.

Item, the prebendaryes house of Frydaythorpe called Tongehall ys in grete decaye.

f.103r.

Item Mr Palmes presentithe and sayethe that/Mr Doctor Wutton deane of the said churche ys not resident, nether feedithe the poor as he is bonde by the Statutes of the sayd churche.

(fols. 103v.–105v. are blank.)

Detectiones et comperta visitacionis Regie in et per civitatem et diocesim Dunelmenses, Anno Domini predicto

Ashe

The churchewardens and parishners doo presente that ther chancell ys in gret decaye. They lacke a curate.

Lanchester

The chauncell is moche in decaye and ruyn for lacke of reparations. *The* have no registor boke.

Chestor in the Strete

The churche is in gret ruyn and decaye.

Gateshede

The churchwardens and parishners doo presente, that ther parson kepithe no hospytalytye.

Item, the churche ys owt of reparations.

Item, Thomas Moorton kepithe a wenche in his howse by whom he hathe had a chylde.

Item, Thomas Jakeson kepithe one Ellyn a semestres in his howse and lyveth with her in fornycation.

Item, John Lowre draper lyvethe in fornycation with Katheryne Foxe and hath gottin her with childe.

Item, one Goodale lyveth incontynently with Katheryne Forman of the same parishe and hathe gottyn her with childe.

Whitborn

The wardens and parishners doo presente that they have no curate. They have no registor boke.

Elwicke

The Bible and all other their bokes used in Kyng Edwardis tyme wer burnned.

Bowdons

The wardens and parishners doo presente that Robert Recberke beyng a maryed man hath had a childe by a nother woman whose compauny he dothe use always.

Stannope

The churchwardens and parishners doo presente that ther parson is not residente. The chauncell owt of reparations. The churche also in decaye.

Item the alehowsekepers doo kepe open their dores in the tyme of dyvyne service
and will not be admonyshed.

Wynston

The wardens and parishners doo presente that they have no registor boke. The
lacke the pormens boxe. The chauncell is not repayred. The churche is in ruyn and
decaye.

Darlington

They lacke the registor boke for the churche. The mansion howse of the parsonage ys in grete decaye.

Steynton

All their bokes that they had in kinge Edwardis tyme were delyvered to the
chauncelor and were burnned.
All the bokes of Longe Newton wer burnned in lyke manner.
All the bokes of Cokefild wer burnned in lyke manner.

Newcastell

The wardens and parishners doo presente that one Thomas Wedderhaulte kepithe
Agnes Jobeson as his wif, she having a nother husbond lyving.
Item that Jane Hodson ys with child.
Item John Ynglishe lyvethe in whordom.
Item in Saincte Nicholas one Robynsons wydoo ys with child unlefully, and also
her mayde ys with childe.
Item that Slaters widoo hath a childe also unlefullye.
Item in Saincte Androes they have no register boke.
Item the churche of Alhallowies is unrepared.

Walshend

Ther vicar ys not residente. They have no registor boke kepte.

Tynmouthe

The wardens and parishners doo presente that Thomas Kyrswelles wif hath borr
too children in adultery. That George Otway liveth suspiciouslye with Jenne
Harswell. That William Denman hath gottin Jennet Whalleis with child. Tha
Robert Ladleye hath a child by Alyce Davy unlefullye.

Hexham

Itt is presented that Henry Coryer kepithe a concubyn in his howse, he beyng
maryede, called Isabell Godfeloo. Nicholas Lycheman lyveth in an adulterye with
a nother woman besides his wif. Hugh Rydleye hathe a childe besides his wife
Richard Collyns lyveth in fornycation, keping a woman not maryed./Jenky
Karyocke kepithe unlefullye one Elizabeth Armystronge. John Horde kepithe
unleafullye one Margaret Stevenson. John Pateson kepithe unleafully one Agne
Stokehall. Robert Caryer kepithe also a woman unleafullye. Jenzen Foster an

nis concubyn. One woman called Ledall is a fornicatrix. Jennet Andro lyveth in adulterye.

Alnewicke

Leonard Farley hathe putt away his wif and kepith a nother. George Farleye aathe putt away his wif and kepithe a nother.

Whetingham

The wardens and parishners doo presente that Gilberte Nicholson hathe begate Iennete Lee with child. John Gibson begate Alice Walker with child unlefullye.

Rotheborn

Their Images stand still in the churche. Ther is no registor boke. Ther is no pormanes boxe.

Emmylton

The churchwardens and parishners doo presente that William Blyve hath gotten ais wifes suster with childe. Rowland Browne kepithe a woman in his house by whom he hath had too children. Ther is no registor boke. Ther is no pormans boxe.

(fols. 110r.–111v. are blank.)

Detectiones et Comperta visitacionis regie in et per civitatem et diocesim Carliolenses.

Morlam
The churchwardens and parishners doo presente that they have no registor boke.

Mickell Sawelte
Ther is no registor boke. The churche is in decaye.

Clibeborn
The wardens and parishners doo presente that Thomas Sutton is maryed to a woman, having a wif lyvyng. Robert Crosby lyveth in adultery and hath a childe by a nother manes wif. That Jennet Wharton hath had too children unlefullye.

Shape
The churchwardens and parishners present that they have no registor boke

Warcope
The churchwardens and parishners doo presente that they lacke a Paraphrases. Item they *have boxe* for the por.

Newbiggin
We the churchewardens and parishners present for adultery:
Edward Hodson and Jennet Newton
John Byrde and Mable Wilson
Cristophor Skolocke and Isabell Harper

Skelton
They have no curate. They have no registor boke.

Churcheandros
They have no curate.

Ecclesia cathedralis Carliolensis
It is presented that the Dean, Edward Mychell and Richard Braundlynge, prebendaries ther, have not byn resident as often as they oughte, nether have they kepte ther quarter sarmones accordyng to the statutes.
Item Hugh Sewell, prebendary ther, hath not byn so often resydent as he oughte
Item Barnabye Kyrkebride hath not byn resident nether kepte his quarter sermones as he oughte to have don.

(fols. 113v.–115v. are blank.)

Detectiones et comperta Visitacionis Regie in et per totam civitatem et diocesim Cestrenses.

Cestrensis
Diocesis

Richemonde

Itt is presented that the poeple com not well to the churche.
Item that Richard Snell was burnned ther, beyng condempned by doctor Dawkyns for religion, xiij° Septembris Anno 1558.[5]

Estwitton

It is presented that the vicarege is in decaye and ruynous. The chauncell is in grete decaye. The vicars lyvynge is so small that it ys not able to fynde him. The churche yard is taken from the vicar contrary to right and conscyence.

Catericke

f.116v.

The wardens and parishners doo presente that Mr Cristophor Wandisforthe was maried to Cecyly Fulthrope withoute askinge of the Banes. And the same Cecyly was adiudged by the ecclesiasticall lawes to be the leafull wif of Mr John Burghe.

Aiskarthe

It is presented that the chauncell is moche in decaye for lacke of reparations.

Crofte

It is presented by the wardens and parishners that Sir Antonny Greane is pre-sented to the sayd parsonage. And he bought it firste of one Henry Wedderall and after redemed it ageyne at one Oswalde Metcalfes handes for lx^{li} payable at Mighelmas nexte. Also he hathe a nother benefice at Cowsbye.

Bolton apon Swale

t is presented that Cuthberte Rudde lyvithe in adulterye having too wiffes.

Bowes

f.117r.

t is presented that the parson is note resydent apon his benefice, nether dothe he distribute the xl^{li} parte to the por.[6]

Gret Langton

It is presented that they lacke a registor boke. They lacke the cheste for the por. The chauncell is in gret decaye. The parson is not residente nether dothe he distribute to the por.

Anderby

t is presented that Sir Henry Malevery, vicar ther, is not resydente nether kepithe e auny hospitalytie nether doth distribute auny thinge to the por.

75

Burton

It is presented that the churche is in grete decaye.

Item all their bokes wer burnned by thofficiall.

Manchester
Deanechurche

It is presented that Elizabeth Condell is withe childe.

Item all the bokes wer burnnede.

Item that John Heton in daunger of losinge of his howse and goodes for taking awaye of a masse boke from the curate sithen the Quenes Majesties procedinges.

Radclife

It is presented that Sir John Chetom dothe not rede the Pistell and Gospell withe the Latanye according to the proclamation.[7]

Ashton apon Marrye Bancke

It is presented that James Masse and Alice Morris doo lyve in fornycation.

It is presented that John Barlowe and Helen Den doo lyve incontynentlye together.

It is presented that the wif of Edmond Lether hathe and dothe lyve in adultery with diverse.

Flexton

It is presented that the parson is not resident nether kepithe hospitalytie.

Cales

It is presented that Margerye the late wif of Thomas Higson cam not to the churche thies xx^{ti} yeres.

It is presented that Elisabeth Modes, Davyd Bordmen and Alice Shallcros have had children in fornycation.

Prestburye

It is presented by the churchwardens and parishners that John Andrewe kepithe a woman named Ann Davye and hathe putt awaye his wif.

Manchestor

It is presented by the churchwardens and parishners that John Androo kepithe a woman unlefully.

Item, Hughe Skaclocke lyvethe in fornycation withe Marion Dissune.

Item, Richard Thorpe lyveth in fornycation with Ann Bowker.

Item, that Mergery Miller lyveth incontynently with dyvers.

It is presented by the said wardens and parishners of Maunchester that Margery Bothe dothe lyve in fornycation with dyvers and hathe had iiij^{or} children, and is supposed to be meynteyned by Henry Bothe her father.

Burie

It is presented that the curate dothe not rede the Gosple, Epistle, the Lordes Prayor and the tene commaundmentes according to the proclamation.

Item, it is presented that Thrustan Rostorn thelder and his wif, Thruston Roscorn the younger and his wif, Olyver Nables and his wif, John Nelson and his wif, lyved incontynently bifore they wer maryed, and also wer maryed without auny Banes askinge.

Prestwiche

It is presented that the Parson ys not residente nether dothe distribute aunny thinge to the powre.

Mottrom in Longesdale

f.119r.

It is presented that Nicholas Garleke dothe live incontinentlie with Margery Batterworthe.

Item, it is presented that Edmound Parker doth live incontinentlie with Agnes Turnor.

Item, it is presented that Raulf Bele doth live incontinentlie with Agnes Abridge.

Item, it is presented that Margaret Toplowe dothe live incontinentlie and hath had a childe.

Item, it is presented that Andrewe Rodes doth live incontinentlie and hath had a childe by a woman that is nowe fledd and gon awaye.

Item, it is presented that John Wilde doth live incontinentlie and hath had a childe by a woman that is not knowen.

Item, it is presented that Jennet Afclesinge hathe lived incontinentlie and hath had a childe, they knowe not by whome.

Item, it is presented that Raulf Acrisshawe hath lived incontinentlie and hath gotten a woman with childe.

It is presented that Isabell Heworth hath lived incontinentlie and hath had a childe.

Myddleton

It is presented that Roger Bradley hath lived incontinentlie and hath committed fornication with Isabell Michelfauth.

Moburley

f.119v.

It is presented by the wardens & parishners that Thomas Bower hath and doth lyve in fornycation with Elizabeth Ridgewaye.

Item, ther is no registor boke.

Saddelworth

It is presented that Elyce Scofylde hath commytted fornycation with Margaret Whithed.

Makesfild

It is presented that the cure hathe byn unserved thies iiij yeres. That the churche and the chauncell be in great decaye. Ther is no registor boke.

It is presented that John Hall hathe lyved in adulterye with Alice Clarke. That Thomesyne Lee hath commyttede fornycation with Jenkyn Damparte. That Elizabeth Jonson hath had a child unlefullye.

f.120r.

It is presented that Emme Wanckelithe hath lyved incontynentlye with Henry Marthrope.

Cusworthe

It is presented that Thomas Dene hath commytted adulterye with Margaret Potte. That William Stubbes hathe commytted adultery with Helen Blacketon. That John Dene hath commytted fornication with Elizabethe Hamond.

Rachedale

It is presented that the vicar is not residente, nether kepithe hospitalytie, nether relevithe the por. Ther is no registor boke in the churche. That James Uttleye hath commytted fornycation with Joan Chadwicke. That Margaret Greve hathe lyved incontynentlye by Thomas Whitacre and hath had a childe.

f.120v.

It is also presented that Francys Keye kepith a woman besides his wif. That Agnes Hill hathe commytted fornication and hath had a child by William Lapper priste. That Agnes Hallowies hathe commytted fornycation with Laurence Hope-woode. That Ellyce Redferne hathe had too children by a woman unlefully whiche he kepithe still.

Alderley

It is presented by the wardens & parishners that Joan Henshawe dothe lyve in fornycation. Jane Henshawe of Nether Alderley dothe lyve incontynentlye with Roger Hegnye.

f.121r.

It is also presented that Nycolas Leghe hathe commytted fornycation with Sibell Fynney.

Ashton under lyme

It is presented by the churchwardens and parishners that the parson dothe no service in the churche, nether dothe he distribute to the por as other parsones have done. That Morice Asheton kepithe a harlote, having a wif. That James Gleydell hath commytted fornication with Agnes Tailor. That John Cocker hath commytted fornication with one Agnes Knangref. That James Berd hath commytted fornication with Isabell Cropper. That Raphe Herste hath commyttede fornycacion with Mergerye Herdman. That Elizabeth Balsha hath don fornication.

f.121v.

Oldam

It is presented that the parson kepithe no hospitalytye. That Richard Downes hathe commytted fornycation with Agnes Geslynge. That Raignold Downes dothe not handle his wif as he shold doo.

Tannye

It is presented by the wardens & parishners that they have no registor boke. That one Mawde Jakeson hath lyved incontynently and is with childe.

Cockermouthe

It is presented by wardens & parishners that Thomas Fisher lyvethe incontynentlye with Marye Toolsone. Ther is no registor Boke.

Dalton

It is presented by the churchwardens and parishners that the chauncell is moche in decay. That ther is no registor boke kepte.

Olverston

It is presented by the wardens & parishners that Jennete Lethum hath had a childe in fornycation. That Isabell Wayneman is likewise with childe.

Oldingham

It is presented that the parson ys not resydente nor kepithe hospitalytie. That the chauncell ys in gret decaye. That the churchyarde walles be fallen down by reson of the sea.

Sainctebees

It is presented by the wardens & parishners that the chauncell is in grete ruyn &c. It is presented that William Singleton hathe had a child by Jennett Lunde. That Antonye Gibson dothe lyve incontynently with Jennette Gibson. Also that Agnes Toubman, William Latons, Jennett Tower, be commen fornicators.

Moncaster

It is presented that Isabell Jackeson hath had a child in fornycation by one John Mere of Myllom. That John Asbore hath putt away his wif without lefull cause &c.

Wiggon

It is presented by the wardens and parishners that the chauncell is fallen down.
Also it is presented that Thomas Sadler is commen drunckarde.
Also it is presented that William Eccleston hathe commytted fornication with Margaret Cadye.
Also that Peter Platte hathe don the like with Jane Ashleye.
Also it is presented that ther is a chauncell whiche Sir Peter Legh knighte shold have buylded whiche nowe ys in sore decaye and a gret hurte to the churche.

Leyland

It is presented by the churchwardens and parishners that Edward Jerrarde hathe taken awaye Jennette Rydyng from her husbond and kepith her as his concubyn at one Roger Blackleches.

Newchurche in Rosindale

It is presented that Dennys Haworth hath had a child by Jennete Hudson. That Thomas Rawson hath put away his wif without good cause. That William Brighte committeth adultery with Marion Ramesden.

Prescote

It is presented that the vicar is not residente nether kepithe hospitalitie. That the churche and chauncell is in sore decaye.

Warrington

It is presented by the churchwardens and parishners that William Bancke hathe commytted fornycation with Margaret Tetlowe. Also that Thomas Morres hathe lyved in fornication with his woman. Also that Thomas Breche, gent., hathe lyved incontynentlye with Alice Southorn. Also that Henrye Kennyon and Alice Hatton doo lyve in fornycation. That James Wrighte is a fornicator and a commen swerer and dronckarde. Also that Thomas Warrynge and Ellyne Clare doo lyve in fornication.

Also it is presented that Thomas Pynkerman kepithe a concubyne. Also that William Wakefild and Ellyn Man doo lyve in fornication. Also that Gilbert Finche is a commen fornicator and a dronckard.

Downeham

The churchwardens and parishners doo presente that ther vicar is not resydent, nether kepith auny hospitalytye.

Also that Thomas Bentam, Jennet Welles, Henry Hellingworthe, Jennet Shettilworthe, Roger Dilworthe, Ann Allyn, be commen fornycators and doth lyve naughtylye.

Clederowe

It is presented by the wardens and parishners that they have had no priste sithen Mighelmas. That the churche is in moche decaye.

Also it is presented that Henrye Wilson, Joan Brigge, John Redde, William Harrison, Alice Giles, Richard Horson, Elisabeth Dutdale, be commen fornicators and doo moche hurte in the contrye.

Witton

Also the wardens and parishners doo present that Roger Jonson and Richard Aderton be commen drunckardes & blasphemers.

Also that Peter Vennables kepith Emme Ayre in adulterye. That Martyn Wiborn and Emme Birchwood doo lyve together in fornication. Also that John Forreste and Margarete Adamson doo lyve in fornication. Also that the sarvaunte of George Holforth and Parnell Adamson be fornicators. Also that Thomas Dudley and Alice Aderton be fornycators.

Also it is presented that William Herthe and Ellyn Breton kepe howses of bawdery.

Middlewiche[8]

It is presented that Henrye Blackborn hath putt away his wif and kepithe a nother woman.

It is presented that the churche and the chauncell lake reparations.

Dennam

It is presented by the churchwardens and parishners that the chauncell and the churche bee in sore decaye.

It is by them also presented that Joan Brodershire, Agnes Acton, Elizabeth

Holland be commen fornicators and have had children. Also one Lucye hathe had a child by Arthure Bleeson and is with child ageyn. Also Richard Deane hathe lived in fornication with Margaret Crocker and made with her a contracte and now is maryed to a nother.

Also that Katherin Holforthe maryed Peter Starkye being a maryed man bifore. And the wif of the said Peter hath maryed Thomas Lestwiche.

It is presented that the parson makithe no distribution to the por.

Marburye
f.126r.

The churchwardens and parishners doo presente that ther parson is not resident nether kepith auny hospitalytye. That Marion Broke by William Whipsted is with childe in fornication. That Blanche Kynsey widoo kepith unlefull compannye with Richard Claighton. That Brigett Furbar and John Flowoode doo lyve in fornication. That William Bentley and Katherin Taylor doo lyve in fornication. That Thomas Taylor and Helen Lecyter have had iij children in fornication. That Griffithe Pole and Agnes Mylner hath lyved together in fornication.

Littell Budworth

The wardens and parishners doo present that John Nykeson kepith Katherin Gorste and Randell Fradsham kepith Helene Mynshill in fornication.

Onver
f.126v.

The wardens and parishners doo presente that Thomas Dalson and Ellyne Maddocke doo lyve together in fornication *and is* with child.

Ronkehorn

The wardens and parishners doo presente that the vicar kepith no residence nor hospitalitie. That the chauncell and the vicarege are verye moche in decaye.

Wisterton

The wardens and parishners doo presente that Hughe Wilkinson and Alice Wilson lyve in adulterye. That William Huccinson and Helen Rode be adulterers. That Charles Eyre and Margerye Janishe have longe tyme & still doo contynewe in adulterye.

Knotforthe
f.127r.

Itt is presented that Grace Este is commen adulteryce and lyveth incontinentlye.

Atton

Itt is presented by the churchwardens and parishners that Roger Watson, John Boteley, Umfry Hupley, Margaret Spencer, Roberte Felcote, Margaret Capper, be commen adulterers and lyve yvill.

Bowdon

The churchwardens and parishners doo presente that Richard Chapman and Katherin Warberton be fornicators. That Ellyn Worthenton is with childe by

John Brochegirdle in fornication. That Elisabeth Mathewe, Richarde Shalcros and Margaret Dayne be commen fornycators.

Wrambury

It is presented that the chauncell is in decaye. That Umfry Barnarde hath gottyn a child by Alice Tyler. That Rafe Henbere hath gottyn his mayde with childe. That Margaret Fisher hath had a child in adulterye.

Midlewiche[9]

The wardens and parishners doo presente that the vicar dothe not his dewtye in the churche and that he is a dronckard. Ther is no registor boke.

Wynbere

It is presented by the wardens & parishners that Robert Bloar kepith yvill rule in his howse and ys a commen recevor of incontynent parsones.

Gunbere

It is presented by the churchewardens and parishners that John Broke, John Simkinge, John Aresmythe, Richard Woodwarpe, one Marce Peres, Elizabeth Eton, be commen adulterers and lyve very yvill. That Randolf Gregorye and Mawde Preste doo lyve in fornication.

Gusterde

The wardens and parishners doo present Roger Amson, John Brodherste, Hugh Rewell, Alice Brundereth, William Carter, Richard Carter, Thomas Carter doo lyve suspiciouslye of incontynencye.

Sandbrige

It is presented that they have no vycar nor curate. Ther is no registor boke kepte.

Breton

The wardens and parishners doo presente that James Carter and Margery Dale doo lyve in fornycation. That Raphe Pencke and Margaret Stubes bee fornycators. That Robarte Hardynge and Heleyne Presberye doo lyve in fornication. That John Rogerson and Helen Beleye doo lyve in fornication. That Sir Richard Hockeneye priste and Elizabethe Sharrocke doo lyve in fornication. That William Masse and Joanne Stubbes doo lyve in fornication. That Randall Fedem and the parson of Breton doo withold vj^s viij^d from the churche, &c.

Lymme

The wardens and parishners doo presente that James Clare and Margaret Blakborn doo lyve in fornycation. That Hewe Clare harboreth unhonest persones.

Nether Pever under Bridward

The wardens and parishners doo presente that John Deane and Margaret Marshe doo lyve in adulterye. That Margaret Widder hath had a child in fornycation.

That Joan Stobbes hath had a childe in fornycation. That Godfreye Breten hath
had a child by Cecylye Cheden in fornication. That Robert Brodye hath had a
chylde by Ellyne Widder.

Frodesham

The wardens and parishners doo presente that Roberte Wrighte of Ynche hath had
a child by Isabell Powghton unlefully. That Richard Mangrove hath had a child
by Katherin Cockeshawe in adultery. That Raffe Nickson hath had a childe by
Joan Twiste in fornication. That Mr Richard Jarrate kepithe a concubin in adulterye in the parishe. That Hue Leche hathe had a childe by Joane Holebricke in
fornication. That Robert Woodworthe hath had a child by Elizabeth Manlye in
fornication. That all the bokes of the churche wer delyvered to the dean and wer
by him burnned at Budworthe.

Thornton

The wardens and parishners doo presente that Thomas Awdecrofte hath committed adultery with one Agnes.

Holt parishe

The wardens and parishners doo presente that Launcelote Hansone hath a
concubyne. That Thomas Bate hath a concubyne. That Richard Farrer and
Katherin Frodsom doo lyve in fornycation.

Northwiche

The wardens and parishners doo presente that Katherin Lawton is an adulterer.
That William Reve is an adulterer. That William Sharman hath commytted adul-
tery with Ellyn Survall. That Mawde Furnewall is suspected for adulterye. That
Helene Prestburye is likewise suspected.

Bangor

The wardens and parishners doo presente that one Robert Jenkyne hathe had a
child by Jane Ellys in fornication.

Tarwyn

The wardens and parishners doo present that Katheryne Wilson hath had a child
unleafullye. That Margaret Dickeson hath had a child unlefully. That Jane More
hath had a childe unlefullye.

Farme

The wardens and parishners doo presente that Thomas Orshawe hathe gottin a
child unlefullye. That Thomas Pulforthe hath also gottin a child in fornication.

Brumboro

The wardens and parishners doo presente that William Irebye hath had a child by
Jennett Bennette.

Bidston

The wardens and parishners doo present that William Buckeston dothe kepe a concubyn.

Womeslowe

The wardens and parishners doo present that James Barrete lyveth in fornycacion with Helen Burges. That John Lambe lyvethe in fornication with Elizabeth Blunstone. That Elizabeth Peerson hath had a childe in fornication with Thomas Blackshaa. That Joan Bradley hath and dothe lyve incontynentlye.

f.131v. It is presented that Ann Damporte hath had a child by Laurence Damporte in fornication. That Margarette Wosingcrofte hathe lyved incontynentlye with Thomas Cashe. That George Walker hath lived incontynentlye with Romesbotom Margery. That William Bennette hathe and dothe lyve incontynentlye with *William Bennette*.[10] That Henry Peerse hath and dothe live incontynentlye with one Grace &c.

Stockeporte

That the churche lackithe reparations. That Raphe Wynnyngton hath committed fornication with Agnes Regwaye. That Margery Danyell lyveth in fornication with
f.132r. Thomas Tailor &c./That the chauncell is ruynous. That Margerye Kempe hathe commytted fornication with Jeffrye Holme. That John Thornleye hath commytted fornication with Alice Warnebye. That John Sydebothom hath commytted fornication with Elizabeth Warnebye. That William Thorneleye hath commytted fornycation with Helen Harrison. That John Rede hathe commytted fornication with Alice Blomleye. That Henry Woode hathe commytted fornication with Margaret Hibbarte. That George Wheywall hath commytted fornication with Cecyly Barleye. That Mawde Robothom hath lyved in fornication with Otmell Hexam.

f.132v. It is also presented that William Sherle hathe lyved in fornication with Margaret Corker. That Helen Browne ys with child by Thomas Coliar in fornication. That Roger Hebbarte hath commytted inceste with Elizabeth Hebberte.

Chadell

The wardens and parishners doo presente that Edmond Jamesson lyveth in fornycation with Emme Arrowsmyth. That William Hunte lyveth in fornication with Mergery Ryle. That Roger Williamson lyveth in fornication with Mawde Asheton. That John Jones lyveth in fornycation with Joan Uproisette.
f.133r. Also it is presented that William Jannye lyveth in fornication with Alice Harrison. That Mawde Blomley hath had a child by Thomas Hayward in fornication.

Ashburie

It is presented that Helen Prestburye hath lyved in fornication with Robert Hardway. That William Sharmond hath committed adultery with Helen Furnvall.

Middelton

The wardens and parishners doo presente that Roger Bradleye hath lyvede incontynentlye with Isabell Mycchell. That William Hancocke lyvethe in fornication with one Katherin Layton.

Saincte Johnes in Chestor

It is presented that the chauncell lackes reperatyones. That An Calcote hath commytted fornication with Thomas Penkes. That Elizabeth Saule hathe committed fornication with Thomas Bildon. That Raphe Bradford was married without Banes askinge.

Trynytie parishe

It is presented that Morres Lane carpynter kepithe a woman named Agnes having a wif. That the same woman is a bawde.

Saincte Oswalds

It is presented that the vicar is not residente and that the curate dothe not declare the chapters accordingelye. That the churche is unrepayred.

It is presented that Thomas Steward kepith a harlot in his house and dothe lyve incontynently with her. That James Barnes kepithe Margaret Croshawe in his howse beynge a commen harlotte. That Elizabeth Newton of Longeleye is a commen harlote and is with child by John Myller her nere kynesman. That the curate redithe necgligentlye. That Jane Hagger beinge excommunicated for her incontynent lyving remeyned still not reconsiled.

Saincte Peters

It is presented that the parson ys not residente &c. That Mistres Dutton kepith secreatlye a Roode, too pictures and a masse boke. That Roger Smythe being a maried man hath commytted adultery.

It is presented that Roger Bryne boccher hath had a childe in adulterye. That Thomas Thorpe beynge a maryed man is suspected to have a woman with child. That Thomas Byldon thelder commethe seldom to the churche.

Saincte Mighelles

It is presented that Sir Thomas Fynlowe curate kepithe one Clarys a suspected woman in his house. That Thomas Hill hath gottin a mayde with child in his masters howse.

Saincte Maries

The wardens and parishners doo presente that ther parson of longe tyme hathe not byn residente with them beinge worthe fivety poundes by yere, nether makithe distribucions. That Sir Henry Snappe curate is a commen haunter of alehouses and besides verye necgligente in readinge of the sarvice &c.

Itt is presented that Robert Caryor being a maried man kepithe Helen Worrall as his concubyne. That Elizabeth Breewood hath had a chyld by one Parcyvall in fornication. That Peter Fleicher hathe certin ymages whiche he kepithe secreatlye.

(fols. 135v.–136v. are blank.)

Processus habiti et facti contra adulteros et fornicatores detectos et compertos in visitacione Regia infra provinciam Eboracensem, prout sequitur:[1]

In ecclesia cathedrali Cestrensi, xxvj^{to} die mensis Octobris Anno Domini Millesimo quingentesimo lix^{no}.

Wrighte

Willelmus Wrighte de Tarwyn, Cestrensis diocesis, detectus de crimine fornicationis cum Katherina Vennables de eadem; personaliter comparuerunt et fatebantur obiecta. Unde moniti sunt ad penitendum se more penitentium solito in ecclesia parochiali ibidem die dominica proxima. Et ulterius iniungitur viro prout sequitur: *That he shall give and contribute to the said Katherin in consideration of her povertye: xx^s, whereof x^s to be payd owt of hand and other x^s at the day of her mariage. And further apon his own costis and chargies he shall repayre and amende the wooddyn bridge that is in the commen hie way betwixte Chestor and Tarwyne.*

f.137v.
Nickson

Thomas Orshawe de Farne detectus est de crimine fornicationis cum Margareta Nickeson de eadem quesitus per apparitorem causa citandi, et certificatum est quod recessit a patria. Mulier personaliter et fatebatur crimen et submisit se, unde imposita est ei canonica penitentia per ipsam peragenda die dominica quarta proxime post puerperium in ecclesia parochiali ibidem. Et certificandum decano rurali &c.

Trafford

Detectum est quod Willelmus Trafforde de Shatwicke vixit fornicatorie cum Emma Ebye de eadem et quod matrimonium inter eos sit contractum &c. Unde evocatus ad iudicium negavit fornicationem et fatebatur contractum. Et assumendo in se ad procurandum solempnizacionem huiusmodi matrimonij die dominica proxima ad quindenam dimittitur si infra mensem certificet Magistro Chetham de solempnizacione.

Detectum est quod Edmundus Watkins de Durdleston vixit in fornicatione *cum*
f.138r.
cum Mergeria Civedale nuper de eadem./Unde vir evocatus ad iudicium fatebatur crimen, allegans mulierum recessisse a patria, et submisit se &c. Deinde imponitur sibi canonica penitentia per ipsum peragenda more penitentis nudis pedibus et capite, ac lineis sive laneis die dominica proxima in ecclesia parochiali antedicta. Et publice declarabit scedulam sibi traditam &c. Et ulterius dabit pixedi pauperum in dicta ecclesia quinque solidos, viz. qualibet die dominica: vj^d &c.

Taperley

Detectum est quod Oliverus Hughe de Tarperley fornicatorie vixit cum Helena Dudeleye qui personaliter comparens fatebatur crimen, et submisit se &c. Unde imponitur ei penitentia, et more penitentis nudis pedibus et capite ac lineis sive laneis per ipsum peragenda per duos dies dominicos proximos sequentes in ecclesia sua parochiali cum declaratione scedule sibi tradite. Et quod tradat ad elemosinariam pixidem: ij^s coram parochianis &c. Et ad certificandum in proximo consistorio post apud Cestr'.

Detectum est quod Joannes Gymesdiche de Thornton fornicatorie vixit cum Alicia Thompson de eadem, et ipse parsonaliter comparens fatebatur crimen et submisit se &c./Deinde imponitur ei penitentia condigna &c per ipsum peragenda more penitentis &c per duos dies dominicos proxime futuros in ecclesia parochiali &c, cum declaratione scedule sibi tradite &c, et quod tradat ad elemosinariam pixidem: iij^s coram parochianis &c, viz. prim*o* die dominic*a*: xij^d, et secundo: ij^s. Et ad certificandum de dicta penitentia in proximo consistorio post apud Cestr'. *f.138v.*

Detectum est quod Willelmus Elham de Thorneton fornicatorie vixit cum quadam muliere eiusdem parochie &c. Dictus Willelmus ad iudicium evocatus et person-aliter comparens fatebatur crimen et submisit se &c, allegans mulierem ab hac luce migrasse &c. Et deinde imponitur viro penitentia condigna &c per ipsum peragenda more penitentis &c in ecclesia sua parochiali &c die dominica proxima cum declaratione scedule sibi tradite &c. Et quod tradat ad elemosinariam pixi-dem coram parochianis: iij^s iiij^d, et ad certificandum in proximo consistorio post apud Cestr'.

Brigitta Furbur de Marberie, uxor Johannis Furburr, detecta est de crimine adulterij cum quodam Johanne Flowod. Dicta Brigitta ad iudicium evocata per-sonaliter comparuit et negavit obiecta &c, et in sua purgatione produxit Margaretam Tailor, Janam Yevenson Margaretam Furburr et Aliciam Whitting-ham que producte et admisse eandem Brigittam/Furburr virtute sui iuramenti ad tacta Dei evangelia prestiti ab eodem crimine purgaverunt &c. *f.139r.*

Detectum est quod Henricus Bradberrie de Plemstone fornicatorie vixit cum Helena Deane de eadem. Dictus Henricus ad iudicium evocatus et personaliter comparens fatebatur crimen et submisit se &c. Unde imponitur ei penitentia pro commissis suis &c per ipsum peragenda more penitentis in ecclesia sua parochiali die dominica proxima et ulterius iniungitur viro prout sequitur, viz: *That he shall geve two shirtes and two smockes to the churchwardens of the same parishe, And they to distribute the same to iiij^{pr} poor folkes of the seide parishe &c, et ad certificandum in proximo consistorio apud Cestr'.*

Apud Manchester, tricesimo die mensis Octobris Anno Domini millesimo quingentesimo quinquagesimo nono.
Detectum est quod Jacobus Barrett de Womeslowe fornicatorie vixit cum Helena Burgies de eadem. Vir evocatus ad iudicium et personaliter comparens fatebatur crimen et assumpsit in se ad solempnizandum matrimonium cum dicta Helena die dominica proxima ad septimanam &c, ad quod faciendum ad tacta Dei evangelia prestitit iuramentum &c, et habet ad certificandum decano decanatus in proximo die iuridico post.

Detectum est quod Joannes Lambe de eadem parochia fornicatorie vixit cum Elizabeth Blinston de eadem que Elizabeth peperit prolem. Dictus Johannes ad iudicium evocatus et personaliter comparens fatebatur crimen. Unde imponitur ei penitentia canonica &c per ipsum peragenda in ecclesia sua parochiali more penitentis &c die dominica proxima ad septimanam cum declaratione scedule sibi tradite &c. Et quod tradat ad elemosinariam pixidem coram parochianis xij^d, et quatuor camisias per iconomos ibidem quatuor pauperibus eiusdem parochie tradendas et distribuendas &c et ad certificandum decano decanatus in proximo die iuridico post &c. Et preterea iniungitur viro, viz. dicto Johanni quod sustentabit victum et vestitum infanti &c, et deinde dictus Johannes Lambe ad tacta Dei evangelia prestitit iuramentum quod posthac non frequentabit consortium dicte Elizabethe.

Detectum est quod Helena Prestburie de Aisheburie fornicatorie vixit cum Roberto Hardinge de Brereton. Partes ad iudicium evocate et personaliter comparentes fatebantur crimen et sub sui iuramenti vinculo ad tacta Dei evangelia prestiti promiserunt ad solempnizandum matrimonium citra diem Lune proximum ad septimanam sub pena iuris.

Willelmus Sharmonde de Asheburie detectus est de crimine adulterij cum/Helena Furnevall de eadem dictus Willelmus ad iudicium evocatus et personaliter comparens certificavit matrimonium inter eosdem solempnizatum fuisse et esse iuxta monitionem alias datam.

Detectum est quod Rogerus Bradley de Middleton incontinenter vixit cum Isabella Michell de eadem. Mulier ad iudicium evocata et personaliter comparens fatebatur crimen et submisit se &c. Unde imponitur ei penitentia canonica per ipsam peragenda more penitentis die dominica proxima in ecclesia sua parochiali cum declaracione scedule sibi tradite &c, et ad certificandum decano decanatus in proximo die iuridico post. Deinde dicta mulier allegavit quod predictus Rogerus Bradley adversa valetudine laboravit cui imponitur similis penitentia per ipsum peragenda ut supra &c. Et preterea ut tradat ad elemosinariam pixidem dicte ecclesie coram parochianis &c: vj^{s}viij^d, citra festum sancti Andree proximum, et ad certificandum decano decanatus in proximo die iuridico post.

Detectum est quod Randulphus Wynnyngton de Stockporte fornicatorie vixit cum Agnete Rigwaye de eadem. Dictus Randulphus ad iudicium evocatus et personaliter comparens fatebatur crimen. Unde penitentia canonica imponitur ei pro commissis &c per ipsum peragenda more penitentis in ecclesia sua parochiali per tres dies dominicos proximos &c cum declaratione scedule sibi/tradite &c et ad certificandum decano decanatus in proximo die iuridico post &c. Deinde ad peticionem dicti Randulphi Wynnyngton dicta penitentia commutata est sub forma sequenti, viz. ut distribuat xl^s pauperibus dicte parochie, viz: vj^s viij^d in pecuniis et xiij^{s}iiij^d in pane egentibus dicte parochie distribuendis citra festum natalis Domini proximum &c, et residuum ad placitum iudicis dicto Randulpho significandum &c.

Detectum est quod Margeria Daniell de Stockporte fornicatorie vixit cum Thoma Tailor de eadem iam mortuo, et dicta Margeria ad iudicium evocata et personaliter comparens fatebatur crimen &c. Unde penitentia canonica imponitur ei pro commissis &c, per ipsam peragenda more penitentis in sua ecclesia parochiali die dominica proxima cum declaratione scedule sibi tradite &c, et ad certificandum decano decanatus in proximo die iuridico post &c.

Detectum est quod Margeria Kempe de Stockporte fornicatorie vixit cum Galfride Holme de eadem. Dicta Margeria ad iudicium evocata et personaliter comparens fatebatur crimen, que monita est ad comparendum in crastino hora octava ante meridiem ad videndum ulteriorem processum &c.

Detectum est quod Joannes Thorneley de Stockporte fornicatorie vixit cum Alicia Warnebie. Dictus Johannes ad iudicium evocatus et personaliter comparens fatebatur crimen qui monitus/est ad comparendum in crastino hora octava ante meridiem ad videndum ulteriorem processum &c. Deinde mulier personaliter comparuit et fatebatur crimen cui imponitur penitentia canonica per ipsam peragenda in ecclesia sua parochiali per duos dies dominicos, viz. die dominica ad septimanam et die dominica ad quindenam more penitentis &c, cum declaratione scedule sibi tradite &c, et ad certificandum decano decanatus in proximo die iuridico post &c. Et deinde consimilis penitentia imponitur viro per ipsum peragenda more penitentis (cum declaratione sibi tradite &c,) die veneris ad septimanam in foro de Stockporte predicto (nisi interim velit ducere dictam Aliciam in uxorem) et ad certificandum decano decanatus ut supra &c.   f.141r.

Detectum est quod Johannes Sidebothom de Stockeporte fornicatorie vixit cum Elizabeth Warnebie de eadem qui evocati ad iudicium et personaliter comparentes fatebantur crimen. Unde penitentia canonica imponitur viro more penitentis per ipsum peragenda die veneris proximo ad septimanam in foro de Stockporte predicto cum declaratione scedule sibi tradite &c, et ad certificandum decano decanatus in proximo die iuridico post et deinde consimilis penitentia dicte Elizabethe iniungitur per ipsam more penitentis peragenda in ecclesia sua parochiali per duos dies Dominicos proximos cum declaratione scedule &c, et ad certificandum ut supra &c nisi interim veluit solempnizare matrimonium &c.

Detectum est quod Willelmus Thorneley de Stockporte fornicatorie vixit cum Helena Harrison qui evocati ad iudicium et personaliter comparentes fatebantur crimen. Unde penitentia canonica/imponitur viro per ipsum peragenda more penitentis die veneris proximo ad septimanam in foro de Stockeporte predicto cum declaratione scedule sibi tradite &c, et ad certificandum decano decanatus in proximo die iuridico post, et deinde consimilis penitentia imponitur mulieri per ipsam peragenda more penitentis in ecclesia sua parochiali per duos dies dominicos proximos et ad certificandum decano ut supra &c, nisi veluit interim solempnizare matrimonium &c.   f.141v.

Detectum est quod Johannes Rede de Stockeporte fornicatorie vixit cum Alicia

Blomeleye. Dictus Johannes ad iudicium evocatus et personaliter comparens fatebatur crimen et assumpsit se ad solempnizandum matrimonium cum dicta Alicia citra festum natalis Domini proximum, et deinde iniungitur dicto Johanni ut solempnizet matrimonium cum prefata Alicia citra diem dominicam ad tres septimanas ad quod faciendum sub sui iuramenti vinculo ad tacta dei evangelia prestiti promisit alioquin ad peragendam penitentiam canonicam more penitentis &c in foro de Stockeporte die veneris proximo et ad certificandum decano decanatus in proximo die iuridico post.

Detectum est quod Henricus Wood de Stockeporte fornicatorie vixit cum Margareta Hibberd que recessit. Dictus Henricus ad iudicium evocatus et personaliter comparens fatebatur crimen cui penitentia canonica pro commissis imponitur per ipsum more penitentis peragenda die veneris ad septimanam in foro de Stockeporte cum declaratione scedule sibi tradite &c, et ad certificandum decano decanatus in proximo die post &c, nisi interim velit ducere eandem Margaretam Hibberd in uxorem &c.

f.142r.

Detectum est quod Georgius Wheywall de Stockeporte fornicatorie vixit cum Cecelia Barley. Dictus Georgius ad iudicium evocatus et personaliter comparens fatebatur crimen cui penitentia canonica imponitur per ipsum peragenda more penitentis in ecclesia sua parochiali die dominica proxima cum declaratione scedule sibi tradite &c, et ad certificandum decano decanatus in *proximo* die iuridico *proximo*. Et deinde dictus Georgius fatebatur se contraxisse matrimonium cum prefata Cicelia. Unde monitus est ad declarandum parochianis &c se ducturum fore dictam Ciceliam in uxorem citra festum pentecost' proximum &c.

Detectum est quod Matilda Robothom de Stockporte peperit per Otiwellum Hexam. Dicta Matilda ad iudicium evocata et personaliter comparens fatebatur crimen cui penitentia canonica pro commissis imponitur per ipsam peragenda more penitentis in ecclesia sua parochiali per duos dies dominicos proximos cum declaratione scedule sibi tradite &c et ad certificandum decano decanatus in proximo die iuridico post &c, nisi interim matrimonium inter ipsam et dictum Otiwellum solempnizatum fuerit.

Detectum est quod Willelmus Sherte de Stockeporte fornicatorie vixit cum Margareta Corker que recessit a diocesi. Dictus Willelmus Sherte ad iudicium evocatus et personaliter comparens fatebatur crimen et assumpsit in se ad solempnizandum matrimonium cum dicta Margareta citra/festum purificationis beate Marie virginis proxime futurum si mulier consentierit &c, ad quod perimplendum prefatus Willelmus Sherte unacum Johanne Burton de Wymeslowe yeoman obligatur in viginti libris ut per obligationem inde confectam plenius liquet e apparet.

f.142v.

Detectum est quod Edmondus Jamesson de Chadwell fornicatorie vixit cum Emma Arrowesmithe. Dictus Edmundus ad iudicium evocatus et personaliter comparens fatebatur crimen cui penitentia canonica pro commissis &c imponitur per ipsum peragenda more penitentis die veneris ad septimanam in foro de Stopporte cum declaratione scedule sibe tradite &c, et ad certificandum decano decanatus in proximo die iuridico post &c, nisi interim eandem Emmam in uxorem ducere velit.

Detectum est quod Willelmus Hunte de Chadell fornicatorie vixit cum Margeria Rile. Dictus Willelmus ad iudicium evocatus et personaliter comparens fatebatur crimen, et deinde penitentia canonica pro commissis ei imponitur per ipsum peragenda more penitentis die veneris ad septimanam in foro de Stopporte et ad certificandum decano decanatus in proximo/die iuridico post, et preterea iniungitur dicto Willelmo ut tradat ad elemosinariam pixidem per iconomos distribuendos: x^s in festo Sancti Michaelis proximo casu quo interim eandem Margeriam in uxorem non duxerit &c.

f.143r.

Detectum est quod Rogerus Williamson de Chadell fornicatorie vixit cum Matilda Asheton. Dictus Rogerus ad iudicium evocatus et personaliter comparens fatebatur crimen. Unde penitentia canonica ei imponitur pro commissis per ipsum peragenda more penitentis in ecclesia sua parochiali die mercurij proximo cum declaratione scedule sibi tradite &c et ulterius iniungitur dicto Rogero ut tradat ad elemosinariam pixidem coram parochianis: x^s et ad certificandum decano decanatus in proximo die iuridico post, &c.

Detectum est quod Johannes Jones de Chadell fornicatorie vixit cum Joanna Up Roistr'. Dictus Johannes ad iudicium evocatus et personaliter comparens fatebatur crimen. Unde ei penitentia canonica pro commissis imponitur per ipsum peragenda more penitentis in ecclesia sua parochiali per duos dies dominicos proximos cum declaratione scedule sibi tradite &c et ulterius iniungitur viro quod mulier, viz. dicta Johanna, consimilem peraget penitentiam more penitentis &c, et ad certificandum in proximo die iuridico post &c decano decanatus &c si interim matrimonium inter eos solempnizatum non fuerit.

Detectum est quod Willelmus Jannye de Chadell fornicatorie vixit cum Alicia Harrison qui evocati ad iudicium et personaliter comparentes fatebantur crimen et deinde dictus Willelmus sub sui iuramenti vinculo ad tacta dei evangelia prestiti promisit ad solempnizandum matrimonium cum dicta Alicia citra festum natalis Domini proxime futurum et ad certificandum decano decanatus in proximo die iuridico post &c, et preterea iniunctum est dicto Willelmo prout sequitur, viz.: *that he shall geve to the poor mens boxe: iij^{s}iiij^d* citra festum purificationis beate Marie virginis proximum &c, *and further shall bake a strike of wheate into bread and geve it to the poor of the seid parisshe* die dominica proxima ad septimanam &c.

f.143v.

Detectum est quod Helena Browne de Chadell fornicatorie vixit et quod sit gravida per Thomam Coliar qui iam adversa valetudine laborat et dicta Helena ad iudicium evocata et personaliter comparens fatebatur crimen sed tamen continuatur causa sub spe maritagij inter eos habendi et solempnizandi &c.

Detectum est quod Elizabeth Peerson de Wymeslowe fornicatorie vixit et quod peperit per Thomam Blackshawe. Dicta Elizabetha/ad iudicium evocata et personaliter comparens fatebatur crimen Unde penitentia canonica ei pro commissis imponitur per ipsam peragenda more penitentis in ecclesia sua parochiali die dominica proxima ad septimanam cum declaratione scedule sibi tradite &c, et ad certificandum decano decanatus in proximo die iuridico post &c, et preterea iniungitur quod dictus Thomas Blackshawe consimilem peraget penitentiam more penitentis &c, in dicta ecclesia &c per duos dies dominicos proximos &c et quod tradat ad elemosinariam pixidem coram parochianis: iij^s iiij^d citra festum natalis Domini proxime futurum et ad certificandum decano decanatus in proximo die iuridico post &c.

Detectum est quod Matilda Blomeley de Chadell fornicatorie vixit et quod peperit per Thomam Haywarde. Unde ad iudicium evocata et personaliter comparens fatebatur crimen cui penitentia canonica pro commissis &c ei imponitur per ipsam peragenda more penitentis in ecclesia sua parochiali per duos dies dominicos cum declaratione scedule sibi tradite &c, et ad certificandum decano decanatus in proximo die iuridico post &c.

Detectum est quod Johannes Bradley parochie de Wymmeslowe fornicatorie vixit cum quadam Elizabethe. Unde ad iudicium evocatus/et personaliter comparens fatebatur crimen et assumpsit in se ad solempnizandum matrimonium cum dicta Elizabeth [   ]^2 citra festum natalis Domini proximum futurum ad quod perimplendum sub sui iuramenti vinculo ad tacta Dei evangelia prestiti promisit &c, et ad certificandum decano decanatus in proximo die iuridico post &c.

Detectum est quod Anna Damporte parochie de Wymeslowe fornicatorie vixit et quod peperit per Laurentium Damporte qui iam recessit; unde dicta Anna ad iudicium evocata et personaliter comparens fatebatur crimen cui pro commissis penitentia canonica imponitur per ipsam peragenda more penitentis in ecclesia sua parochiali die dominica proxima ad septimanam cum declaratione scedule sibi tradite &c et ad certificandum decano decanatus in proximo die iuridico post &c.

Detectum est quod Margareta Wosingecrofte de Wymeslowe fornicatorie vixit cum Thoma Cashe qui iam recessit. Unde dicta Margareta ad iudicium evocata et personaliter comparens fatebatur crimen, cui pro commissis penitentia canonica imponitur per ipsam peragenda more penitentis in ecclesia sua parochiali die dominica proxima ad septimanam cum declaratione scedule sibi tradite &c et ad certificandum decano decanatus in proximo die iuridico post &c.

Detectum est quod Georgius Walker de Wymeslowe fornicatorie vixit cum Margeria Romesbotom. Unde dictus Georgius ad iudicium evocatus et personaliter comparens fatebatur crimen cui pro commissis penitentia canonica imponitur per ipsum peragenda more penitentis in ecclesia sua parochiali per duos dies dominicos proximos &c, cum declaratione scedule sibi tradite &c, et ad certificandum decano decanatus in proximo die iuridico post, &c.

Detectum est quod Willelmus Bennet parochie de Wymeslowe fornicatorie vixit cum Elizabetha Davie. Unde dictus Willelmus ad iudicium evocatus et personaliter comparens fatebatur crimen et assumpsit in se ad solempnizandum matrimonium cum dicta Elizabetha citra festum natalis domini proximum futurum &c, ad quod perimplendum sub sui iuramenti vinculo ad tacta dei evangelia prestiti promisit &c et ad certificandum decano decanatus in proximo die iuridico post &c.

Detectum est quod Henricus Peerse de Wymeslowe fornicatorie vixit cum quadam Gratia [   ]³ que iam habitat apud Donham. Unde dictus Henricus ad iudicium evocatus et personaliter comparens fatebatur crimen cui penitentia canonica pro commissis imponitur/per ipsum peragenda more penitentis in ecclesia sua parochiali per duos dies dominicos proximos cum declaratione scedule sibi tradite &c, et ulterius iniungitur dicto Henrico ut tradat ad elemosinariam pixidem coram parochianis: xij^d, et ad certificandum decano decanatus in proximo die iuridico post &c.

f.145v.

Rogerus Hebbert parochie de Stockeporte detectus est de crimine incesti cum Elizabetha Hebbert. Unde dictus Rogerus ad iudicium evocatus et personaliter comparens fatebatur crimen cui pro commissis penitentia canonica iniungitur per ipsum peragenda more penitentis in foro dicte parochie de Stockporte et ad penitendum se simili modo in ecclesie sua parochiali die dominica proxima cum declaratione scedule sibi tradite &c, et ulterius dicto Rogero iniungitur prout sequitur, viz.: *that in the market he geve asmuche bread to the poor as shalbe baken of a strike of wheate and likewise apon Soundaie in the church to the poor half so muche bread*, et ad certificandum decano decanatus in proximo die iuridico post &c.

Detectum est quod Katherina Layton de Stockporte fornicatorie vixit cum quodam/Willelmo Hancock de Astburie qui iam recessit, unde dicta Katherina ad iudicium evocata et personaliter comparens fatebatur crimen cui pro commissis penitentia canonica imponitur per ipsam peragenda more penitentis in ecclesia sua parochiali per duos dies dominicos proximos cum declaratione scedule sibi tradite &c, et ad certificandum decano decanatus in proximo die iuridico post &c.

f.146r.

Detectum est quod Georgius Holme de Manchester fornicatorie vixit cum quadam Elizabeth Robinson. Unde dictus Georgius ad iudicium evocatus et personaliter comparens fatebatur crimen cui penitentia canonica pro commissis imponitur per ipsum peragenda more penitentis in ecclesia sua parochiali per tres dies dominicos proximos post festum sancti Andree cum declaratione scedule sibi tradite &c, et ad certificandum decano decanatus in proximo die iuridico post &c.

Detectum est quod Katherina Robothom de Stockeporte fornicatorie vixit cum quodam Thoma Holliworthe qui iam recessit. Unde dicta Katherina ad iudicium evocata et personaliter comparens fatebatur crimen cui imponitur penitentia canonica pro commissis per ipsam peragenda more penitentis in ecclesia sua parochiali per duos dies/dominicos proximos cum declaratione scedule sibi tradite &c, et ad certificandum decano decanatus in proximo die iuridico ex tunc sequenti &c.

Apud Novum Castrum, decimo octavo die mensis Decembris[4] Anno Domini millesimo quingentesimo quinquagesimo nono.

Detectum est quod Cuthbertus Turnor de Morpeth incontinenter vixit cum Elizabeth Ambrie de eadem unde dictus Cuthbertus ad iudicium evocatus et personaliter comparens fatebatur crimen cui penitentia canonica pro commissis imponitur per ipsum peragenda more penitentis in foro ibidem die Sabbati proximo &c cum declaratione scedule sibi tradite &c, et ad certificandum magistro Sherwood Surrogato &c citra diem Sabbati proximum ad septimanam. Et ulterius iniungitur dicto Cuthberto quod posthac penitus se a consortio dicte Elizabethe abstineat nisi in locis publicis &c, ad quod perimplendum ad tacta Dei evangelia prestitit iuramentum. Et deinde consimilis penitentia iniungitur dicte Elizabethe per ipsam peragenda more penitentis in ecclesia sua parochiali die dominica proxima cum declaratione scedule &c, et ad certificandum ut supra &c.

Detectum est quod Robertus Marton de Gateshedd fornicatorie vixit cum Johanna Atkinson de eadem. Unde ad iudicium evocati et personaliter comparentes fatebantur crimen. Deinde dicto Roberto penitentia canonica imponitur per ipsum peragenda more penitentis die Sabbati proximo in foro de Novo Castro &c et ad certificandum magistro Sherwood Surrogato &c in proximo die iuridico post, et preterea consimilis penitentia mulieri pro commissis suis imponitur per ipsam peragenda more penitentis in ecclesia sua parochiali per duos dies dominicos &c cum declaratione scedule sibi tradite &c, et ad certificandum magistro Sherwoode ut supra. Et ulterius iniungitur dicto Roberto quod posthac penitus se abstineat a consortio et a cohabitacione cum dicta Elizabetha ad quod perimplendum ad tacta dei evangelia prestitit iuramentum &c.

Detectum est quod Johannes Lore de Gateshed incontinenter vixit cum Katherina Foxe de eadem qui ad iudicium evocati et personaliter comparentes fatebantur crimen. Unde dicto Johanni penitentia canonica pro commissis iniungitur per ipsum peragenda more penitentis in foro de Novo Castro die Sabbati proximo cum declaratione scedule sibi tradite &c, et ad certificandum magistro Sherwood Surrogato in proximo die iuridico post &c, et deinde iniungitur dicto Johann quod posthac penitus se abstineat a consortio dicte *Elizabethe* nisi in locis publicis ad quod perimplendum/ad tacta Dei evangelia prestitit iuramentum &c, et ulterius penitentia dicte *Elizabethe* respectuatur pro tempore quia gravida sit &c.

Detectum est quod Margareta Stercke de Gateshed fornicatorie vixit cum Johanne Davison de eadem. Unde dicta Margareta ad iudicium evocata et personaliter comparens fatebatur crimen cui penitentia canonica pro commissis imponitur per ipsam peragenda more penitentis in ecclesia sua parochiali die dominica proxima &c, cum declaratione scedule sibi tradite &c, et ad certificandum magistro Sherwood Surrogato &c in proximo die iuridico &c.

Detectum est quod Thomas Jackson de Gateshed fornicatorie vixit cum Helena Maye de eadem qui ad iudicium evocati et personaliter comparentes crimenque negantes matrimonium inter eos esse contractum fatebantur et assumpserunt in se ad solempnizandum matrimonium huiusmodi citra diem lune proximum ad septimanam &c, ad quod perimplendum ad tacta Dei evangelia iuramentum prestiterunt &c, et ad certificandum magistro Sherwoodd Surrogato &c.

(fols. 148r.–v. and 148A r.–v. are blank.)

Sequuntur nomina[1] **omnium** absentium qui Regiam visitacionem infra diocesim Ebor' minime subierunt, &c.

Nottingham

Bingham	Dominus Oliverus Lecetor, rector ibidem
Cotgrave	Magister Willelmus Perpoincte, rector
Widmerpole	Dominus Edmundus Stubbes, rector
Broughton	Dominus Joannes Normavell, rector
Broughton iuxta Kynnalton	Dominus Joannes Fishe, rector
Hawkesworth	Dominus Christophorus Sandforthe, rector
Colston Basset	Dominus Willelmus More, vicarius

Clifton	Dominus Edmundus Thurlond, rector
Barton	Dominus Jacobus Wheatleye, rector
Bonington[2]	Dominus Thomas Staveley, rector
Grete Leeke	Dominus Ricardus Walker, rector
Gotham[3]	Dominus Ricardus Walker, rector
Eperstone	Dominus Willelmus Wetherall
Kirkebee in Ashfild	Antonius Wiclife, rector
Adenborowe	Dominus Robertus Bagley, vicarius

Decanatus Aynstie

Brotherton	Laurentius Diconson, vicarius
Braiton	Dominus Robertus Turner, rector

Byrkyne	Magister Willelmus Brokden, rector
Wigishall	Dominus Robertus Byas, vicarius
Tadcaster	Dominus Thomas Swane, vicarius
Spofforthe	Magister Alanus Percy, rector
Swillington	Magister Franciscus Mallet, rector
Saxton	Dominus Willelmus Cowper, curatus
Garforthe	Dominus Thomas Vavizer, rector
Monkefriston	Dominus Joannes Norffolke, curatus
Barwicke	Dominus Thomas Greyne, curatus

Bulmer

Turrington	Dominus Edwardus Otbye, rector
Kylborn	Dominus Christophorus Rayner, curatus

Topclif	Dominus Joannes Jake, vicarius
Sesey	Dominus Thomas Barne, rector

Craike	Dominus Willelmus Garnette, rector
Thurmanby	Dominus Thomas Cayle, rector

Hallifax

Hallifax	Dominus Joannes Harrison, vicarius
Kirkeburton	Dominus Henricus Sowthill, vicarius
Emlaye	Dominus Thomas Barnbye, rector
Bristall	Dominus Willelmus Taylor, vicarius
Eland	Dominus Rogerus Walker, curatus
Hudderfild	Dominus Hugo Gledle, vicarius
Haworthe	Dominus Arthurus Rowlinge, curatus

Decanatus Redford et Laneham   f.151r.

Carleton in Lindricke	Magister Leonardus Stafford, rector ibidem habens plura beneficia nunquam comparuit.
Wyrkesoppe	Dominus Joannes Thornleye, vicarius
Warsoppe	Dominus Joannes Peerson, rector
Estdraiton	Dominus Edwardus Herling, vicarius
Egmanton	Dominus Joannes Oton, vicarius
Laneham	Dominus Willelmus Wetherall, vicarius
Gameston	Magister Thomas Thurland, rector
Bole	Dominus Edmundus Wyngrene, vicarius
Sandbye	Dominus Ricardus Woode, rector
Misterton	Dominus Joannes Mershall, vicarius
Gringlaye	Dominus Jacobus Barton, vicarius f.151v.
Claworthe	Magister Rogerus Dallison
Mathersaye	Dominus Willelmus Mershe, vicarius
Fynnyngley	Dominus Joannes Richardson, rector
Harworthe	Dominus Georgius Fisher, vicarius

Decanatus Southwell

Beckingham	Dominus Robertus Apeleye, vicarius
Sowth Whetley	Dominus Georgius Lane, vicarius
Northleverton	Dominus Henricus Prise, vicarius
Rampton	Dominus Willelmus Pickard, vicarius
Northmuskham	Dominus Ricardus Fisheborn, vicarius
Crophilbisshop	Dominus Ricardus Thompson, vicarius

Decanatus Newarke   f.152r.

Halton iuxta Newarke	Dominus Joannes Malberye, rector
Thorpe in Glebis	Dominus Thomas Shipman, rector
Alston	Dominus Joannes Normanvell, rector
Rolston	Dominus Thomas Luddington, vicarius
Crumwell	Dominus Thomas Thurland, rector
South Scarley	Dominus Willelmus Arsleye, vicarius

South Collingham	Dominus Willelmus Coseleye, rector
Fledburgh	Dominus Thomas Wasshington, rector
Normanton	Dominus Galfridus Lodge, vicarius

Decanatus Malton

Sutton[4]	Dominus Joannes Poisegate, rector
Marske	Magister Willelmus Rokebye, vicarius
Ormysbye	Dominus Ricardus Stapleton, vicarius
Hawnebye	Dominus Joannes Sympson, rector
Thurmanby[5]	Dominus Marmaducus Tesedale, curatus
Kyrkbye in Clevelond	Dominus Willelmus Burye, rector, habens plura beneficia nunquam comparuit.
Nydd	Dominus Henricus Shawe, vicarius
Acklond	Dominus Joannes Jakeson, curatus
Kirkebee	Magister Thomas Thwaites, rector
Ingleby Greno	Dominus Georgius Gowland, curatus
Ottrington	Dominus Rolandus Otford, curatus
Sherborn	Dominus Thomas Watson, vicarius
Westowe	Dominus Robertus Snell, vicarius
Bugthorpe	Dominus Jacobus Creton, vicarius
Scawbye	Dominus Henricus Keye, vicarius
Folcketon	Magister Joannes Dacye, rector
Willerbye	Dominus Thomas Markindale, vicarius.
Langtofte	Dominus Robertus Scalinge, vicarius
Ruesbye[6]	Dominus Antonius Maxwell, vicarius
Speton	Dominus Martinus Stevenson, curatus
Gilling	Dominus Edmundus Tyndall, rector
Salton	Dominus Radulphus Westcrope, vicarius
Stangrave	Dominus David Owen, rector
Hooton Busshell	Dominus Joannes Newsome, vicarius
Apleton	Dominus Willelmus Houghton, vicarius

Beverley et Hull

Welton	Dominus Robertus Twenge
Hovenden	Dominus Willelmus Skelton, curatus
Walkington	Dominus Thomas Wrighte, rector
Etton	Dominus Willelmus Calverd, curatus
Northcave	Dominus Reginaldus Dene, curatus
Kirkeborn	Dominus Willelmus Bell, vicarius recusat venire
Huggette	Magister Abraham Robinson, rector habet plura beneficia
Wressill	Dominus Edwardus Stampe, vicarius
Burnholme	Dominus Edwardus Wormmall, rector
Thornton	Dominus Willelmus Harte, vicarius
Hooton in Cranswick	Dominus Willelmus Ellys, vicarius
Kylnwicke	Dominus Joannes Mershall, vicarius

f.152v.

f.153r.

f.153v.

Goodmandham	Dominus Robertus Cleving, rector	f.154r.
Southdalton	Dominus Robertus Ringrose, rector	
Awborn	Dominus Joannes Raignold, curatus	
Lowthorpe	Dominus Thomas Fugall, rector	
Owgthorn	Dominus Thomas Hopkinson, rector	
Holme	Dominus Joannes Lyster, curatus	
Garton	Dominus Ricardus Harde, curatus	
Mapleton	Dominus Joannes Besakell, vicarius	
Sutton	Dominus Vincentius Donnaye, curatus	
Swyne	Dominus Joannes Huyton, curatus	
Rosse	Dominus Willelmus Gowle, curatus	
Welwicke	Dominus Joannes Fisher, vicarius	
Ryston	Dominus Joannes Rudde, rector, non resident	
Goxhill	Dominus Willelmus Parkin, curatus &c.	

Otteley[7] f.154v.

Mylton	Joannes Burgyn, rector est etatis xiiij annorum; Radulphus Halworth vicarius	
Arneclife	Dominus Thomas Wilson, vicarius	
Long Preston	Dominus Thomas Hall, vicarius	
Hubbrame[8]	Dominus Thomas Preston, curatus	
Skipton	Stephanus Ellys, ludimagister	
Kirkesmeton	Dominus Joannes Waynehowse, rector	
Sprotburghe	Dominus Petrus Silles, rector	
Tankerseye	Dominus Thomas Cockeson, rector	
Rawmershe	Dominus Willelmus Nutte, rector	
Thornescoo	Magister Henricus Malevery habet plura beneficia	
Sheffild	Dominus Ricardus Hayward, vicarius	
Hymesworth	Dominus Vincentius Crofte, rector, non residet.	
Baddisworthe	Dominus Joannes Greane, rector, non resident	f.155r.
Rothewell	Dominus Joannes Hagger, vicarius ibidem; Laurentius Huccinson, curatus	
Metheleye	Dominus Antonius Askam, rector Georgius Tailor, curatus	
Normanton	Dominus Ricardus Snytall, vicarius	
Sandall magna	Brianus Jakeson, vicarius	
Croston	Dominus Jacobus Brodebente, rector	
Alworthe	Dominus Thomas Huntington, rector	
Wormeslaye	Magister Willelmus Brogden habet duo beneficia in diocesi Ebor' et unum Londini &c.	
Snothe	Dominus Joannes Harrison, curatus	
Adlingflete	Dominus Willelmus Ellys, vicarius	
Escrycke	Dominus Willelmus Holmes, rector	
Crambu'	Dominus Robertus Myddilton, curatus	
Foston	Dominus Joannes Durham, curatus &c.	
Ricall	Dominus Milo Yarrowe, vicarius	f.155v.

Over Helmsley	Dominus Willelmus Smythson, rector
Bulmer	Dominus Joannes Jakeson, rector
Elvington	Dominus Christophorus Ustler, rector
Strensall	Dominus Philippus Machell, vicarius
Huntington	Dominus Joannes Heworthe, vicarius
Bisshophill[9]	Dominus *Willelmus* Mores, rector
Sancte Trinitatis	
Ebor'	Dominus Thomas Borrowe, curatus
Sancti Salvatoris	Dominus Thomas Leither, rector
Sancti Laurentij	Dominus Jacobus Jonson, vicarius.

f.156r.

Cestrensis Diocesis

Sequuntur nomina non comparentium in visitacione Regia infra diocesim Cestrensem

Richemond Borowbrige et Catericke

Copgrave	Dominus Georgius Lambe, rector
Fanham	Dominus Joannes Pockeson, vicarius
Kyrbee super	
moram	Dominus Willelmus Graye, vicarius
Aldebroughe	Dominus Robertus Mershall, vicarius
Usborn magna	Dominus Robertus Redshawe, vicarius
Usborn parva	Dominus Edwardus Dickonson, vicarius
Cundall	Dominus Joannes Ellerkar
Staneleye	Dominus Willelmus Gascoyne
Grynton	Dominus Willelmus Dowson, vicarius non residet
Ripley	Magister Robertus Parcivall non residet
Moncketon	Dominus Davidus Bell, curatus
f.156v. Arkindall	Dominus Ricardus Langfellowe, vicarius
Scruton	Dominus Franciscus Jagger
Bedall	Dominus Henricus Ylkins, rector
Patrikbrompton	Dominus Joannes Helme, vicarius
Mensleye	Dominus Reginaldus Hindmere, rector
Wathe	Dominus Jacobus Seller, rector
	Dominus Joannes Dickeson, curatus
Tanfilde	Magister Joannes Tunstall, rector non residet sed postea comparuit et subscripsit
Kyrklington	Magister Joannes Wadforthe, rector
Kirbefletam	Dominus Christophorus Sympson, vicarius
Burnston	Dominus Christophorus Beckewith, vicarius
Aiskrigge	Dominus Rogerus Thomlinson, rector
Aiskerthe	Dominus Joannes Backehouse, vicarius

f.157r.

Decanatus Copeland

Brigham	Magister Ricardus Parr, vicarius non residet
	Dominus Henricus Wooddall

Arleckden	Dominus Willelmus Barker, curatus
Whitbecke	Dominus Michael Braithwayte, curatus
Whitham	Dominus Willelmus Towreson, rector
Harrington	Dominus Robertus Ladd, rector
Sancti Bege	Dominus Jacobus Grindall, curatus, *postea comparuit*[10]
Hayle	Dominus Nicolaus Copeland vicarius
Gosforthe	Dominus Willelmus Stringer, rector
Moncaster	Dominus Willelmus Tobman, curatus

Decanatus Vici *Ablani*[11]

Bartumley	Dominus Robertus Kynsey, rector
Badeley	Dominus Joannes Olyver, vicarius
Wybunburye	Dominus Matheus Woode, vicarius
	Dominus Thomas Dickson, stipendiarius

Decanatus medij vici   f.157v.

Ashburye	Magister Hugo Apowell, rector
Sonbage[12]	Dominus Petrus Prestland, vicarius
Breerton	Dominus Thomas Smyth, rector
Swetnam	Dominus Robertus Plante, rector
Goscre	Dominus Ricardus Swayne, curatus
Davenham	Magister Simon Sheppard, rector
Whitgate	Dominus Ricardus Baven, vicarius

Decanatus Leyland et Blackborn

Croston	Dominus Thomas Lemyng, vicarius
Leylond	Dominus Carolus Wainwrighte, vicarius
Ecclieston	Dominus Joannes Woddye, rector

Decanatus Werrington

Wynwecke	Magister Thomas Stanley non residet
Wiggan	Reverendus pater episcopus Sadren' rector non residet.
Prescote	Dominus Robertus Nelson, curatus f.158r.
Aighton	Dominus Edwardus Morecrofte, rector
Halsall	Magister Ricardus Halsall, vicarius
	Dominus Henricus Halsall curatus
Sefton	Dominus Robertus Ballarde, rector
Ormyskirke	Dominus Elizeus Ambros, vicarius
Walton	Magister Antonius Mollyneux, rector

Decanatus Frodisham et Furnes

Aisheton	Dominus Joannes Robinson, rector
Aldingham	Dominus Robertus Brocke non residet
	Dominus Robertus Gardener curatus ibidem
	Dominus Thomas Dickinson stipendiarius
	Dominus Edwardus Pirrey, stipendiarius

Dominus Leonardus Fell, stipendiarius

Hauxhedd   Dominus Ricardus Harris curatus ibidem *postea comparuit*

Dominus Thomas Syngilton, stipendiarius

Dominus Ricardus Warde, stipendiarius *postea comparuit*

Dominus Hugo Kellete, stipendiarius

f.158v.

Decanatus Cestr' Wirrall et Bangor

Sancte Marie   Dominus Carolus Duckes, rector
Cestr'

Torporley	Magister Alanus Charleton, rector
Crisilton	Magister Willelmus Collingwood, rector
Plemstowe	Dominus Joannes Walker, vicarius
Ince	Dominus Henricus Roper, curatus
Barrow	Magister Henricus Sudall, rector
Malpas	Magister Willelmus Hill, rector unius medietatis
	Magister Arthurus Dudeley, rector alterius medietatis
Tatnall	Magister Rannulphus Wymeslowe, rector
Aldeford	Magister Willelmus Wybram, rector
Bangor	Magister Willelmus Charleton, rector
Hanmer	Dominus Rannulphus Philipe non residet
Walezey	Dominus Thomas Tassye, vicarius
Kyrkebye	Magister Ricardus Walker, rector, non residet
Backeford	Dominus Thomas Davye vicarius

f.159r.

Decanatus Mancestrie

Prestwiche	Dominus Willelmus Longleye, rector *postea subscripsit*
Rachedale	Dominus Joannes Hawson, curatus
Gawesworthe	Magister Willelmus Lee, rector
Chedill	Magister Thomas Buckleye, rector
Wymeslowe	Dominus Jacobus Broke, curatus
Moburley	Magister Jacobus Davison non residet
Stopeford	Magister Arthurus Lowe, rector
	Dominus Thomas Clarke, curatus

(fol. 159v. is blank.)

f.160r.
Dunelmensis
Diocesis

Sequuntur nomina omnium et singulorum clericorum non comparentium in Regia visitacione infra diocesim Dunelmensem &c.

Darlington	Dominus Willelmus Sheppard, curatus
Langnewton	Dominus Ricardus Hartburn, rector
Billingham	Dominus Robertus Crawforthe, curatus
Cockefild	Dominus Georgius Rayne, curatus
Eggiscliffe	Dominus Brianus Baynes, rector non residet
	Dominus Willelmus Stevenson curatus

Stockborn	Dominus Robertus Peterson, rector
Elton	Dominus Joannes Sare, curatus
Myddleton in	
Tesedale	Magister Wilelmus Bell, rector non resident
Stranton	Magister Joannes Semer, vicarius
	Dominus Jacobus Lakynby curatus
Wolsington	Dominus Thomas Sparke, rector
Branspethe	Dominus Nicolaus Foster, rector
Edmondbiers	Dominus Joannes Foster, rector
Mugliswicke	Dominus Joannes Watson, curatus
Westspittell	Dominus Joannes Ramys, custos
Masindewe	Dominus Thomas Halman, magister
	Gilbertus Lewen, magister hospitii Marie Magdalene
	Cuthbertus Ellison, procurator capelle super pontem
Tynmowth	Dominus Oliverus Selbye, vicarius
Chollerton	Dominus Christophorus Lewes, curatus
Newborn	Dominus Egidius Robinson, vicarius
Ponteland	Dominus Thomas Halman, vicarius
Corbrige	Dominus Ricardus Mershall, vicarius, non resident
	Dominus Radulphus Eltringham, curatus
Wardon	Dominus Antonius Barrowe, curatus
	Dominus Nicolaus Mawen, stipendiarius, recusavit venire
Knaresdell	Dominus Robertus Tesedall, rector
Bedlington	Dominus Willelmus Watson, vicarius
Morpeth	Dominus Joannes Daker, rector, non resident
	Dominus Edwardus Trowtbecke, curatus
Shipwashe	Dominus Thomas Ogle, rector, non resident
Bothall	Dominus Robertus Passe, rector
Forde	Magister Willelmus Collinwood nullo modo comparuit
Hotghton	Dominus Thomas Thomson, vicarius
Alnchan	Dominus Georgius Hymners, vicarius &c.

f.160v.

f.161r.

(fol. 161v. is blank.)

f.162r.
Carliolensis
Diocesis

Nomina contumaciter absentium tempore visitacionis
Regie infra diocesim Carliolensem &c.

Kirkebesteven	Magister Petrus Vanes, rector non resident
Musegrave	Dominus Joannes Kirkebecke non resident
Burghe	Dominus Joannes Murrey, curatus
Warcope	Dominus Willelmus Gargate, curatus
Marton	Magister Willelmus Burye, rector, non resident
Duston	Magister Rolandus Threlket, rector
	Dominus Joannes Benson, curatus
Kyrby Thurer	Mighell Crakinthorpe, rector, non resident
	Dominus Robertus Nutthide, curatus

	Shape	Dominus Robertus Shalfild, curatus
	Banter	Dominus Joannes Harrison, curatus
	Cliburner	Edwardus Knyppe, rector, habet plura beneficia
		Dominus Georgius Barton, curatus
f.162v.	Barton	Dominus Thomas Smythe, rector
		Dominus Hugo Barton, curatus
		Dominus Adam Dawson, stipendiarius
	Crostwayte	Dominus Joannes Ratclif, vicarius
		Dominus Lancelotus Levagies, stipendiarius
		Dominus Lancelotus Murreye, stipendiarius
	Irebye	Dominus Jacobus Nicolson, curatus
	Bolton	Magister Georgius Nevill, rector
	Plumbland	Magister Willelmus Porter, non residet
	Bownes	Magister Joannes Robinson, rector
	Denton	Dominus Edwardus Bell rector
	Beamond	Dominus Robertus Thompson, rector
	Thuresbye	Magister Radulphus Brandlinge, vicarius
		Ricardus Hogeson, curatus
	Orton	Magister Ricardus Place, rector, non residet
		Thomas Twentyman, curatus
f.163r.	Kirkeanders	Dominus Thomas Rumney,[13] rector
	Kirkeoswald	Dominus Joannes Scales, vicarius
	Hutton	Dominus Ricardus Towson, rector
	Graystocke	Dominus Joannes Dane, rector
	Skelton	Dominus Hugo Hodgeson, rector
	Ranwicke	Dominus Stephanus Bowman, curatus

(fols. 163v.–167v. are blank.)

Recognisauncis takyne to the
Quenes Majestis use bifore the
Visitors of the Province of Yorke[1]

A certificat of suche recognisauncies as wer taken bifore Edwyn Sandis doctor of Divinitie and Henry Harvye doctor of Lawe, Commissioners generall emonge other appoincted by the Quenes Majestie for thexercisinge of her highnes visitacion within the Province of Yorke, Anno Regni Domine nostre Elizabethe Dei gracia Anglie Francie et Hibernie Regine fidei defensoris primo.

Venit Edwardus Baker de Newarke in comitatu Notingham husbondman et recognovit se debere Domine nostre Regine viginti libras, levandas de bonis terris et catallis suis &c ad usum Domine nostre Regine &c.

The condicion of this recognisaunce is suche, That if the said Edward Baker obedyently doo suche pennaunce as now be and hereafter shalbe appoincted unto him by the quenes majestis Commissioners for his offences detected in the visitacion, and doo also make certificate therof at suche tyme and place as shalbe also appoincted unto him, That then the recognisaunce to be voyde &c.

Memorandum that this recognisaunce   Capta erat hec recognitio
is discharged[2]   coram Henrico Gates Milite,
                                                           Edwino Sandis et Henrico Harvy
                                                           xxv[to] die Augusti Anno Domine
                                                           Regine primo.

Venerunt Thomas Cowdrye de Herpynton in comitatu Ebor' yeman, et Gilbertus Stanfild clericus, et recognoverunt se debere Domine nostre Regine quadraginta libras &c, levandas de bonis terris et catallis suis &c.

The condicion of this recognisaunce is suche, that if they doo personally appere bifore the Quenes Majestis Commissioners in the parishe churche of Hallifax tomorowe in the mornynge by viij of the clocke, and that Cowdrye at that tyme doo personally bring in his wif and then doo receive and performe suche ordre as the said Commissioners shall take and appoyncte tocching the matters detected in the visitacion, That then the Recognisaunce to be voyde &c.

Memorandum that this recognisaunce   Capta erat hec recognitio coram
is discharged   Thoma Gargrave milite, Edwino
                                                           Sandis et Henrico Harvye &c, primo
                                                           Septembris Anno Regni Domine
                                                           nostre Regine primo.

Venerunt Willelmus Boyes clericus rector de Giesley Ebor' diocesis, Willelmus Hawkisworthe armiger, Gabriel Grene, Stephanus Passelewe et Cristophorus Mawde generos' et recognoverunt se debere Domine nostre Regine quingentas libras legalis monete Anglie, levandas de bonis terris et catallis suis &c, ad usum Domine nostre Regine.

The condicion of this recognisaunce is suche, that if the said William Boyes doo personally appere bifore the quenes Majestis Commissioners at London appoincted for ecclesiasticall matters, either in the consistory of Paules at London or at suche other place and places as the said Commissioners shall fortune to sytte and be in or aboute the said Citie of London, then and ther to aunswer to all suche matters as shalbe obiected ageinst him, betwixt the first and the vijth daies of Novembre nexte commynge, and further that he doo not departe from thence withoute speciall lycence of the said Commissioners, That then the recognisaunce to be voide &c.

Memorandum that this recognisaunce ys discharged

Capta erat hec recognitio coram Thoma Gargrave Milite, Edwino Sandis et Henrico Harvy quarto die Septembris Anno Regni primo &c.

Venerunt Rogerus Mershall clericus prebendarius ecclesie cathedralis Ebor', et ipse per se recognovit debere Domine nostre Regine centum libras legalis monete Anglie, & Thomas Clarke de civitate Ebor' generosus et recognovit se debere dicte Domine nostre Regine per hanc recognitionem quadraginta libras, levandas de bonis terris et catallis suis ad usum eiusdem Domine Regine &c.

The condicion of this recognisaunce is suche, that yf the sayd Roger Mershall doo personally appere from tyme to tyme bifore *the these the* Quenes Majestis Commissioners or suche other as her Majestie hath or shall appoincte, at all suche tyme and places as apon notyce or commaundment therof geven or signified to the sayd Roger Mershall or the sayd Thomas Clarke shalbe lymytted and assigned, That then this recognisaunce to be voyde &c.

Memorandum that this recognisaunce is discharged

Capta erat hec recognitio coram Thoma Gargrave et Henrico Gates Militibus, Edwino Sandis et Henrico Harvy, nono die mensis Septembris Anno Regni Dicte Domine nostre Regine primo.

A Calendar of the remaining recognisances:[3]

George Palmes, *legum doctor*: £200.   f.171r.
   George Palmes of Bugthorpe, gent., and Richard Goldthorp of York, gent.:
£100 each.
      To appear before these or other commissioners, *at all suche tyme and places*
as apon notice or commaundment to him geven or to auny of his sureties.
   Before Gargrave, Gates and Sandis, 9 September.
   Memorandum of discharge.

Robert Pursglove, *clericus, archidiaconus Notingham*: £200.   f.171v.
   Arthur Dawkynes of York, gent., and Edmund Ayne of Bradfield, Yorks.
gent.: £100 each.
      Pursglove, *clarke and suffregan of Hull*, to appear before these or other
commissioners at all suche tyme and *places and when he shalbe therunto*
required or apon notyce or warnyng geven to him or to his sureties, and then
and ther to aunswer to suche Articles as shalbe obiected ageinst him.
   Before Gargrave, Gates and Sandis, 9 September.
   Memorandum of discharge.

Geoffrey Downes, *clericus*, prebendary at York: £100.   f.172r.
   Robert Barthrope,[4] *clericus*, £100 and John Tyndall of Brotherton gent., 100
marks.
      To appear before these or other commissioners, *so that the said Galfrid*
Downes or auny of his sureties have reasonable warnynge or knowledge
therof, then and ther to aunswer to suche matters as shalbe obiected against
him.
   Before the same, 9 September.
   Memorandum of discharge.

Alexander Jennynges, *clericus*, vicar of Bingley: £40.   f.172v.
   Oswald Wilkinson of York, gent., and John Marvyll of Bingley, husbandman:
£20 each.
      To appear before these or other commissioners after reasonable warning.
   Before the same, 9 September.
   Memorandum of discharge.

SAME DATE AND CONDITIONS:

Robert Woode, *clericus*, vicar of Otley: £40.   f.173r.
   Humphrey Ellis of York, innholder, and Thomas Kyrkebye of York, draper:
£20 each.

f.173v.   Thomas Jeffrison, *clericus*, of Ledsham, Yorks.: £40.
            Alexander Thorpe of York, scrivener, and William Sawre of Ledsham, yeo-
            man: £20 each.

f.174r.   Henry More, *clericus*, rector of St Martin, Micklegate, York: £40.
            William Fairewether and John Wilson of York, yeomen, and Thomas
            Pikkeringe of York: £20 each.

(*f.174v. blank*)   ————————————

f.175r.   John Crawforthe, *clericus*, prebendary of first prebend, Durham: £200.
            Roger Clakeson of the parish of St Oswald, Durham, gent., and Laurence
            Hayley of the parish of St Margaret there, yeoman: £100 each.
                To appear as above, *and further doo not departe from the place so
                appoyncted without speciall lycence.*
            Before Evers, Gargrave, Sandis and Harvey, 15 September.
            Memorandum of discharge.

            SAME DATE AND CONDITIONS:

f.175v.   William Bennette, *sacre theologie doctor*, prebendary of the fourth prebend,
            Durham: £300.
                Robert Meynell, serjeant-at-law, and James Parkinson of Easington, gent.:
                £100 each.

                                          ————————————

f.176r.   Roger Thompson, *clericus*, vicar of Ampleforth: £40.
            John Smythe of Ampleforth, yeoman, and William Speighte of York, gent.:
            £20 each.
                To appear before these or other commissioners as above, and to answer *to all
                suche matters as shalbe obiected.*
            Before Gates, Sandis and Harvey, 14 September.
            Memorandum of discharge.

                                          ————————————

f.176v.   Thomas Robertson, *sacre theologie professor*, Dean of Durham: £500.
            Robert Menell, serjeant-at-law, William Lawson of Washington, gent. and
            Thomas Whithede of Wearmouth, gent.: £100 each.
                To appear as above, *and further doo not departe from the place so
                appoincted except he have speciall lycence of them bifore whom thappar-
                aunce of him the said Thomas Robertson shalbe taken.*
            Before the same, 25 September. (No memo. of discharge.)

SAME DATE AND CONDITIONS, BEFORE THE SAME (DISCHARGED):

Robert Dalton, *clericus*, prebendary of Durham: £300.   f.177r.
   John Howton of Auckland, gent., and Robert Dalton of the same, gent.: £100
each.

Stephen Marley, *clericus*, prebendary of the sixth prebend, Durham: £200.   f.177v.
   Thomas Tempest of Lanchester, esquire, and William Hogeson of the same,
gent.: £100 each.

John Tuttyn, *clericus*, prebendary of the eighth prebend, Durham: £300.   f.178r.
   Robert Maynell, serjeant-at-law, and Gerard Salvyn of Croxdale (*Crokisted*),
gent.: £100 each.

George Cliffe, *clericus*, prebendary of the twelfth prebend, Durham: £200.   f.178v.
   Christopher Athe of the parish of St Mary, Durham, and Nicholas Thornell
of Auckland, gents.: £100 each.

Nicholas Marley, *clericus*, prebendary of the ninth prebend, Durham: £200.   f.179r.
   Robert Tempest of Holmeset, esquire, and Thomas Tempest of Lanchester,
gent.: £100 each.

Anthony Salvyn, *clericus*, prebendary of the eleventh prebend, Durham: £300.   f.179v.
   Gerard Salvyn of Croxdale, gent. and Thomas Salvyn jun. of Hemingbrough,
gent.: £100 each.

William Carther, *clericus*: £300.   f.180r.
   William Holmes of Bishop Wearmouth and Thomas Smythe of the same,
yeomen: £100 each.

Thomas Segiswicke, *sacre theologie doctor*: £300.   f.180v.
   Thomas Blackete of Stanhope in Weardale and Arthur Myers of the same,
yeomen: £100 each.

26 SEPTEMBER, OTHERWISE THE SAME:

George Bullocke, *clericus*, prebendary of Durham: £300.   f.181r.
   John Burton of Horton, husbandman and Robert Car of South Shields, gent.:
£100 each.

William Whitehead, vicar of Heighington: £100.   f.181v.
   Thomas Whithed of Monk Wearmouth, gent., George Smythe of Durham,
yeoman, and George Blackeston of Bishop Wearmouth, yeoman: 100 marks
each.

f.182r.   Richard Salvyn, *clericus*, rector of Hinderwell: £40.
                 Gerard Salvyn of Croxdale, gent. and Robert Birkehed of Branspeth, yeoman:
                 £20. (No memo. of discharge.)

(f.182v. blank)

f.183r.   Peter Bee of Allanton, yeoman: £40.
                 Lancelot Walles of Laseby, *clericus*: £20.
                 To appear at Hexham *bifore the surrogates of the Quenes Majestis visitors
                 in those partes when he shalbe therunto requyred apon reasonable warnynge,
                 and then to aunswer to suche matters as shalbe obiected ageinst him.*
                 Before Sandis, Harvey and Browne, 4 October.
                 Memorandum of discharge.

(f.183v. blank)

f.184r.   Richard Harte of Manchester, *clericus*: £300.
                 Sir John Sowthworthe, knight, and John Massye esquire: £100 each.
                 To appear *bifore the lorde electe archbishope of Caunterburye and suche
                 other the Quenes Majesties Commissioners as be joyned with him for ecclesi-
                 asticall cawses the xxth day of November next commyng either at his howse
                 at Lambehith or at suche other place and places as he or they shall sytte
                 or be within the Citie of London or nere unto the same, and also doo not
                 departe from thence excepte he obteyne speciall lycence for the same.*
                 Before Sandis, Harvey and Browne, 18 October.
                 Memorandum of discharge.

FOOTNOTES TO INTRODUCTION

1. Borthwick, Reg. 28 (Lee), f. 101v.
2. S. E. Lehmberg, 'Supremacy and Vicegerency: a re-examination', *EHR* lxxxi, (1966), 225; G. R. Elton, *Policy and Police* (Cambridge 1972), 247; *Wriothesley Chronicle*, (Camden Soc. 1877), 11; see also C. J. Kitching, 'The probate jurisdiction of Thomas Cromwell as vicegerent', *BIHR* xlvi, (May 1973), 102.
3. Frere, i, 121 ff. and references cited there.
4. *LP*, x, 364. The lack of any surviving Articles for a general visitation could also be explained by the absence of parochial business.
5. Frere, ii, 19. The Injunctions were said to have been 'by his Grace's commissaries given in such places as they in time past have visited'.
6. Frere, ii, 1. The Injunctions have been widely noted and discussed. See for example, P. Hughes, *The Reformation in England* (3 vols., New York 1951), i, 353 ff; G. R. Elton, *England under the Tudors* (reprint, 1967, Cambridge), 153.
7. Borthwick, Reg. 28 (Lee), ff. 134-5. The scribe there has *1537*, but this is impossible if the chronology given for the visitation is correct in calling 4 April a Tuesday.
8. 28 Henry VIII, c. 7, s. 15. The Register thus provides important proof that the oath of succession was generally administered.
9. Borthwick, DRP. RV. The document also suggests that a register was kept of the visitation proceedings.
10. Borthwick, Reg. 28 (Lee), f. 101. The year is omitted, but 1538 is most probable.
11. Frere, ii, 34. Some of the bishops went further than the crown in reforms, see for example, Lee's Injunctions for York, *ibid.*, 44.
12. *Ibid.*, i, 134 ff; ii, 114.
13. BM, MSS. Cotton Titus B. IV, f. 77.
14. BM, MSS. Stowe 153, f. 2.
15. Frere, ii, 153. Also printed in *York Cathedral Statutes* (1900), 58-67.
16. Some of the wills proved before the visitors in the London circuit are preserved among the PCC 'Original Wills' (i.e. registered copies) at the PRO, PROB 10/Box 16.
17. Much has been written about the settlement, see particularly, J. E. Neale, 'The Elizabethan Acts of Supremacy and Uniformity', *EHR*, lxv, (1950), 304-32; R. B. Manning, 'The crisis of episcopal authority during the reign of Elizabeth', *J. Brit. Studies*, xi, (Nov. 1971), 1; W. P. Haugaard, *Elizabeth and the English Reformation* (Cambridge 1968); Claire Cross, *The Royal Supremacy in the Elizabethan Church* (London 1969).
18. T. Rymer, *Foedera*, (20 vols., 1704-35), xv, 518-9.
19. The patents were not enrolled, and the text copied into the beginning of the Act Book is the only surviving copy.
20. PRO, State Papers Domestic, SP 12/6, no. 22. On image-breaking see also J. Strype, *Annals of the Reformation* (4 vols. in 7, Oxford 1824) I, i, 254. In the London circuit the precentor of Ely, a favourer of images, had to collect them together, burn them and declare his lack of faith in them: PRO, Special Jurisdictions, PROB 34/1 f. 112r.
21. i.e. excluding a session held by surrogates at Alnwick on 30 Sept.
22. C. G. Bayne, 'The visitation of the Province of Canterbury', *EHR*, xxviii, (1913), 660.
23. below, 21v, *concionator visitacionis*.
24. J. A. Venn, *Alumni Cantabrigienses*, (part I, 4 vols, Cambridge 1922-7), iii, 19; C. H. Garret, *The Marian Exiles* (Cambridge 1938); see also I. P. Ellis, 'Edwin Sandys and the settlement of Religion, 1558-1588 (unpublished thesis, Oxford B.Litt. 1962).
25. J. A. Venn, *op. cit.*, ii, 323.
26. J. A. Venn, *op. cit.*, iii, 27.

111

27. SP 12/6 f. 30. See Appendix I.
28. below, 43r.
29. The Articles are described below, p. xxviii
30. The rigours of a visitation are admirably described by Prof. R. M. T. Hill, 'The Labourer in the Vineyard', (Borthwick Paper 35, Univ. of York), 1. Miss Hill also notes (p. 17) that visitation books were often destroyed once penances &c had been performed.
31. cf. those for the Lincoln and London circuits in Lambeth Palace CM XIII, 57, 58.
32. The comparable register of wills and licences for the London circuit is now at the PRO, Special Jurisdictions, PROB 34/2/1.
33. The curious statement by R. B. Manning, *Religion and Society in Elizabethan Sussex* (Leicester 1969), 50, that the visitors concerned themselves only with the administration of the oath of Supremacy, is quite clearly untrue.
34. SP 12/10.
35. See Appendix III.
36. Quite apart from the work of Burnett, Cardwell and Strype, the more recent pioneers were H. Gee, *The Elizabethan Clergy and the Settlement of Religion* (Oxford 1898); H. N. Birt, *The Elizabethan Religious Settlement*, (London 1907); R. W. Dixon, *A History of the English Church since the Reformation*, (Oxford 1878–1902) vol. V.
37. cf. G. I. O. Duncan, *The High Court of Delegates* (Cambridge 1971), 127–8.
38. below, 54.
39. It is not clear whether all the commissioners present presided jointly over every activity or whether they split up, some to hear the clergy, some the laity.
40. At Durham and Carlisle (below, 38r, 45r), these are said to have been printed.
41. below, 35v.
42. below, 43r.
43. below, 52v.
44. A further session was planned for Doncaster in late October, but the case was settled out of court, below, 60r. Sandys wrote disconsolately to Peter Martyr the following year that up to the beginning of November he had been 'in a constant discharge of the duties entrusted to me and with excessive fatigue both of body and mind', *Zurich Letters* (Parker Society 1842), i, no. 31.
45. below, 10r, 23r, 23v, 24v.
46. ed. Gladys Hinde, Surtees Society clxi, 123. Watson was the only prebendary of Durham to subscribe (below, 32r).
47. Bayne, *art. cit.*, 640, 643.
48. See Appendix III. The text used in London by Horne is given in Strype, *Annals*, I. i. 249: 'Who is then that faithful and wise servant whom his Lord hath set over his household to give them their meat in due season?' (Matthew xxiv, 45).
49. See note by 'J.B.' in *The Cheshire Sheaf*, 3rd series, iii, 27.
50. see, for example, W. F. Irvine, 'Clerical changes in 1559', *The Cheshire Sheaf*, 3rd series, iii, 38–9.
51. below, 6r, 6v, 7v. See also Salvyn 6v, Raby 6v, 7r; Iveson, 19r, Clarke 20.
52. But Harte of Manchester was ordered to appear before the Archbishop of Canterbury at Lambeth, 184v.
53. respectively, 17v, 18r, 29r, 35r, 39r.
54. Dalton, Tuttyn, N. Marley, Bullock and Cliffe. Robertson's temporary escape may have been because the visitors knew he would be deprived to make way for the restoration of Robert Horne as Dean.
55. At Southwell and York the Act Book omits some of the details of subscription, but a comparison with the register of recognisances suggests that no further sequestrations were imposed.
56. below, 170r.
57. below, 13v.
58. Bonds issued for re-appearance at a later stage of this visitation itself have also disappeared though they were definitely issued, see for example 29v below, *cassantes priorem recognitionem*.
59. For a discussion of the oath see Hughes, *op. cit.* iii, 38.
60. Gee, 77.
61. e.g. for Palmes 171r, Dalton 177r, Whitehead, 181v, Salvyn 179v, 182r.

62. e.g. Thomas Clarke, later actuary of the High Commission, 170v; Alexander Thorpe, 173v; and Robert Meynell sergeant-at-law, 175v, 176v, 178r.

63. 171r, 172v.

64. Fletborough, 9v; Edingley, 5r. For a general account of sequestration see R. M. Haines, *The Administration of the Diocese of Worcester in the first half of the Fourteenth Century* (1965), 202–3.

65. These are often named in the text.

66. Percival, 75v.

67. If the outcome was a foregone conclusion it was clearly too expensive. But some other proctors were called in, see below, 65r, 66v, 68v, 71v(2), 72v, 75v.

68. below, 58r.

69. Umfrye, 57r; Huddleston, 76r.

70. 79r–87r.

71. 137–147.

72. Only 2 instance causes were begun, and both were referred to other courts, 10r, 27r. Of the other causes, only 1 records the presence of any witnesses, 8v.

73. See particularly, J. S. Purvis, *A Medieval Act Book at York* (York 1943), 3. In the jurisdiction of the Dean and Chapter alone there were 3236 moral charges out of 3640 brought in the century before 1485.

74. below, 10r, 41r.

75. 8v.

76. 22r: *dum maior fuerit populi multitudo.*

77. Greene, 22v; Lamb, 139v.

78. see index *sub* poor.

79. 41v, a fortnight; 40r, a month; 138v, at the next deanery court.

80. below, 140r.

81. e.g. Smith, 23v.

82. Pavyer, 24v.

83. Wheywall, Robothom, 142r.

84. Sherte, 142v.

85. May, 41r; Otway, 42v; Yedding, 43v; Barrett, 139r; Prestbury, 140r.

86. 141v.

87. 23r, 28v, 139r. On compurgation see J. S. Purvis, *Tudor Parish Documents* (1948), 17n.

88. Frere and Kennedy, iii, 1.

89. It is (of course) highly improbable that the two scolds reported at Hull (99r) and the seven at Bridlington (102r) were the only ones in the province!

90. below, 124v.

91. for matters discussed in this paragraph, see index *sub* books, church goods, and church fabric.

92. SP 12/7 no. 79. The only surviving impression of the northern seal is a fragment on the will of Richard Large of Skerne, proved by the visitors 5 Sept. 1559, Borthwick Institute (no reference number).

93. PROB 34/1 records sessions in London on 16 and 24 Oct., 4 and 25 Nov. and 4 December, but these were clearly only tidying up the business. Bayne, *art. cit.*, 646.

94. Bayne, *art. cit.*, 657.

FOOTNOTES TO SECTION I *(fols. 1–54)*

1. *sic*; the remaining names appear in the dative.

2. see Frere, iii, 8 *et seq.*

3. No deprivations are recorded on these grounds in the Act Book.

4. One line left blank.

5. interlined.

6. Half a line left blank.

7. Deprived as vicar of Newark next day, see below, 58r.

8. *etc*: The performance of the penance had to be certified to the rural dean. See also recognisance below, 169r.
9. Robert Pursglove.
10. i.e. the commissary himself.
11. incomplete entry.
12. Subsequently deprived of his rectory of Ordsall to allow the restoration of William Denman, see below, 64r.
13. text has *fama'*.
14. text is blank.
15. below, 170r.
16. There is no subsequent report of their appearance at York, but the recognisances indicate that Wood and Jennings at least were brought there; see below, 172v.
17. For a recent analysis of the religious persuasions of the York Chapter, see J. C. H. Aveling, *Catholic Recusancy in the City of York, 1558–1791*, (Cath. Rec. Soc. 1970), Appendix II, 293–306.
18. i.e. not accepting the Prayer Book and Injunctions.
19. below, 172r.
20. The words *sequestranda fore* should be understood.
21. below, 171v.
22. below, 171r.
23. below, 170v.
24. Probably a mistake for £100, see below, 170v.
25. interlined.
26. *recte* Cleveland.
27. This entry was overlooked by Aveling, *op. cit.*, 301.
28. Overlooked by Aveling, 299.
29. Overlooked by Aveling, 301.
30. A notary, and later actuary of the High Commission, see Aveling, 318.
31. The special Injunctions for York have not survived, but examples for other dioceses may be seen in Frere, iii, 30 *et seq.*
32. 14 September.
33. see also below, 95r.
34. *non* should be understood.
35. see below, 95v., where he is called Robert.
36. i.e. with four other people.
37. see also below, 95v.
38. see also below, 96r.
39. Possibly a mistake for Whitgift, judging by the surrounding entries.
40. below, 96r.
41. below, 174r.
42. below, 173v.
43. The text has *di'*.
44. The Act Book is strangely silent about Thomas Fugall, vicar of Hessle, who was later alleged to have been told to 'recant his wilful errors' by the commissioners; see J. S. Purvis, *Tudor Parish Documents*, 204–207, citing Borthwick R VII G1041.
45. below, 176r.
46. The incumbent is reported absent below, 153r.
47. below, 182r.
48. *i.e.* with five others.
49. *recte* Hugh.
50. Regius Professor of Divinity at Cambridge, Venn I, iv, 40. See also below, 180v.
51. There follows the word *dicte* crossed out.
52. Editor's italics: the English portion of the text is in exactly the same script as the Latin.
53. below, 177r.
54. below, 175v.
55. below, 181v.

56. *pretensus* anticipates the restitution of Robert Horne as Dean. The word is used widely in the following section.
57. below, 176v.
58. below, 175r.
59. below, 177v.
60. below, 178r.
61. below, 179r.
62. Bullock was master of St John's College Cambridge and Lady Margaret Professor of Divinity, Venn I, i, 253. John Rudd had been deprived of this prebend by Mary and successfully sought restitution, see below, 68r.
63. *primo* crossed out.
64. below, 181r.
65. *rath* crossed out.
66. below, 179v.
67. below, 178v.
68. blank in text.
69. word obscured by blot.
70. These recognisances are omitted from the register.
71. This recognisance is also omitted from the register.
72. interlined.
73. Extracts from the Injunctions for Durham are to be found in a book of chapter business used by Toby Mathew as Dean of Durham: Borthwick, R VI C Delta, fo. 50, cited by Purvis, *Tudor Parish Documents*, 10–11.
74. below, 180r.
75. words omitted in text.
76. Heighington already lacked a vicar owing to the sequestration imposed on William Whitehead, see above, 31r.
77. The first five cases appear again below, 146v–147v.
78. Sherwood was a Surrogate, see below, 146v.
79. *sic*: the crime is omitted.
80. *sic*: the verb is omitted.
81. The text has *emaᵗ*, which is used on only one other occasion, on fo. 47v. in the phrase *et emanavit sequestracio*. If the same word is intended here, the sentence would appear to be incomplete.
82. interlined.
83. He was nevertheless deprived to allow the restoration of Sir Thomas Smith to the deanery, though not without some opposition from Cecil and the queen, see M. Dewar, *Sir Thomas Smith* (1964), 82.
84. Bury had already been deprived of his mastership of a hospital at Richmond, see below, 65r.
85. interlined.
86. The word *Pilkington* appears, crossed out, after *Sandis*.
87. *sic*.
88. omitted from text.
89. below, 184r.
90. The words *Edmundum Scambler* appear, crossed out, before *Johannem*.
91. The word *Joannes* appears, crossed out, before *Edwardus*.
92. The word *post* appears, crossed out, after *die*.
93. In fact it had only been vacant since Cuthbert Scott's deprivation in June.
94. The former dean had only been dead one year, though it is uncertain whether he had previously resigned, see notes by 'F.S.' in *The Cheshire Sheaf*, 3rd series, iii, 20–1.

FOOTNOTES TO SECTION II *(fols. 57–76)*

1. On the Marian deprivations of married clergy, see A. G. Dickens, 'The Marian Reaction in the diocese of York', 2 parts, *Borthwick Papers* 11 and 12 especially part I, Appendix A.

2. *Ibid.* I, 27 and sources there cited.
3. *Ibid.* I, 26: Dickens notes that Monson was restored to sacerdotal functions by Mary after apologising for his marriage, but this was clearly not to his former rectory.
4. October is more likely, see session reported above, 54r.
5. *sic.*
6. Dickens, *op. cit.*, I, 22 and sources there cited.
7. *Oct* appears, crossed out, before *Septembris.*
8. *recte* Johannes.
9. An unusual occurrence of the singular form. The commissaries may have separated to hear causes.
10. *decreverunt* is understood.
11. Dickens, *op. cit.*, I, 29 notes that Yokesall died in 1559.
12. There is no mention of a fourth article.
13. Presumably the Delegates.
14. Almost certainly 25th, as the 24th was a Sunday. The following entry refers to the *aforesaid 25th.*
15. A contraction meaning, as before, that he exhibited his proxy.
16. *Clif,* crossed out, appears before *Bullocke.*
17. Dickens, *op. cit.*, I, 25, and sources there cited.
18. omitted.
19. *Domini,* crossed out, appears before *quam.*
20. Dispensations were vested in the archbishop of Canterbury by the Statute 25 Henry VIII c. 21.
21. Dickens, *op. cit.*, I, 27 and sources there cited.
22. *ree* should be understood.
23. Verb omitted.

FOOTNOTE TO SECTION III *(fols. 79–87)*

1. Osmotherley.

FOOTNOTES TO SECTION IV *(fols. 90–135)*

1. see also 101v.
2. see also 102r.
3. see also 99v.
4. Already entered on 99v.
5. See A. G. Dickens, *Marian Reaction,* ii, 14.
6. As he was bound to do by Injunction 11 of 1559 if non-resident in a benefice worth over £20 p.a., see Frere, iii, 12.
7. See article 55 of 1559 (Frere, iii, 7). The text of the proclamation is printed in Hughes and Larkin, *Tudor Royal Proclamations,* ii, (New Haven, 1969), no. 451.
8. see also 127v.
9. see also 125r.
10. *recte* Elizabeth Davye: see 145r.

FOOTNOTES TO SECTION V *(fols. 137–147)*

1. All these causes are for a date after the end of the main visitation, and were therefore heard by surrogates. Others are reported in section I above.
2. Blank in text.
3. Blank in text.
4. The following cases are all first reported above, 40r *et seq.*

FOOTNOTES TO SECTION VI (*fols. 149–163*)

1. These were listed, with some errors and omissions noted below, by Gee, *op. cit.*, 83–88.
2. Sutton Bonnington; Gee has *Dunnington.*
3. omitted by Gee.
4. Gee has *Salton*, but this is represented below, 153r. One John Postgate was rector of Sneaton, see 'Tudor Crockford' at Borthwick Institute.
5. Thornaby; Gee has *Thormanby*, but this is represented above, 150v.
6. Gee has *Ainsby*, but Maxwell was vicar of Rudston, see 'Tudor Crockford'.
7. This section also includes the deanery of Doncaster.
8. Hubberholme; omitted by Gee.
9. York, St Mary Bishophill senior, not *Bishop's Hull* as suggested by Gee. The rector's name was *Robert* Morres, not William, see Aveling, *op. cit.*, 326.
10. This and similar additions on fos 158 and 159 are in another hand.
11. *recte* Albani: Nantwich.
12. Sandbach; Gee has *Soulby.*
13. Or possibly *Riverney*, as in Gee.

FOOTNOTES TO SECTION VII (*fols. 168–184*)

1. A separate book, now bound into the same volume, with a parchment cover now numbered *168* and bearing this legend.
2. This and similar entries on subsequent recognisances were written later.
3. The calendar is set out to correspond with the format of the preceding folios which have been fully transcribed. Italics indicate *verbatim* quotations from the original for the status of the persons bound over, and for the conditions of the bond where they vary significantly from the preceding examples. The first name is that of the person bound over, with a note of the sum pledged. There follow the names of the sureties and the sums in which they were held. Finally there is a note of the commissioners before whom the recognisance was made, and the date.
4. Almost certainly *recte* Ba*b*thorpe.

INDEX OF SUBJECTS

Note: *This index refers only to the text, and does not include the Introduction. Index entries for items such as adultery, fornication, incontinence, illegitimate children, etc. are subsumed under the entry* moral offences. *Where a cause extends over two or more consecutive folios, only the first folio is indicated.*

alchemy *see* calculation

alehouses, inns, 51r, 107r, 134v
   innholder, 173r
   drunkenness, 122v, 123v, 124r, 124v;
    (of clergy) 127v, 134v

appeal to Delegates, 67r

Articles, Royal:
   subscription to (text of), 15v; refusal of
    see benefices: sequestration
   verbatim answers to, 30r, 32v, 33r–v,
    34r–v

benefices:
   deprivation from, 2r, 17v, 18r, 29v, 35r,
    39r; (by Mary) 57r *et seq.*
   impropriation of, 91r
   institutions to, 2v, 79r *et seq.*
   presentation, purchase of, 116v
   restitution to, 2v, 57r *et seq.*
   dispensation to hold two, 72v
   oath of fealty for, 79r *et seq.*
   sequestration of (for refusal to sub-
    scribe), 2r, 13r–v; 16v *et seq.*, 24r–v,
    26r, 29v, 30r–v, 31r, 33r–v, (46r?)
   vacant and unserved, 2r, 4v, 5r(2), 9v(2),
    10v(2), 11r, 12v, 25r–v, 26v(2), 27r,
    39v, 42r, 47r, 91v(2), 92r(2), 93v,
    94r, 94v(2), 97r, 119v, 124v, 128v;
    see also under institutions, *above.*

blasphemy, 124v

books:
   burning of, 91r(2), 92r(2), 92v, 93r,
    94r, 96v, 97r, 107r–v, 117r, 117v,
    129v
   lack of, 90r, 91v(2), 98r, 112v
   removal or detention of, 92r, 98r, 117v,
    134r

Erasmus *Paraphrases*, 91r, 92r, 94r,
   112v
   homilies, 91r
   Registers, lack of, 90–135 *passim*

burial fees *see* clergy, income of

'calculation', 'conjuration', 99r

cathedral and college Statutes:
   Carlisle: 113r
   Durham, 37v
   Manchester, 51v
   York, 15v, 103r

church fabric:
   dilapidations, 41v, 90–135 *passim*
    caused by the sea, 122r
   repairs, 48v
   windows lacking glass, 90r, 97r, 97v,
    98r

church fittings:
   altars not pulled down, 102v
   images, removal of, 134r, 135r
    detention of, 97v, 100v(3), 109v
   pulpit lacking, 100v
   Rood, removal of, 134r
    retention of, 101r

church goods:
   detained, 100v, 101r
   inventories of, 4v, 37v

churchyard, vicar dispossessed of, 116r

clergy:
   absentees from visitation, 6v–7v, 19v–
    20r, 44v, 51r, 149 *et seq.*
   non-resident, 91r, 93v, 95r, 97v, 101v,
    107r, 113r, 117r(3), 118r, 118v,
    119v, 120r, 122r, 123v, 124r, 126r,
    126v, 133v, 134r, 134v, 154r, 154v,
    156r(2), 156v, 157r, 157v(2), 158r,

punishments—*cont.*
    payment to woman, 137r
    repair of bridges, 137r
    repair of highway, 96r
    see also benefices (deprivation, sequestration)
purgation, 23r, 28v, 139r

recognisances, 13v(2), 16v *et seq*, 24r–v, 26r, 29v, 30r–v, 31r, 32v, 33r–v, 51v, 142v, 168 *et seq.*

scolds, 99r, 102r
seal *ad causas ecclesiasticas*, 38r
sermons, 4r, 8r, 10r, 12r, 13r, 15r, 21r, 21v, 25r, 25v, 26r, 27v, 29r, 32r, 38v, 39v, 43r, 44r, 45v, 46r, 47r, 48r, 49r, 49v, 50r, 52r, 53r, 54r, App. III.
    see also preaching, licenses for
    not preached, 103r, 113r

services:
    at inconvenient times, 95r
    disturbances in, 90r, 95r
    neglected (by clergy), 90v, 121r, 127v; (by laity), 96v, 116r, 118r, 134v
statutes *see* cathedral and college statutes
Supremacy:
    Act of, 16r
    oath of, 15v
    see also Articles; benefices (deprivation, sequestration)
surrogates, 3r, 10r, 23r, 23v, 60r, 76v, 183v, App. III
swearing, 123v
synods, 2v
synodals, 2v

tithe, 42r

witnesses, 8v, 74v; *see also* purgation
witchcraft, 95r

INDEX OF PERSONS

Note: *As far as practicable, names appear below in their nearest modern spelling, ignoring expletive* es *and converting many* ys *to* i. *Significant variants found in the text appear in brackets. Clergy are indicated by asterisks, and the names of active visitation commissioners are in block capitals. References are to folios of the original document, as indicated in the margins of this edition.*

Abridge, Agnes, 119r
Acrisshaw, Ralph, 119r
Acton, Agnes, 125v
Adam, Agnes, wife of Richard, 97v
*Adams, John, 76r
Adamson,
   Margaret, 125r
   Parnell, 125r
Aderton,
   Alice, 125r
   Richard, 124v
Afclesing, Janet, 119r
Alexander, Alice, 10r
Alice, a beggar, 28v
Allyn, Ann, 124r
Althan, Thomas, 98v
*Ambroze, Elizeus, 158r
Ambry (Ambrie), Elizabeth, 40r, 146v
Amon, George, 25r
Amson, Roger, 128r
Andrew (Andro, Androo),
   Janet, 109r
   John, 118r
*Apeley, Robert, 151v
*Apowell, Hugh, 157v
*Abbot, William, 80r
*Ardern, Thomas, 19v
Armstrong (Armystronge), Elizabeth, 109r
Armistead (Armysted), Jane, 98r
Arrowsmith (Aresmythe, Arrowsmyth),
   Emma, 132v, 142v
   John, 128r
*Arsley, William, 152r
Asbore, John, 122v
Ashley,
   Jane, 123r

   William, 97r
Ashton,
   Elizabeth, 95v
   Matilda (Maud), 132v, 143r
   Maurice, 121r
*Askam, Anthony, 155r
Atclif, Roger, 27r
Athe, Christopher, 178v
Atkin, Robert, 42v
Atkinson,
   Joan, 40r, 147r
   *John, 62r
   Robert, 72v
   Roger, 67v
   *Thomas, 67v, 70r, 72r
   Thomas, 98v
Auckland (Aykelande), Edward, 96v
Auley, William, 95r
*Austin (Austyne), John, 44v
Awdecrofte *see* Oldcroft
Awood,
   Agnes, 12r
   Lawrence, 12r
Ayne, Edmund, 171v
Ayre *see* Eyre
Aykelande *see* Auckland

*Babthorpe (?also Barthrope), Robert, 18v, (?172r)
*Backhouse, John, 156v
*Bagley, Robert, 149v
Baker, Edward, 5v, 92v, 169r
*Baldwin, Richard, 65r
*Ball, William, 37r
*Ballard, Robert, 158r
Balsha, Elizabeth, 121r

122

Marvel (Marvyll), John, 172v
Marton, Robert, 40r, 147r
Mass,
  James, 117v
  William, 128v
Massey (Massye), John, 184r
Mathew,
  Elizabeth, 127r
  *Toby, 38r (n)
Mawde, Christopher, 170r
*Mawen,
  Nicholas, 161r
  Master, (?same), 94r
*Maxwell, Anthony, 153r
May, Helen, 147v
Menson, William, 102r
Mere, John, 122v
Mershe see Marsh
Mershall see Marshall
Mesle, William, 102r
Metcalfe,
  Francis, 62r
  Oswald, 116v
Meynell, Robert, 175r, 176v, 178r
*Middleton (Myddilton), Robert, 155r
*Midgley (Mygley), Christopher, 13v
Mill (Myll), George, 41r
Miller,
  John, 134r
  Margery, 118r
Milner, Agnes, 126r
Minshill, Helen, 126r
Mitchell (Michell),
  *Edward, 44v, 113r
  Isabella, 140r
Mitchelforth (Michelfauth), Isabell, 119r
Mitchelson, Elizabeth, 102r
Modes, Elizabeth, 118r
*Molyneux, Anthony, 158r
Monk (Moncke),
  *Henry, 44v
  Margery, 54v
*Monkton (Monckton), Thomas, 76v
*Monsum, George, 59r
Moorton, Thomas, 106v
More,
  *Henry, 24r, 174r
  Jane, 130v
  *William, 149r
*Morecroft, Edward, 158r

*Morland, Christopher, 85r
*Morlay, Geoffrey, 20r
Morres,
  *Robert, (*William*), 83r–v, 155v
  Thomas, 123v
Morris, Alice, 117v
MORTON, WILLIAM, 52v, 53r, Appendix III
*Mowse, William, *Ll.D*, 6v
Murrey,
  *John, 162r
  *Lancelot, 162v
Mygley see Midgley
Mynnet, Thomas, 8v
Myers (Myres), Arthur, 180v

Nables, Oliver, 118v
Nelson,
  John, 118v
  *Robert, 158r
*Neville, George, 162v
*Newsom, John, 153r
Newton,
  Elizabeth, 134r
  Janet, 112v
Nicholson (Nicolson),
  Gilbert, 109v
  *Henry, 79r
  *James, 162v
Nixon (Nickson, Nykeson),
  John, 126r
  Margaret, 137v
  Ralph, 129v
*Norfolk (Norffolke), Thomas, 150r
*Norman, Richard, 19v
*Normanvel (Normavell), John, 149r, 152r
Northumberland, Thomas Earl of, 1v
*Norton, Baldwin, 19v
*Nuthide, Robert, 162r
*Nutt, William, 154v

*Ogle, Thomas, 161r
*Oglethorpe, William, 81v
Oldcroft (Awdecrofte), Thomas, 130r
*Oliver, John, 157r
Orshaw, Thomas, 130v, 137v
Orton, William, 91r
Ostler, Ralph, 100v
*Otby, Edward, 150r
*Otford, Roland, 152v

INDEX OF PLACES

Note: *References are to folios of the original document, as indicated in the margins of this edition.*

As far as possible, placenames have been identified and indexed under their modern form, with cross-references where this differs significantly from that in the text. Counties and Ridings are not included unless this seemed essential to identify one of several places with the same name.

Estralsey *see* East Harlsey
Estwaite *see* Eastwood
Eton *see* Eaton
Etton, 153v
Eversham, 71v
Eyton *see* Eaton

Fanham *see* Farnham
Farme [?Farndon], 130v
Farndon, Farne, 137v, *see also Farme*
Farnham, Fanham, 156r
Felkirk, 96v
Fenton, prebend of (York), 19r
Finningley, 151v
Fishlake, 95r
Fledborough, Fledburgh, Fletborough, 9v, 152r
Flixton, Flexton (Ches.), 118r
Folkton, 26v, 153r
Ford, 161r
Foston, 101r, 155r
Fridaythorpe, prebend of (York), 102v
Frodsham, Frodisham, 87r, 129v
  deanery of, 158r
Fryston, Fuiston, 98r
Furness, deanery of, 48r, 158r
Fuiston *see* Fryston

Gainsford, 29r
Gamston, 151r
Garforth, 160r
Garton, 154r
Gateshead, 106v, 147r–v, 181r
Gawsworth, 159r
Giggleswick, 22v
Gilling, 153r
Givendale, prebend of (York), 19r
Goodmanham, 154r
Goostrey, Goscre, 157v
Gosforth (Cumb.), 157r
Gosforth (Northumb.), 42r
Gotham, 149v
Goxhill, 154r
Great Langton, 85r, 117r
Great Leake, 149v
Great Ouseburn, 156r
Great Salkeld, Mickell Sawelte, 112r
Greystoke, 163r
Grindale, prebend of (York), 20r
Gringley, 151v

Grinton, 156r
Grove, 80v
Guiseley, 13r, 170r
Gunbere (unidentified), 128r
Gusterde (unidentified), 128r

Hale, 157r
Halifax, 150v
  session at, 12r, 169v
  deanery of, 150v
Halloughton, Halton iuxta Newark, Howton, 93r, 152r
  prebend of (Southwell), 6v
Halsall, 158r
Halsham, 84r
Haltemprice, 83r
Halton iuxta Newark *see* Halloughton
Hanmer (Flints.), 158v
Harpington, 169v
Harrington, 157r
Harworth, 151v
Hawkshead, 158r
Hawksworth, 149r
Hawnby, 152v
Haworth, 150v
Heighington, 39v, 181v
Hemingbrough, 179v
Hemsworth, Hymesworth, 95r, 154v
Hexham, 108v
  session at, 183v
Hickleton, Hicketon, 97r
Hinderwell, 28r
Hockerton, 76r
Holme, 154r
Holme archiepiscopi, prebend of (York), 19v
Holmside, Holmeset, 179r
Holt, 130r
Horton *see* Houghton-le-Spring
Hothersfilde *see* Huddersfield
Houghton (Cumb.), 161r
Houghton-le-Spring, Horton, 181r
Hovenden [?Hovingham], 100r, 153v
Hoveringham, 91r
Hovingham (?), *see* Hovenden
Howton *see* Halloughton
Hubberholme, Hubbrame, 154v
Huddersfield, Hothersfilde, 12v, 97v
Huggate, 153v

142 INDEX OF PLACES

Hull, 99r
  session at, 25r, 84r
  bishop of, 6r, 16v
  deanery of, 153v–154r
Huntington, 155v
Hutton (dioc. of Carlisle), 163r
Hutton Buscel, 153r
Hutton Cranswick, 76v, 153v
Hymesworth see Hemsworth

Ince, 158v
Ingleby Greenhow, 152v
Ireby, 162v

Kellington, 81v
Kendal, session at, 48r, 71r–v, 72r, 73v
Keyingham, 25v, 99v
Keyworth, 79v
Kilburn, 150r
Kildwick, 13v
Kilnwick, 101r, 153v
Kirbefletam see Kirkby Fleetham
Kirby (Wirral), 158v
Kirby on the Moor, 156r
Kirby Underdale, Kirkby, 84r, 152v
Kirk Andrews, Churcheandros, 112r, 163r
Kirkburn, 101r, 153v
Kirkburton, 150v
Kirkby Fleetham, Kirbefletam, 156v
Kirkby in Ashfield, 91r, 149v
Kirkby in Cleveland, 68v, 152v
Kirkby Malhamdale, 98v
Kirkby Overblow, 98r
Kirkby Stephen, 162r
Kirkby Thore, Kyrby Thurer, 162r
Kirklington, 156v
Kirk Oswald, 163r
Kirk Sandal, Churchesandall, 81r, 96r
Kirk Smeaton, 154v
Knapton, 101v
Knaresborough, prebend of (York), 19v
Knarsdale, 161r
Knotforthe see Nutsford
Kyrby Thurer see Kirkby Thore

Lambeth palace, 184r
Lancaster, session at, 49r, 63r, 63v, 64v
Lanchester, 106r, 177v, 179r
Laneham, 151r
  deanery of, 8r, 151r–v

Langtoft, 153r
  prebend of (York), 19v
Langton see Great Langton
Laseby see Lazenby
Lastingham, Lestingham, 100r
Latheley (unidentified), 63r
Lazenby, Laseby, 183r
Ledsham, 24r, 173v
Leeds, 79r
Lenton, 92r
Lestingham see Lastingham
Leyland, 123r, 157v
  deanery of, 157v
Liethe see Lythe
Little Ouseburn, 156r
London, benefice in diocese of, 155r
  royal commissioners in, 31r, 32v, 33r–v,
    34r–v, 35r–v, 37v, 51r, 51v, 69r, 89r,
    184r
  S. Paul's Cathedral, consistory of, 170r
Long Newton, 107v, 160r
Long Preston, 154v
Lowdham, 79v, 91r
Lowthorpe, 154r
Lymm, 129r
Lythe, Liethe, 27r

Macclesfield, Makesfild, 119v
Malpas, 158v
Maltby, 10v
Malton, session at, 26r, 84v
  deanery of, 152r–153r
Manchester, 50r, 74r, 75r–v, 118r, 139r,
    146r, 184r
  session at, 50r
  College, session at, 51r
  Deanchurch, 117r
  deanery of, 159r
Mansfield, 86r
Mappleton, 154r
Marbury, 126r, 138v
Marske, 152r
Marton, 46r, 162r
Mattersey, Mathersaye, 151v
Melton [?on the Hill], 97r
Mensleye see Wensley
Methley, 155r
Mickell Sawelte see Great Salkeld
Middleton (unidentified), 119r, 133r, 140
Middleton in Teesdale, 160r

Whittingham, Whetingham, 109v
Whorlton, 100r
Widmerpool, 149r
Wigan, 122v, 157v
    session at, 49v, 86v
Wighill, Wigishall, 150r
Wighton *see* Weighton
Wigishall *see* Wighill
Willerby, 153r
Wilmslow, 131r, 139r, 142v, 144r, 144v,
    145r, 159r
Winston, 107v
Winteringham, 101v
Winthorpe, 5r–v, 92v
Winwick, 157v
Wirral, deanery of, 158v
Wistaston, Wisterton, 126v
Witton, 124v
Wollaton, 79v
Wolsingham, Wolsington, 160v
Womeslowe *see* Wilmslow
Woolley, Woulley, 97r
Worksop, 151r
Wormsley, Wormeslaye, 155r

Woulley *see* Woolley
Wrenbury, Wrambury, 127v
Wressle, 153v
Wybunbury, Wynbere, 127v, 157r

Yedingham, 84v
York, 170v–176r
    cathedral, sessions in consistory of, 14r,
      15r, 22r, 58v, 59v, 61v, 62v, 64r–v,
      76v, 82v
    dean and chapter of, 69r
    prebends of, 15v *et seq.*, 170v *et seq.*
    parishes:
    All Saints, Pavement, 21r
    Holy Trinity, Micklegate, 155v
    S. Lawrence, 155v
    S. Martin, Micklegate, 24r
    S. Mary's Abbey, advowson attached
      to, 82v
    S. Mary Bishophill senior, 83r, 155v
    S. Michael, Ouse Bridge, 21v, 61v
    S. Olave, 98v
    S. Saviour, 155v
    church courts at, 27v, 58v, 98v